M

THE HANDBOOK
OF ITALIAN
RENAISSANCE PAINTERS

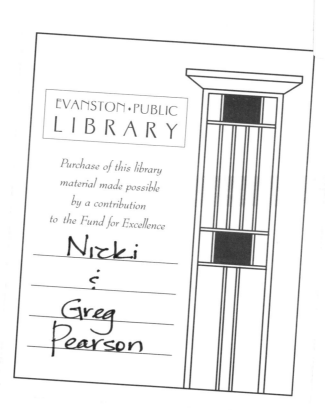

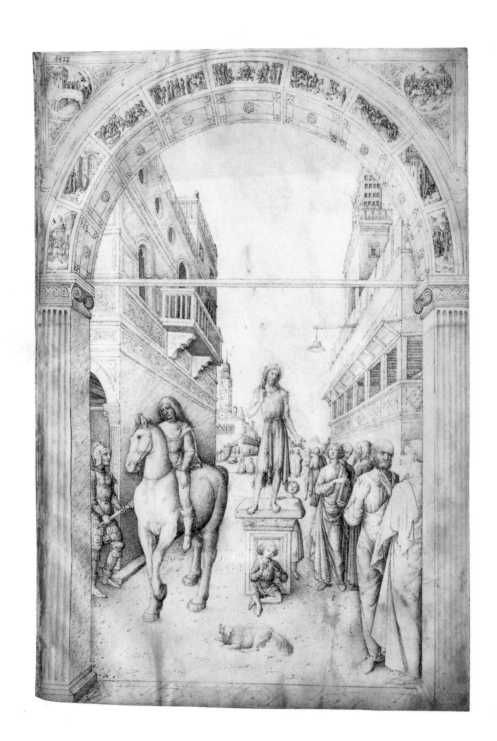

THE HANDBOOK
OF ITALIAN
RENAISSANCE PAINTERS

Karl Ludwig Gallwitz

Prestel
Munich · London · New York

Front cover: Sandro Botticelli, *Primavera* (detail)
Back cover: see plates 6, 16, 10, 106 and 7

Translated from the German by Michael Ashdown
Copyedited by Kate Garratt

Library of Congress Catalog Card Number: 99-65363

© Prestel Verlag, Munich · London · New York, 1999

Prestel Verlag
Mandlstrasse 26 · 80802 Munich
Tel. (089) 38 17 09-0, Fax (089) 38 17 09-35;
16 West 22nd Street · New York, NY 10010
Tel. (212) 627-8199, Fax (212) 627-9866;
4 Bloomsbury Place · London WC1A 2QA
Tel. (0171) 323 5004, Fax (0171) 636 8004

Prestel books are available worldwide.
Please contact your nearest bookseller
or one of the above Prestel offices for
details concerning your local distributor.

Designed by Matthias Hauer
Font: Dante by Monotype
Lithography by ReproLine, Munich and
Repro Ludwig, Zell am See
Printed and bound by Spiegel Druck, Ulm

Printed in Germany on acid-free paper

ISBN 3-7913-2227-3

Table of Contents

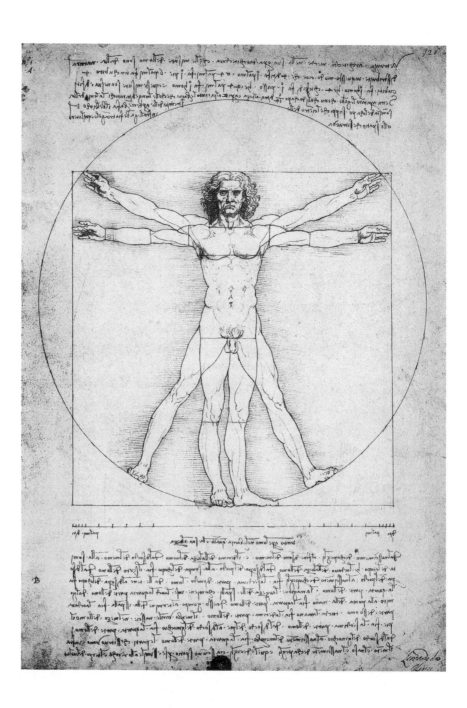

Introduction

This handbook is aimed at art historians and students, especially as a help in classifying lesser-known masters in terms of their importance and interdependencies. It is also intended as a *vade mecum* for travellers in Italy and museum visitors who wish to study the painting of the Italian Renaissance in greater detail. In particular, the graphic section of the book will help guide them through the plethora of names and schools that Italy's cultural and artistic revival produced between the beginning of the fifteenth and the end of the sixteenth centuries. After all, it is not always possible to run around with a copy of the 'Bénézit' under one's arm.

At first glance, the graphic overviews may seem bewildering, but the user will very quickly become aware of the advantages of such a representation. A restriction on the number of symbols and the inclusion of an aid to location in the tabular section ensures that the status of the individual artists within the network of interrelationships among the various schools can be quickly traced and understood.

Both the tabular and graphic sections extend far back into the Gothic Age. Likewise, the line between the Late Renaissance (Mannerism) and the Baroque Age has not been drawn too distinctly; the question of whether the so-called Mannerists (or which of them) should still be regarded as Renaissance artists should remain open. In particular, however, it has been taken into account that the significance and achievements of an artistic epoch can be properly understood only when set against the epochs that preceded and followed it. The graphic representation – not only of the interdependencies and influences among the masters of a school, but also the relationships among their artistic predecessors and descendants – facilitates

such a comparison, and is presented here in this manner for the first time. The special appeal of studying a particular school of painting lies in following the expression of specific stylistic devices back to their roots. In any case, it is almost impossible to delimit artistic and cultural epochs distinctly in chronological terms. On the one hand, these cover different periods in different locations; on the other, we repeatedly come across important artists who, untouched by the artistic currents of a new age, continue to live in the 'old world' and hold fast to its rules and ideas, just as we encounter lonely pioneers who anticipate the achievements of an epoch without ever really becoming exponents of the new style. They remain isolated forerunners, because their time has not yet come. Moreover, the problem in making a chronological distinction between the Gothic Age and the Renaissance is compounded by the fact that we occasionally encounter artists who, using the creative means of the Gothic Age, produced works that were in many respects already well and truly imbued with the spirit of the Renaissance. Heinrich Wölfflin has referred to this phenomenon in connection with the different development of the Renaissance in Italy and Germany. Besides, we should not attribute too much significance to the question of whether, for example, Bronzino (pl. 19) should be assigned to the High Renaissance or already to Mannerism, since the artist himself could hardly have answered this question satisfactorily. The tendency to classify and categorize, which is at the root of all academic study, does not stop at the arts and here, too, can be fully justified. It should never, however, make us lose sight of the fundamental aspects, namely the objective appreciation of an artist and his œuvre in a chronological context.

In particular, this handbook is intended to identify the stylistic interdependencies and interrelationships between the Italian schools of painting, as well as those within the individual schools. To this end, their elucidation using graphic charts not only serves a broad overview, but also – with regular use – makes it easier to remember them. It is important to note, however, that this method can only be used efficiently for the painting of the *Italian* Renaissance. Conditions were much less favourable for the development of comprehensible paths of stylistic tradition in the far more strongly individualistic art north of the Alps. In Italy, by contrast, a highly developed system of workshops, strict rules concerning collaborative works and partnerships, exacting, demanding, and prosperous clients with refined tastes, a lesser tendency to break with proven tradition and, in particular, better possibilities for an artist to become informed on the artistic production of his contemporaries (this, in turn, conditioned by climate, means of transport and political factors) favoured the formation and development of a 'stylistic map'. It is the diversity and uniformity of this 'stylistic map' that make up the special quality of Italian Renaissance painting. Towards the end of the Cinquecento, the traditional distinguishing characteristics of the individual schools become blurred, and only the truly great masters retain an individuality that conspicuously raises them above the average.

Since the classification of an artist to an era is essentially based on stylistic characteristics, or, to put it better, since the accumulation of stylistic characteristics in a majority of concurrent artists makes it possible to define an artistic period, it seems logical to identify individual artists as typical representatives of a stylistic epoch – rather than draw timelines across the page – and, in so doing, set fixed points to aid stylistic orientation. For the user of this handbook, it should be pointed out that the choice of artists has been made with a concen-

tration on activity between 1410 and 1590. Hence, representatives of the transition to the Baroque or Early Baroque are included only if they clearly represent the endpoint of a stylistic tradition.

The following artists may be considered typical of the Italian schools of painting, and, at the same time, as the outstanding representatives of an epoch who serve as points of orientation in the graphic overviews:

GOTHIC

Florence: *Cimabue* (1240–1302)
Siena: *Guido da Siena* († mid-thirteenth century)

LATE GOTHIC

Florence: *Giotto* (1266–1337)
Siena: *Simone Martini* (1283–1349)
Marches: *Gentile da Fabriano* (circa 1375–1427)
Venice: *Paolo Veneziano* (circa 1300–circa 1360),
Nicolò di Pietro (doc. 1394–1427)
Verona: *Altichiero da Zevio* († 1395)

EARLY RENAISSANCE

Florence: *Masolino* (circa 1383–1447),
Fra Angelico (circa 1387–1455), *Masaccio* (1401–1428),
Fra Filippo Lippi (1406–1469), *Piero della Francesca*
(1416/20–1492), *A. Pollaiulo* (1433–98),
Domenico Ghirlandaio (1449–94)
Umbria: *Benozzo Gozzoli* (1420–97),
Perugino (1446–1524), *Pinturicchio* (1455–1513)
Bologna: *Francia* (circa 1450–1517)
Ferrara: *Cosmé Tura* (circa 1430–95),
Francesco Cossa (circa 1435–77), *Ercole Roberti*
(circa 1456–96), *Lorenzo Costa* (1460–1535)
Lombardy: *Vincenzo Foppa* (circa 1427–1516/17),
Bernardo Zenale (1436–1526)
Verona: *Pisanello* (1395–1455)
Padua: *Mantegna* (1431–1506),
Carlo Crivelli (1468–93/95)
Venice: *Giovanni Bellini* (1431–1516),
Antonello da Messina (circa 1430–79),

Alvise Vivarini (circa 1445–1504), *Vittore Carpaccio* (circa 1455–1526), *G.B. Cima* (1459–1517/18)

HIGH RENAISSANCE

Florence: *Leonardo da Vinci* (1452–1519), *Michelangelo* (1475–1564), *Botticelli* (1445–1510), *Piero di Cosimo* (1462–1521), *Fra Bartolommeo* (1472–1517), *Lorenzo Credi* (1459–1537), *Andrea del Sarto* (1486–1530), *Luca Signorelli* (1441–1523)
Umbria / Rome: *Raphael* (1483–1520)
Emilia: *Correggio* (1489–1534), *Garofalo* (1481–1559)
Ferrara: *Dosso Dossi* (1480/90–1542)
Lombardy: *Borgognone* (circa 1453–1523), *Bernadino Luini* (circa 1480–1532)
Piedmont: *Guadenzio Ferrari* (1470–1546)
Brescia: *G. Romanino* (1470–1562), *Moretto* (circa 1495–1554)
Verona: *Francesco Caroto* (circa 1480–1555)
Venice: *Giorgione* (circa 1478–1510), *Titian* (circa 1489–1576), *Sebastiano del Piombo* (1485–1547), *Palma Vecchio* (1480–1528), *Lorenzo Lotto* (circa 1480–1556)
Friuli: *Pordenone* (1484–1539)

LATE RENAISSANCE (MANNERISM)

Florence: *Jacopo Pontormo* (1494–1557), *Rosso Fiorentino* (1494–1540), *Angelo Bronzino* (1503–72), *Giorgio Vasari* (1511–74), *Alessandro Allori* (1535–1607)
Verona: *Paolo Veronese* (1528–88)
Bologna: *Primaticcio* (1504–70), *Nicolò dell' Abate* (circa 1509–71), *Annibale Carracci* (1560–1609)
Umbria: *Federigo Baroccio* (circa 1535–1613)
Lombardy: *Parmigianino* (1503–40), *G.B. Crespi* (1557–1633)
Venice: *Paris Bordone* (1500–71), *Jacopo Bassano* (circa 1515–92), *Tintoretto* (1519–94)

EARLY BAROQUE

Florence: *Ludovico Cardi da Cigoli* (1559–1613)
Bologna: *Giovanni Guercino* (1591–1666)

Lombardy: *Caravaggio* (1560/65–1610)
Venice: *Palma Giovane* (circa 1550–1628)

This listing does not take account of the fact that many artists spanned different stylistic periods in the course of their creative lives. For example, it is necessary to count the later *Michelangelo* (pl. 14) and the later *Titian* (plates 21, 29, 20) among the Mannerists, likewise the inventive *Pordenone*, whose paintings exhibited strongly Mannerist traits even in the 1520s.

The appended chronological table, in which culturally and artistically important events and works are placed in historical context, similarly extends far back into the Middle Ages. It raises no new discussion as to whether the end of the Middle Ages and the beginning of modern times, i.e., the Renaissance, should be set at around 1300 (establishment of the independent city states), or not before 1453 (conquest of Constantinople by the Turks). References to events and works of art within the chronological table should not necessarily be equated with pre-eminence in terms of their historical implications or art-historical importance. Instead, the table is based on dates, events and works of art that have claims to a certain degree of fame, and so assist with orientation and association to help the user gain an overview. In academic studies of history and art, we are often confronted with the same misunderstanding, namely, that importance and value are confused with degree of fame. Here, too, the bold type in the tables should be taken with a pinch of salt; it is not the intention of this *vade mecum* to become involved in a scholarly debate as to whether *Raffaelino del Garbo* might have deserved a bolder type than *Lorenzo Credi*.

Hints for the use
of the graphic representations

To ensure that the charts and the symbols used are properly understood, it is necessary to make some basic introductory remarks. The charts give an overview and allow interrelationships to be recognized, but they cannot, and are not intended to be, a substitute for artists' biographies. They can only give limited information on the degree of dependence or the intensity of an influence, for example by the use of bold arrows where a corresponding relationship in the work of an artist is conspicuous or undisputed in academic terms. Beyond this aspect, bold type is used particularly to emphasize interrelationships among the outstanding masters of a school, in order to make the chart clearer and easier to remember. Hence, the bold arrows reflect both the intensity and art-historical importance of the relationship. There will seldom be doubt concerning the latter, while the degree of external influence on an artist's œuvre can only be determined when he is studied in greater depth. This is precisely what the charts are intended to encourage. Of course, a more differentiated representation would also be possible, but apart from the fact that this would be at the expense of clarity, it is doubtful whether the user would be helped in this way. The charts are based on the findings and assumptions of numerous experts who are anything but unanimous in their judgements. Hence, to draw one line thick and another thin would mean to side with one or the other opinion. To do so would be beyond the scope of this handbook.

In any case, it is wise to use the terms 'dependence' or 'influence' sparingly. It is generally more accurate to say that certain stylistic characteristics of one artist can be found again in the pictures of another. In this way, we always take account of the possibility that the supposed influences of a great painter in an artist's œuvre can, in fact, represent an independent achievement by that artist. Moreover, we consider that, in contrast to the widely-held view, the defined achievements of a particular school of painting are not necessarily attributable to an initial external impetus, but may have arisen autonomously. In art, especially, we should not underestimate the possibility of two artists at different locations, each without any influence on the other, arriving at similar results.

The symbols for *immediate influence* do not necessarily imply a particularly strong interdependence. Many painters were more influenced by the œuvre of masters whom they had never met than by their own tutors. In isolated cases, however, the tutor-pupil relationship can be most revealing, and is hence worthy of mention. While the pupil's stylistic acquisitions can be lost very quickly, for example through contact with the art of other workshops and schools, what he learned from his master in terms of draughtsmanship, painting technique and solutions to specific problems of rendering (e.g. the depiction of the hands, nose, or eye region) remains long evident. This can often lead to difficulties in attributing the pictures. For those who have developed an eye for such details, it is fascinating to track them down. A repeatedly cited example of the 'transmission' of a facial type over three generations of painters is that of the *Madonnas* of Fra Filippo Lippi (plates 5, 6), his pupil Botticelli (plates 7, 8), and, in turn, Botticelli's pupil Filippino Lippi (pl. 9). Since, however, Filippino was only twelve when his father, Fra Filippo, died, an immediate stylistic influence by the latter can be discounted. The gleaming, light pink, and slightly swollen tips of the noses in a delicate, oval face – sometimes the figures give the impression of having just recovered from a cold – and also the high, arched forehead of Fra Filippo's *Madonna and Child with Two Angels* (Uffizi) are found time and again in Botticelli's *Madonnas* and portraits of women, and also in Filippiono's *Adoration of the Child* (likewise in the Uffizi).

The charts also substantiate the fact that large workshops, such as that of Vincenzo Foppa (pl. 63) in Pavia, or of Verrocchio in Florence, produced very different artistic personalities. From this, we may conclude that, even at that time, training left enough scope for the individual expression of a talent. The faithful imitation of a master is by no means a phenomenon that is restricted to his pupils and assistants. The great masters also had their tenacious imitators many years later. To be fair to the latter, however, we must point out that imitation was in no way despised five centuries ago. On the contrary, it was desired by many clients, and was rewarded just as well as a truly independent work. This practice, too, may have contributed to a comprehensible, continuous development of style in Italy. However, many of the countless minor artists who made no secret of their dependency on established masters also contributed to this phenomenon, thus helping to spread and consolidate the artistic legacy of the latter. This, too, had to be taken into account in designing the charts. If the graphic representation were to be restricted to the interrelationships among the famous masters alone, this would create a very deceptive impression of the true complexity involved. By designing the charts as we have, it is shown that great masters were not necessarily the products of the workshops of other great masters. Sometimes, indeed, as in the case of Caravaggio (pl. 77), we know nothing about them at all.

The term 'School of painting' refers to one or more generations of painters who, within a defined geographical region, exhibit common stylistic features or develop these further in an independent manner. Here, external influences are digested in such a way that they enrich or modify the artists' own tradition, amongst other things, but do not obliterate its essence. The more general the stylistic criteria, the larger the geographical region covered by a school. With respect to the Gothic Age and the Renaissance, we repeatedly encounter fundamental differences between the *Italian* and *Flemish* Schools, which, in the Italy of five hundred years ago, tended towards the designation as *Flemish* of all stylistic innovations that came south from transalpine regions. Moreover, within the Italian School, there are many schools that can be classified on a regional basis, e.g. the *Tuscan* and *Lombard Schools*, and within these the *Florentine*, *Milanese* or *Cremonese Schools*, covered by the term 'Local School'. As a rule, the schools also feature one or more outstanding master, whose œuvre is a typical expression of the school's distinguishing features, or whose exemplary creativity and teaching laid the foundation for the formation of a school. Within the local schools, there are also schools of individual painters, such as the *Squarcione* or *Leonardo Schools*. These refer to circles of pupils and imitators that were clearly and formatively influenced by a master. However, there are also great masters who, despite having had a considerable influence on other artists, never led to the formation of a school, e.g. Correggio (plates 78, 88, 89), Savoldo (pl. 102), Crivelli (pl. 37).

On the basis of the above criteria, it is not possible in the Renaissance to speak of either a *Roman* or a *Neapolitan School*, even though these terms occasionally turn up and can be useful in a specific connection. As a melting-pot of the most diverse of artistic currents, Rome never developed an independent artistic tradition, but instead always owed the flourishing of its art to the achievements of 'foreign' masters. The great commissions awarded by the Pope and his entourage led in Rome to a concentration of outstanding artists whose mutual stylistic enrichment (especially in the Late Renaissance) produced works that have necessitated the use of descriptive terms such as *Tusco-Roman* or *Umbro-Roman*. In Naples, both the political circumstances as well as the Neapolitan mentality and lifestyle hindered the formation of an artistic practice that could grow beyond its boundaries in such a way that it could develop an independent significance and character.

Comments on the graphic representations

The graphic representation of the most important schools of painting of the Italian Renaissance in eight charts is by no means intended to be a definitive classification. Other solutions using more or fewer charts are also conceivable. For example, we could classify Brescia to Lombardy, or also to Venice, or integrate the Veronese School into the Venetian chart. On the other hand, however, the achievements of the Bergamasque, and in particular the Sienese Schools, might have been worthy of a separate presentation. The solution adopted here is a compromise that takes account of various factors: stylistic affinity and interdependence, art-historical importance and impact, traditional classification and, last but not least, technical design considerations. Except in those cases where it is difficult to make a statement about affiliation to a specific or local school of painting, the tabular index contains details concerning the masters' more intimate artistic milieux. Hence, it can also happen occasionally that a painter who is classified to the Paduan School, for example, is noted in the Venetian or Emilian chart, since various circumstances, whether they concern training, centre of activity, or the traditional claims of local historians, suggest such a solution.

The question of a school's importance can be answered in many different ways, depending on the point of view. Objective, measurable criteria, such as the number of 'grand masters' a school has produced, its productivity and its geographical range, contrast with aspects that are largely subjective in their appraisal. For example, it is not always possible to make a unanimous judgement with respect to innovative power, impacts on other schools, expression of specific stylistic devices, and aesthetic value. We only need to imagine that a Florentine argues with a Venetian about which School should have precedence in order to imagine where such a discussion can lead.

It is undisputed, however, that Florence and Venice – drawing on different intellectual and formal sources – produced the two most important schools of painting of the Italian Renaissance, so that a distribution of all Italian painting over two charts would have been quite justifiable. The other schools are always stylistically orientated to one or the other of these two schools, with some exceptions for which here, too, this coarse screening is inadequate.

In making an art-historical assessment of the various schools, both contemporary taste and also the respective authority of outstanding art critics have played an important role. Of course, this also applies to the œuvre of individual painters, of whom even the most famous have been subject to shifts in taste over the centuries. This applies just as much to Raphael (plates 41, 50, 51, 52) as it does to Pontormo (pl. 18) or Correggio.

As already indicated above, there is not always agreement among art historians over the classification of certain masters. Carlo Crivelli is just as much part the Venetian School as of the Paduan School, or that of the Marches. In the case of the painter families of the Bembi or Campi, it is debatable who should appear in the Lombard chart and who in the Bolognese chart. The same is true for the Boccaccini (pl. 73), who, depending on the point of view, are assigned to Venice, Bologna or Lombardy. Antonio Allegri, who was from Correggio and who became famous under that name, is often classified to the Lombard School, or to the 'Lombard School of Parma', while Piero della Francesca (pl. 10) is caught between art-historical fronts merely because of his place of birth, San Sepolcro, on the border between Tuscany and Umbria. Leonardo (plates 1, 12, 13), born in Vinci in Tuscany and trained in Florence, was not only influenced by the local painting there but was also formatively influenced during his long stay in Milan in such a way that it would also have been possible to integrate him into the Lombard chart. Occasionally, art historians make do with attributes such as *Roman-Tuscan* or *Umbro-Florentine*, the latter used particularly in connection with Piero della Francesca, Luca Signorelli (pl. 11) and Melozzo da Forlì (pl. 85). The master's style is not more precisely defined in this way; it indicates, rather, the difficulty of accurate classification. The more famous an artist became, the more willing local researchers were to lay claim to him, lending more weight to the length of his stay in their own city than to questions of formative training and stylistic breadth. Naturally, it is not possible to assign the Bellini (plates 23, 24) to the School of Padua merely because they worked there for some years; similarly, one would hardly count Lorenzo Lotto (pl. 32) as a member of the Venetian School just because he died in the Marches. However, in the case of Baldasare Peruzzi or Civerchio, the subtleties involved are of little consequence in terms of the scope of this handbook, which in particular is intended to show lines of interdependence and influence, and is not concerned with pigeon-holing the artists on stylistic grounds. Because of the regional information given in the tabular index, the question of whether Peruzzi should be represented in chart V (Lombardy) or III (Umbria, Marches), and Civerchio in chart VIII (Brescia) or V (Lombardy) does not make it more difficult to locate these artists. Moreover, where their

artistic formation took place, and where they worked or were influential, is in any case made plain.

The following criteria were crucial for the classification made here: a) traditional, undisputed affiliation to a school and/or distinct association with a stylistic tradition; b) place of formative painterly training; c) location of own workshop/local sphere of influence; and d), distinct stylistic dependence on individual painters. As a rule, the place of birth plays only a minor role. Rather, the inclusion of the place of birth in the tabular index is principally an indication that the artist was not born in the region of the school of painting to which he undisputedly belongs. For example, Domenico Veneziano is counted as one of the outstanding artists of the Tuscan School; likewise, Giovanni da Milano is counted as a member of the Tuscan School (Giotto circle (pl. 2) and T. Gaddi), and not of the Lombard School, as his name might imply. In contrast, Jacobello del Fiore, whose name is indicative of a Venetian origin, is correctly found in the Venetian chart.

Where it serves clarity and seems justified on the grounds of manifold influences, some artists have been included in different charts (e.g., Carlo Crivelli in charts II and IV). This has been taken into account in the tabular index.

The Italian Schools of Painting

The combination of the Sienese and Florentine Schools in one chart is justified both on the basis of their strong interdependence and also by the fact that an independent Renaissance School barely developed in Siena, in contrast to the outstanding role that this city played in the painting of the Trecento. This is hardly changed even by the outstanding achievements of Matteo di Giovanni (*La Maestà*; *Adoration of the Shepherds*, both in the Pinacoteca Nationale, Siena), Benvenuto di Giovanni or Francesco di Giorgio Martini (*Coronation of the Virgin*, Pinacoteca Nazionale, Siena), nor by the brief appearance of the great Sodoma, who kept a workshop there from 1506. By contrast, the Sienese painting of the Late Gothic (Simone Martini, both Lorenzetti) had a great influence on Florentine masters, as can clearly be seen in the intricate network of interrelationships in the uppermost part of chart I. The fusion of the Sienese style – endowed with grace, soft outline and sweet colouring – with the self-confident and realism-directed painting of the Florentines (Taddeo Gaddi, Andrea Orcagna), taking Giotto as a point of departure, paved the way for Renaissance painting in Tuscany (Giotto: *St Francis Cycle* in the Upper Church of Assisi; *frescoes in the Scrovengi Chapel*, Padua). In the Quattrocento, Florence took the lead and produced painters whose influence extended beyond Tuscan borders. Here, the transition from the Middle Ages to modern times, from Gothic to Renaissance, took place earlier than it did elsewhere.

Masaccio (pl. 3), with his *frescoes in the Brancacci Chapel* (S. Maria del Carmine, Florence) begun by his tutor, Masolino, bridged the gap between Giotto and Michelangelo. On the basis of deep religious feeling, Fra Angelico, still drawing from the Sienese heritage, produced works of tender intimacy. Reserved in his depiction of strong movement, and using the finest outline and a softly luminous colouring, he was able to achieve nuances of feeling that few after him would ever match. The *frescoes in the monastery of S. Marco* (Florence) are considered among the greatest artistic treasures of the Tuscan capital. His painterly interpretation is still echoed in the pictures of Fra Filippo Lippi where, however, they are enriched with an element of genre and, in part, a somewhat coarse type of human figure in which we can perhaps recognize a profanation of the figures created by Masaccio (*Coronation of the Virgin*, *Madonna and Child with Saints*, Uffizi; *Adoration of the Magi*, London, N.G.). We find the Madonnas of Filippo (*Madonna and Child with St John*, London, N.G.) in the fantastic world of his pupil, Sandro Botticelli, yet the tender sentimentality that emanates from Botticelli's female figures, their unearthly grandeur, projecting aloofness, makes them unmistakable highlights of a highly poetic art (*Madonna of the Pomegranate*, *Madonna of the Magnificat*, *Annunciation*, Uffizi). We again encounter Filippo's *Madonna* type in Botticelli's allegorical representations (*Birth of Venus*, *Pallas Athene and the Centaur*, *La Primavera*, Uffizi), in which an indefinable sadness is present even in otherwise cheerful themes. These pictures have occasionally made us forget that Botticelli was a very pious man on whom Savonarola's heart-stirring sermons made a profound impression. The powerful modelling of his male figures reveals his contacts with the workshop of Verrocchio (*Coronation of the Virgin*, Uffizi). Filippino Lippi, the son of his tutor Filippo Lippi, is regarded as the greatest pupil that Sandro's workshop produced, and nowhere can the interplay of artistic tradition and independent subsequent development be better seen than in the works of these three masters. Especially revealing in this respect is a study of Filippino's *Madonna Enthroned with Saints* in the Uffizi and the *Madonna and Child Enthroned with SS Martin and Catherine of Alexandria* in S. Spirito (Florence).

Essential characteristics of Tuscan painting crystallize in the work of Piero della Francesca: command of form, a tendency towards scientific precision, measuredness in expression and movement and restraint in colouring. Piero's influence can be felt not only in Tuscany, but also in the neighbouring schools of Umbria, Bologna, and Ferrara, his *frescoes in S. Francesco* (Arezzo) in particular serving as a model for several generations of painters to come (Michelangelo, too, took inspiration from them). He embodies a direction in Tuscan art that made great progress in the quest for technical perfection in perspective, treatment of light and anatomical accuracy. Also beginning with sculptors such as Lorenzo Ghiberti and Donatello, and continuing with Uccello, Piero, Castagno (whose figures, which look like painted sculptures, are nevertheless full of dramatic movement and natural posture), the Pollaiuolo brothers (who were exemplary in their depiction of the naked body in particular), Verrocchio (*Tobias and the Angel*, London, N.G.), and Luca Signorelli, right up to Michelangelo, this direction represents the attempt by Renaissance artists to link up with the tradition of Classical antiquity. Signorelli represents this interpretation the most consistently, his figures distinguished from those of his tutor Piero by a still more distinct plasticity and increased movement (*Crucifixion with Mary Magdalene*, Uffizi). His tondi, *Virgin and Child* and *Holy Family*, both likewise in the Uffizi, may also have inspired Michelangelo's famous *Doni Tondo* (Uffizi). Parallel to this an idealistic

direction asserted itself, thematically drawing more from Classical mythology and reflected in the work of Botticelli and Piero di Cosimo in particular (*Death of Procris*, London, N.G.; *Perseus Frees Andromeda*, Uffizi).

The pictures of Domenico Ghirlandaio and his large workshop are convincing by way of their exemplary composition and an endearingly faithful reproduction of detail. While Domenico's saints are nearly always lacking in expression (*Adoration of the Magi* and *Madonna and Child with Saints*, both in the Uffizi), his portrait art is exquisite. (Who does not know the touching *Portrait of an Old Man and a Boy* – the old man with a bulbous nose – in the Louvre?) Domenico greatly influenced his contemporaries with his *frescoes in the Sasetti Chapel* (S. Trinità, Florence) and his *wall paintings in the S. Maria Novella* (Florence).

Leonardo da Vinci's training in the workshop of the highly sophisticated and versatile Verocchio is only in part an explanation for the diverse influences that determined his artistic formation. Leonardo's always inquisitive eye, his scientific sense and his love of nature – something that was far from being a matter of course at the time – led him in a direction which no-one had marked out before him, but which many generations of painters after him would follow. His painterly œuvre, of which only little has come down to us, cannot be adequately dealt with here, but its impacts and his vision deserve to be emphasized in terms of the interrelationship structures within the Italian School. For us, da Vinci's name is associated in particular with the portrait of the *Mona Lisa* in the Louvre and the *Last Supper* in the Refectory of the Santa Maria delle Grazie monastery in Milan. For his contemporaries, however, every work that Leonardo completed (*Virgin of the Rocks*, Louvre and London, N.G.), or even left uncompleted (*Adoration of the Magi*, Uffizi; *Battle of Anghiari*; *equestrian monument of Francesco Sforza*) was regarded as an artistic revelation. Moreover, the fact that no doubts were ever expressed about his outstanding ability – despite his tardiness, pigheadedness and repeatedly criticized unreliability – was testimony not only to his genius, but also to the ability of his time to recognize such genius. Among the Florentine painters who are unmistakably dependent on Leonardo are in particular Lorenzo Credi, Fra Bartolommeo, Andrea del Sarto (pl. 16), Pontormo and, in later years, Ridolfo Ghirlandaio. All of these have taken much from him in terms of design, treatment of light and landscape interpretation. Piero di Cosimo (*Death of Procris*, London, N.G.), too, is more indebted to Leonardo than to his own tutor, Cosimo Roselli. Through Andrea del Sarto, who was able to combine the Leonardesque *sfumato* with an even more joyful colour rendering (*Madonna and Child Enthroned with SS Francis and John the Evangelist*, Uffizi; *Disputation on the Trinity*, Pitti), and his pupil Rosso Fiorentino (*Moses Defending the Daughters of Jethro*, Uffizi), the legacy of the great master extended as far as the School of Fontainebleau. Leonardo's impact on Lombard painting is made clear in chart V.

A graphic representation can do as little justice to Michelangelo's stylistically formative influence as it can to Leonardo's. We may assume that all subsequent generations of painters, going as far back as the Schools of Venice and Milan, were more or less strongly influenced by both these extraordinary artistic figures, or by their painterly and sculptural œuvre. The charts should also be studied with this in mind. In these, an influence by Leonardo or Michelangelo has been indicated only when it is particularly strongly expressed in an artist's œuvre. In the case of Michelangelo, it was the *ceiling frescoes in the Sistine Chapel* (Vatican), dating from between 1508 and 1512, and also his sculptural works (*David*, 1501–04, *Medici Tombs*, 1521–34) that showed the way for many of his contemporaries. Not only a circle of admiring young painters, but also the aesthetic sensibilities of open-minded clients, took their cues from Leonardo's *Virgin of the Rocks* and *Anna Selbdritt*. It is characteristic that his cartoon for the *Battle of Anghiari*, for the wall painting of the Palazzo Vecchio (not executed), was divided up, and, even in his lifetime, the individual sections were treated as precious collector's pieces.

After a stay in Venice, Fra Bartolommeo, who for a time kept a workshop with his friend Albertinelli (pl. 7), fused a style of painting influenced by Credi and Leonardo with what he had learned from Bellini. Later, he produced the atmospheric altarpieces in which he was successfully able to combine Bellinesque design, Venetian colouring and Leonardo's *sfumato* (*Mystic Marriage of St Catherine of Siena*, Accademia, Florence; *Lamentation of Christ with SS Peter and Paul*, Pitti, Florence). Of Mariotto Albertinelli's pictures, the best-known is probably the *Visitation* in the Uffizi which, with its magnificent design and warm colouring, became a model for many depictions of the same theme by other painters.

Jacopo Pontormo, too, spent time in the workshops of Albertinelli and Bartolommeo. However, he probably spent the greatest part of his apprenticeship with Andrea del Sarto. He synthesized the examples of Leonardo and Michelangelo to produce his own 'expressionistic' style, which, with its ecstatically elongated figures, recalls El Greco (*Supper at Emmaus*, Uffizi; *The Legend of the Ten Thousand Martyrs*, Pitti). Pontormo is perhaps wrongly counted as one of the Mannerists, for the eclectic element in his pictures always remains the instrumentation of a highly unconventional and independent art.

Agnolo Bronzino, trained and fostered by the serious and deeply introspective Pontormo, also has his place in the circle of the Mannerists. In particular, his Court portraits, painted in a distanced fashion, stand out among the works of his rich œuvre. In their interpretation and painterly subtlety, they have become unmistakable examples of his art (*portraits of Piero and Cosimo I de Medici*, London, N.G.; *Eleonora of Toledo and her Son*, Uffizi; *Deposition from the Cross*, Palazzo Vecchio, Florence). Bronzino's influence on Alessandro and Cristofano Allori (pl. 20) is similarly immense. Alessandro, much in demand as a church painter, reveals all the characteristics of the Late Renaissance in his paintings. He is of lesser artistic importance than his son, Cristofano, whose *Judith with the Head of Holofernes* (Pitti) counts as one of the most famous paintings from the turn of the Seicento in Florence. The essential formal elements of the Tuscan Renaissance again assert themselves in the transition to the Baroque, in spite of the Venetian colouring: assured, centrally orientated design, marked contours and a well-considered outline.

Among the Mannerists, Giorgio Vasari, founder of the Uffizi and author of the famous artists' biographies, also had a far-reaching impact. With his all-round training at many different locations, he left an extensive body of frescoes and paintings which nevertheless hardly concealed the lesser-valued qualities of the later style, such as imitation, exaggeration and occasional carelessness in execution. However, it should also be remembered that he executed many commissions, for example for the *decoration of the Palazzo Vecchio* in Florence, with the help of a large number of assistants. Among Vasari's many assistants were in particular Candido, B. Buontalenti, and also Jacopo Zucchi, who in his colour and careful draughtsmanship approached Vasari's style very closely (*Circumcision*, fresco in San Silvestro al Quirinale, Rome). Vasari also had a considerable influence on Bronzino's pupil Santi di Tito, who counts as one of the more important masters of the Tusco-Roman School. He excelled in his rich architectures and carefully chosen perspectives, yet the hands in his pictures are more expressive than the faces, a trait that he has in common with most Late Renaissance artists (*Depos-*ition from the Cross with John the Baptist, St Catherine and the Commissioner Baldassare Suarez*, Accademia, Florence).

As a pupil of Santi di Tito and an imitator of Correggio, the versatile Lodovico Cigoli carried over many of the achievements of the Renaissance into a new age. The decrees of the Council of Trent (1545–64), directed amongst other things against the intellectualization of sacral art and excesses of courtly and decorative elements therein, were ultimately also reflected in the wishes of the ecclesiastical clients. In religious painting, narrative content again came to dominate over decorative depictions of biblical events that were iconographically hedged by clauses and picturesque, sometimes unconventional interpretations of theological statements. The pictures by Cigoli (*Sacrifice of Isaac*; *Ecce homo*, both Pitti) and his contemporaries Jacopo Chimenti, Francesco Vanni, Francesco Salviati, Jacopo Empoli, Gregorio Pagani and others must be seen in this context. Set in diagonal or tortuous compositions, their saints occupy unreal spaces that no longer have any visible point of reference. Ever-richer colours and limbs modelled with light and shade stand out against a dark background (L. Cigoli: *Deposition from the Cross*, Pitti; Alessandro Allori: *Christ and the Adulteress*, S. Spirito, Florence; Jacopo da Empoli: *St Ivo*, Pitti). With renewed strength, Rome now attracted artists from all Italian schools and regions. For the majority of the painters, this contributed through mutual artistic enrichment, stylistic adaptation and the formation of a complex network of mutual interdependencies to an obliteration of individual characteristics and those typical of the schools. In the years that followed, only the truly great masters retained a distinctiveness in their style that raised them above the masses and enabled them to produce an unmistakable painting legacy.

This chart comprises the schools of painting of the Republic of Venice, except for those of Padua, Verona, and Brescia, each of which is dealt with in a separate chart. Despite the extensive geographic region that it covers, the Venetian School, including the centres of Venice, Treviso, Vicenza, Bergamo, Udine and Bassano, to mention only the most important, gives a more uniform impression than the Tuscan School. There are at least two reasons for this, the second possibly being due to the first. On the one hand, the centralist structure of the Venetian polity automatically substantiated Venice's role as a cultural centre. Even established masters from the more remote corners of the Republic could only be sure of their fame if they had been able to assert themselves in the metropolis, and had taken on commissions there. The unique city, whose inhabitants tended towards sensuality and displays of pomp, and who above all adored splendour and beauty while despising ugliness and disharmony, had no difficulties in attracting masters from the provinces. And those few artists who found the strength to leave Venice after a stay there left changed by comparison with what they were upon their arrival, taking with them something that made them unmistakably *Venetian* from then on.

The stylistic coherence of the Venetian School is also due to something else, however: a chain of ingenious masters (some of whom lived to a very great age), who, in a continual development of tradition and with an assured appropriation of everything new, ensured that the painterly tradition remained uninterrupted over 150 years. It will never be possible to say for sure whether the line of *immediate* influence that extends from Bellini via Giorgione (plates 27, 28) and Titian, right up to Tintoretto (plates 33, 34), is responsible for the self-contained nature of this School, or if, on the other hand, it was the unity of the painterly interpret-

ation, the rapid assimilation of innovations from other schools and the unchallenged position of Venice as a political and cultural centre that was ultimately responsible for this string of pearls of artistic tradition.

Venetian painting addresses our sense of beauty more than our intellect. It revels in colours and forms, avoids hard contours and harsh contrasts and, contrary to the slightly mannered Tuscans, it is imbued with a refreshing, unaffected naturalism.

Venice freed itself from the Gothic-Byzantine tradition much later than Florence. The luminous Venetian colour already shines forth from the pictures of Paolo Veneziano; the first attempts at characterization can be found in his faces, but the dark, iconic flesh tone still reveals his proximity to Byzantine art (*polyptych: Coronation of the Virgin*, Accademia, Venice). In his pupil, Lorenzo Venetino, we first encounter stylistic elements of the International Gothic and distinct borrowings from Emilian examples, to which his use of naturalistic motifs can probably be traced (*Polyptych of the Annunciation with SS Anthony Abbas, John the Baptist, Paul and Peter; Annunciation with St John the Baptist, Gregory, Jacob and Stephen*, both Accademia, Venice).

Gentile da Fabriano (pl. 42) influenced Venice from a completely different direction. The merits of his pupil Jacopo Bellini lie less in his painterly abilities than in his openness to new ideas and techniques. His temporary collaboration in Padua with Squarcione, who was similarly inclined, is therefore not surprising. He transmitted his adventurous artistic sense to his sons Gentile and Giovanni, the latter laying the foundation for everything that characterizes the Venetian School today. The Vivarini, too, the outstanding representatives of the Murano School of painting, were led on to their path by external factors. Antonio Vivarini shows the influences of Masolino and Uccello in his figures, and also experimented with perspective and imaginative architectures (*Triptych:*

Virgin and Child with SS Jerome and Gregory, Ambrose and Augustine, Accademia, Venice). His son, Bartolommeo (pl. 22), softened the earnest dignity of his saintly figures with a move towards sentimentality and a portraiture that was directed towards individuality (*Polyptych for the Arte dei Tagliapietra*, Accademia, Venice). Bartolommeo is certainly the most remarkable offspring of the Vivarini artistic family. However, by contrast with his peer Giovanni Bellini (also Giambellino), he never entirely renounced the Byzantine tradition.

However, this tradition also lies hidden and dormant in the early work of Giambellino. Anyone who can visualize Byzantine icons of the Virgin will recognize them in Giovanni's *Madonnas* – robbed of their gold background or silver mounting – as the sublime of pure humanity from the depiction of saints become ritual (*Madonna with Blessing Child*; *Madonna of the Little Tree*, both Accademia, Venice). In Giovanni Bellini's painting, the influence over the years of his brother-in-law, Mantegna, is reflected more clearly than that of Antonello da Messina, who was in Venice only briefly (plates 25, 26) (*Virgin Annunciate)*, Museo Nazionale, Palermo; *Portrait of a Man* known as *The Condottiere*, Louvre), even though some of Giovanni's portraits are unimaginable without the ingenious Sicilian's example (*Portrait of Doge Loredan*, London, N.G.; *Portrait of a Venetian Nobleman*, Washington, Kress Collection, N.G.). While his brother Gentile (*Legend of the True Cross*, Accademia, Venice), no less famous in his time, was hardly influential, and his reputation is due to his (in terms of city history) revealing, large-format *vedute* and historical scenes, Giovanni absorbed influences from Padua and the north (Dürer), and developed an independent style in the last decade of the fifteenth century. This style, liberated from Mantegna's (plates 55, 57, 58, 59) severity, with its mild beauty and compositional balance, was a formative influence on Venetian painting from then on, attaining perfection in the

works of Titian (*Lamentation of Christ with Joseph of Arimathea, Madonna, Mary Magdalene and Filippo Benizzi*, Accademia, Venice; *Calvary*, Louvre; *Agony in the Garden*, London, N.G.). Giovanni lived to a great age, and his workshop produced many gifted artists. The greatest of these was Giorgione da Castelfranco who, in his short life, had a profound influence on more than just the master himself and Venetian painting. Even during his lifetime, he was considered to have been the first to accommodate the aesthetic wishes of secular clients. In so doing, he no longer treated the landscape as a mere background for religious or mythological scenes, but instead discovered its potential as an independent subject for depiction in painting (*Tempest*, Accademia, Venice; *Three Philosophers*, Kunsthistorisches Museum, Vienna). Art historians have ascribed to him only a few pictures (some of which are still disputed), which today are among the most precious of museum treasures.

Before we study Giorgione's immediate heirs, Titian, Palma Vecchio (pl. 31), and Lorenzo Lotto, we should briefly examine some of Bellini's other pupils. Bartolommeo Cincani – called Montagna (pl. 35) – was convincingly able to insert human figures into architectural spaces with well-designed perspective (*St Magdalene between SS Hieronymus, Paul, Monica and Augustine*, S. Corona, Vicenza; *Blessing St Peter with a Donor*, Accademia, Venice; *St Zeno, John the Baptist and a Martyr*, London, N.G.). He is harsher than his tutor in his outline and modelling, and J. Burckhardt once described him as "rather sullen". The same applies to Giovanni Battista Cima (pl. 36), who nevertheless greatly surpasses Montagna. His *Madonna* pictures, with their picturesque landscape backgrounds, are completely imbued with Giambellino's spirit and are not always easy to distinguish from the latter's paintings. Where Bellini seems pensive and contemplative, however, Cima is terribly earnest; his *Madonnas* never smile (*Madonna of the Orange Tree*,

Accademia, Venice; *Madonna and Child*, *Incredulity of Thomas*, both London, N.G.).

Vincenzo Catena (actually Biagio) remained close to the painting style of his tutor; influences from Giorgione and Titian are recognizable only in his later pictures. He left an extensive œuvre that brought him fame and prosperity in his own lifetime (*St Hieronymus in the Study*, *Holy Family with a Warrior Adoring the Infant Christ*, both London, N.G.; *Supper at Emmaus*, Accademia, Venice). Less important is his co-pupil of roughly the same age, Andrea Previtali, who faithfully imitated his mentors Bellina and Cima without, however, showing much inventive spirit in his composition (*Virgin and Child with Donor* and *Salvator Mundi*, both London, N.G.). Marco Basaiti is of the same generation, and trained under both Giovanni Bellini and Alvise Vivarini. In particular, his atmospheric landscapes should be mentioned, of which the *Calling of the Sons of Zebediah* in the Accademia in Venice gives a good impression.

In addition to the Bellini and Vivarini, Carlo Crivelli, originally from the Marches, also worked in Venice, having trained under both Squarcione in Padua as well as the masters of Murano. Both workshops are evident in his peculiar œuvre, which stands somewhat in isolation. We have already encountered the powerful, controlled faces of his saints in the work of Antonio Vivarini (*SS Peter and Paul*, London, N.G.), while the graphic modelling and his favoured use of intricately ornamented pilaster and arches for the division of space recall Mantegna (*Annunciation*, London, N.G.; *Coronation of the Virgin with Saints*, Brera, Milan). Completely his own are the garlands of fruit that frame his *Madonnas*, but, above all, a careful painting technique that make his paintings look like precious enamel works (*Madonna and Child*, Washington, N.G.; *Immaculate Conception*, London, N.G.).

Via the line of Giambellino-Montagna, we encounter Francesco da Ponte the Elder, founder of the renowned artistic dynasty that made famous the name of its native city Bassano beyond the borders of the Veneto. Its most outstanding representative, Jacopo Bassano (pl. 39), added a new element to the Venetian School with his naive, pastoral scenes. Already mannered in the depiction of his saints and shepherds, he was able, owing to his precise observation of nature, to produce atmospheric, harmonious images in which the lovingly reproduced animal world in particular counteracted any impression of contrivance (*Two Hunting Dogs*, Uffizi; *Adoration of the Shepherds*, Accademia, Venice). Of Jacopo's four sons, Leandro is more deserving of mention than his brother, Francesco the Younger.

Titian owes his unchallenged position at the centre of the Venetian School not only to his genius, but also to his long life. His alleged year of birth, 1477, should probably be brought forward by twelve years if it is to correspond with other details of his life. In particular, a tutor-pupil relationship between the Castelfranco master Giorgione and Titian, which goes as far back as a mutual period in the Giambellino workshop, would be almost inconceivable if both were of the same age. Moreover, Titian, who had a high opinion of himself, never made a secret of his admiration for Giorgione and the latter's influence on his own formation. Even without this admission, his dependence on Giorgione until around 1515 is clearly evident in his work (*Concert Champêtre*, Pitti, Florence). Nevertheless, Titian never attained the fantastic splendour of Giorgione's landscapes, nor was he able to surpass him in terms of the exquisiteness of his interpretation. With his *Assumption* in the Frari Church in Venice, Titian freed himself from his mentor for the first time, and was able to attain a conception that anticipated the essential design characteristics of the Baroque. In the 1530s, Titian won the friendship of the Emperor, of whom, in the years that followed, he was to paint some of the most impressive sovereign portraits that we know (*Charles V at Mühlberg*, Prado; *Portrait of Charles V*,

Pinakothek, Munich). Two generations of painters, and not those just of the Venetian School, took their cues from his portraits of women (*Flora*, Uffizi; *La Bella*, Pitti Palace, Florence), while his mythological scenes feature an animation and splendour of colour to which the Baroque can add only little (*Bacchus and Ariadne*, London, N.G.). His later works bear witness to a deep-seated break with familiar painting technique. Eschewing any definite contouring, the elderly Titian now designed his pictorial themes using only patches of light and colour that shine forth out of dark shadows and lend highly dramatic accents to the handling (*Christ Crowned with Thorns*, Louvre and Pinakothek, Munich; *Pietà*, Accademia, Venice).

Only one artist challenged Titian's position in his time. After a period in Rome, Giovanni Antonio de Sacchis (called Pordenone), from Pordenone in Friuli, delighted Venetians with his frescoes in the style of Raphael and Michelangelo. Yet he, too, later succumbed to Titian's influence (*Noli me tangere*, Cathedral, Cividale del Friuli; *Disputa di S. Caterina*, S. Maria di Campagna, Piacenza). The other masters of the Friulian School, such as the Grassi, Giovanni da Udine, Gianfrancesco da Tolmezzo, and Pellegrino da San Daniele, never matched Pordenone's ability and had to be satisfied with their role as successors to Giambellino. They are all represented in exemplary fashion in the churches of Friuli.

Palma Vecchio (actually Jacopo Negretti), already mentioned above, and Lorenzo Lotto have in common not only their (occasionally disputed) training under Giovanni Bellini, but also the later unmistakable influence of Titian. Palma, born in Bergamo, always remained bound to his native home and its landscape in his painterly interpretation. Hence, the seeds of Giorgione's inspiration bore fruit in him. In balanced compositions, his figures, enveloped in luminously coloured robes, lie in deep-green landscapes illuminated by warm sunlight (*Sacra Conversazione*, Accademia, Venice; *Adoration of the Shepherds with a Donor*, Louvre).

Palma's preferred blonde, somewhat buxom, female figures became proverbial for his portrait art (*Judith with the Head of Holofernes*, Uffizi; *The Three Sisters*, Gemäldegalerie, Dresden). He had only a few pupils, of whom Bonifazo de' Pitati (called Bonifazio Veronese), however, occupies an outstanding position in the Venetian School. He was unlucky in that his pictures were so similar to Giorgione's and Titian's that they long appeared in galleries under the latter's names. Both the anecdotal elements and also the figures and faces glimmering out of dark corners (typical of his pupil, Jacopo Bassano), are already hinted at in Bonifazio's work (*Feast of the Rich Man*, Accademia, Venice).

Lorenzo Lotto also followed the path indicated by Giorgione; his palette is even richer however, and strives for more powerful contrasts, than that of Palma. His compositions bear witness to a great inventiveness, with biblical events enriched by original ideas and brought closer to us (*Lucia Altar*, Jesi). The so-called *Lucrezia* in London (N.G.) in which he strives to achieve psychological depth, is one of the best known of Lotto's numerous portraits.

Bonifazio was probably also one of the tutors of the last outstanding master of the Venetian Cinquecento, whose training under Titian is disputed (apparently he only stood it for a few days), and his apprenticeship with Paris Bordone (pl. 40) is likewise open to question. Jacopo Robusti, called Tintoretto, may nevertheless have taken from Bordone his gloomy skies and his attempts to achieve spatial depth by means of fantastic architectural constructions (compare Bordone's *Presentation of the Ring to the Doge* with Tintoretto's *Removal of the Body of St Mark*, both in the Accademia), though he remained faithful to Titian (colour) and Michelangelo (draughtsmanship) in particular throughout his œuvre. Michelangelesque plasticity is even more distinct in his paintings with mythological themes (*Venus, Vulcan and Mars*, Pinakothek, Munich; *Ariadne and Bacchus*, Accademia, Venice) than in his works of religious content (*Christ Washing the Feet of the Disciples*, London, N.G.). Foreboding skies, harsh light reflections, fluttering garments and wildly animated figures, often spread over giant picture spaces in surging masses (e.g. *Paradise* in the Doge's Palace in Venice), produce a sense of drama that leaves no viewer unmoved (cf. also the decoration of the *Scuola Grande di San Rocco* in Venice). Tintoretto is the Expressionist among the Venetians. El Greco was never able to disclaim his apprenticeship with this outstanding painter.

Cima's pupil Sebastiano Luciani (pl. 38), later famous under the name of Sebastiano del Piombo, occupies an exceptional position in the Venetian School. Greatly influenced by his tutor, Giorgione, whose legacy he took with him to Rome, he may be regarded as one of those who inspired Raphael towards a more intensive use of colour. After quarrelling with Raphael, he became enthusiastic about Michelangelo, to whom he is greatly indebted but whom he nevertheless never imitated. He was much too self-centred to lose himself completely to others. Hence, despite leaning heavily towards the greats of his time, he was able to achieve individual greatness in his work (*Fornarina*, Uffizi; *Pietà*, Viterbo; *Martyrdom of St Agatha*, Pitti).

We must finally mention Jacopo Palma, called il Giovane to distinguish him from his great-uncle. He is represented in many churches in Venice (e.g., *Messa di Pasquale Cigogna*, Oratorio di Crociferi; *ceiling frescoes* in San Giovanni Paolo; *Betrothal of St Catherine*, Frari Church, and many others). His extensive œuvre identifies him as a typical eclectic, but also as a painter of great ability. He drew unhesitatingly from the works of Giorgione, Titian, and Tintoretto, without ever adding anything of his own stylistically.

III UMBRIA, MARCHES

The Umbrian and Tuscan Schools should always be viewed in connection with one another. It was Florentine and Sienese artists who decorated San Francesco in Assisi and who served local painters as an example in the fourteenth century. Even in the first half of the fifteenth century, it was the Florentines Domenico Veneziano (*Madonna and Child Enthroned with SS Francis, John the Baptist, Zenobius and Lucy*, Uffizi) and Piero della Francesca who executed commissions in Perugia for the ruling families. Allegretto Nuzi and Gentile da Fabriano, from the Marches, had an influence on the slowly-forming School of Perugia.

With his *Adoration of the Magi* (Uffizi), Gentile di Nicolò Massi, called Gentile da Fabriano after his native town, produced a Renaissance picture at a time when the Gothic Age was still in full flower among his contemporaries (Agnolo Gaddi, Lorenzo Monaco) and those who came after him (Jacobello del Fiore). He worked in Venice (unfortunately, his frescoes in the Doge's Palace were destroyed in the great fire of 1577), Florence, Siena, Orvieto, and Rome, and had considerable influence on the arts of those cities. There are clear indications of an influence from the north in his *Adoration* (1420–23). We cannot, however, rule out the possibility that this may have been the master's independent achievement, his genius forming parallel to that of van Eyck and, far removed from the latter, developing in a completely independent manner. Whatever the case, Gentile's status as one of the truly great Italian masters remains uncontested.

However, the early masters of the School of Perugia were most influenced by the Florentine Benozzo Gozzoli (pl. 43; for this reason also included in chart III), who steered the tradition of Fra Angelico towards the Umbrian School, and who must be considered one of their early points of crystallization. Benozzo's most important work is considered to be the frescoes in the chapel of the Medici-Ricardi Palace in Florence; his *Medici family as the Magi* includes depictions of famous members of the House of the Medici. The painters whom he trained and influenced include in particular Bene-detto Bonfigli (pl. 44), Bartolommeo Caporale (pl. 46), Nicolò da Foligno (called Alunno) and, not least, Fiorenzo di Lorenzo (pl. 47). Only in Florence, how-ever, did the native masters Pietro Vanucci – called Perugino (plates 48, 49) – and his pupil, Raffaelo Santi, develop into the artistic personalities to whom they would owe their future status in the world of art. From the manifold influences of the neighbouring artistic regions, these grand masters of the older School developed an independent Umbrian style that is typically expressed in the pictures of, in particular, Benedetto Bonfigli and Fiorenzo (*Adoration of the Shepherds*, Galleria Nazio-nale, Perugia). In these, Fra Angelico's intimacy and tenderness are combined with Benozzo's somewhat upright narrative tone to produce endearing, slightly old-fashioned representations (Bonfigli was a con-temporary of Mantegna after all – see also Bonfigli's *Adoration of the Magi* in Perugia), with almost exclusively religious themes.

Fra Angelico's Madonnas are not far from our minds when we contemplate Bonfigli's *Polyptych of the Dominicans* or his *Annunciation with St Luke*, both in the Galleria Nazionale in Perugia. In Giovanni Boccati's early work, too (including the *Madonna del pergolato* in Perugia, pl. 45), there are unmistakable echoes of Fra Angelico and Filippo Lippi, while he later leaned towards Paduan models and probably also Domenico Veneziano as well (*Madonna dell'Or-chestra*, Galleria Nazionale, Perugia). The influences from Gentile da Fabriano – which were probably due to the intercession of Ottaviano Nelli – are pronounced in the drawing of the garments and in his landscapes, but less so in his figures and physiognomic aspects. Nicolò da Foligno seems less bound to the Gothic than Boccati and Caporale, whose saints, with their marked nimbuses – Boccati liked to paint them from an oblique angle, so that they hung golden above the heads of his saints and *Madonnas* – often look odd in the already Classical

architectural spaces, even though, in a decorative sense, he had also not yet overcome the discrepancy between Gothic tracery and Classical moulding (cf. *Gonfalone dei Legisti*, Galleria Nazionale, Perugia). He managed to surpass his tutor in terms of his expression, movement and treatment of light. The sense of genre and child-like trust in God that we see in the pictures of the Umbrian School are absent in those of the solemn Alunno, but not, however, in those of Fiorenzo. Initially still under the influence of his tutor Benozzo, he became open to the anatomical 'achievements' of Signorelli and the Pol-laiuoli brothers (*St Sebastian*, Galleria Nazionale, Perugia). In her delicate, youthful beauty, the *Ma-donna* in his *Adoration of the Shepherds* surpasses all of Perugino's depictions of the Virgin, as well as a number of Raphael's.

Pietro Perugino's training under Fiorenzo has not been substantiated, and seems doubtful given their difference in age. Nevertheless, a certain affinity with Fiorenzo is recognisable in his nude depictions and in certain physiognomic characteristics. Perugino essentially owes his artistic formation to periods in Florence. Even when his role as assistant in Verrocchio's workshop has likewise not been documented (unless we treat Vasari's claim in this respect as proof), there can be no doubts as to a profound influence by this famous master and his entourage. With his fresco of the *Christ Giving the Keys to St Peter* in the Sistine Chapel, Perugino produced one of his masterpieces in which the virtues, but also the weaknesses, of his art are shown. A grand design of space that draws the eye into its depths is counteracted by the unnatural, dance-like postures of the individual figures, whose expressionless faces reveal hardly any participation in the events. Anyone who seeks movement, strong feelings and restrained inner excitement will hardly find these in Perugino's saints, who look more apathetic than pensive (*Assumption of the Virgin*, Accademia, Florence). Fantasy and empathy were probably unable to compensate fully for his lack of faith. Pietro's portraits are impressive however, as are his landscapes, which mirror his Umbrian native land (*Francesco dell' Opere*, Uffizi; *Self-portrait*, Galleria Borghese; *Vision of St Bernard*, Pinakothek, Munich).

From his place of birth near Urbino, the versatile 'man of the world' Donato Angelo (called Bramante) is to be found in the Umbria/Marches chart. He worked in Milan and Rome, where he became famous as the architect of St Peter's. He is much less important as a painter. His *Christ at the Column* (Brera, Milan) identifies him as a frustrated sculptor, and what he transmitted of this plastic interpretation to his pupil Bramantino (pl. 67) was mitigated under the influence of Leonardo.

Strengths and weaknesses similar to those of his tutor Perugino are shown by Pinturicchio (actually Bernardino di Betto), several years his junior. He was even less concerned with psychological depth and characterization than was Pietro. Whereas Pietro's *Madonnas* and saints still stare into the void in a somewhat dreamy and absent-minded manner, his pupil's figures look away from us without thought. For all that, he fascinates us with a feeling for space and a naive pleasure in narrative which, combined with his preference for magnificent garments and architectures, made him a highly respected artist in Rome (*frescoes in the Borgia Apartments*, Vatican). He proved to be the ideal illustrator of Papal biographies (*frescoes in the Piccolomini Library*, Siena) and Christian legends (*Miracle of St Bernard*, Galleria Nazionale, Perugia).

Of the many artists who directly or indirectly influenced Raffaelo Santi (Raphael) – who was open to innovation – the most important is Perugino. Apart from his father, Giovanni Santi, who owes the preservation of his name more to his son's art than to his own, Raphael's tutor is considered to have been Pietro. He was undoubtedly a great influence on Raphael's initial development (*Betrothal of the Virgin [Lo Sposalizio]*, Brera; *Madonna del Granduca*,

Pitti), but it was only Raphael's contact with Michelangelo and the Venetians in Rome (including Sebastiano del Piombo) that aroused in him the creative strength on which his fame is grounded (*frescoes in the Stanze*, Vatican; *Sistine Madonna*, Gemäldegalerie, Dresden; *Transfiguration*, Pinacoteca Vaticana). Weaker in movement than many of his contemporaries, and by no means profound in his psychological analysis, the greatness of his achievement lies in particular in his grandiose ability in the design of space, and in his sense of beauty. His *Madonnas* (*Madonna della seggiola*; *Madonna del Granduca*, both Pitti), and also his portraits of women (*Donna velata*, Pitti), express the latter especially well. However, we are also indebted to him for his impressive portraits of men, in which his keen eye and precise reproduction of the visually perceptible world also make the more profound aspects apparent (*Pope Leo X*, Uffizi; *Baldassare Castiglione*, Louvre). There is no need to include here the Tommaso Inghirami in the Pitti.

Raphael, who learned from many others and taught many more, is at the centre of the Umbrian chart (chart III), but he is not at the centre of the Umbrian School. This position is more appropriate to Fiorenzo di Lorenzo or Perugino, who always remained Umbrian in spite of their Tuscan dependencies. In a sense, Raphael became a Roman, which at that time in the world of art meant nothing less than cosmopolitan.

Raphael's greatest pupil, friend and heir, Giulio Pippi – called Giulio Romano (pl. 53) – is to be found in chart III, because he carried on the former's tradition rather than because he can be regarded as one of the Umbrian School in a real sense. His early *Madonnas* and those of his tutors are confusingly similar (*Madonna and Child*, Uffizi; *Madonna*, Palazzo Barberini), and yet Giulio is no imitator. The fact that Raphael shines through time and again, despite Giulio's independent, fanciful pictorial inventions, may be due to the meeting of two kindred spirits, with no special energy being required on the part of the stronger, nor a particular willingness on the part of the weaker to form or to be formed. After the death of his friend, Giulio, together with Giovanni Francesco Penni, Raphael's other heir, completed several works by his master before being summoned to the Gonzaga Court. Here, in Mantua, he produced his principal works as an architect (*Palazzo Te*) and as a painter (*frescoes in the Palazzo Ducale and Palazzo Te*). What distinguishes him is his inventive power and Classical education. Despite his great versatility, he is not always satisfying in his execution. His mythological female figures seem lascivious and not particularly distinguished, which does not, however, make them any less attractive. It was from Giulio that European Mannerism took its point of departure.

Only a very few of Raphael's many pupils and assistants were Umbrian. Here, we encounter the core of the painters' circle which – equally influenced by Michelangelo – initiated the notion of the 'Roman School'. As a mediator of the Umbro-Roman tradition, the highly gifted Florentine Perino del Vaga, amongst others, is worthy of mention. After the Sack of Rome by the Imperial *Soldateska* (1527), he moved to Genoa and founded a school of painting there. He was an excellent draughtsman and was also highly regarded for his grotesques and decorations. He retained a stylistic affinity with Michelangelo in his depiction of nudes (*Judgement of Zaleucos*, Uffizi).

The last important master of the Umbrian School, whom Rome was ultimately unable to hold, was Federico Baroccio from Urbino. Venetian trained, influenced by Raphael and an admirer of Michelangelo, he was later profoundly influenced by Correggio. He tried to bring the demands made by ecclesiastical reforms on religious art in line with the painterly principles of Mannerism (*Madonna del popolo*, Uffizi). His gestures are less contrived than those of other Mannerists, and he reinforces the illustrative character of his pictures by a complicated composition that catches the eye of the beholder. Apart from his sacral themes, he also painted exquisite portraits (including *Portrait of Francesco Maria II della Rovere*, Uffizi). Baroccio had a particularly strong influence on Guido Reni, Salimbeni and the Carracci (pl. 92).

IV PADUA

The Paduan School owes its importance to two personalities in particular: the theoretician and organizer, Francesco Squarcione (pl. 56), and his brilliant pupil, Andrea Mantegna. If we were to add a third, it would most deservedly be the Florentine sculptor Donatello (1386–1466), whose work in Padua over many years (*equestrian monument to Gattamelata, high altar in S. Antonio*) had a lasting influence on the art of Mantegna and his counterparts. The academic spirit of the university city of Padua also infected the rather mediocre painter Squarcione (there is a *Virgin and Child* by him in Berlin) and awoke his enthusiasm for Classical antiquity – or at least what he understood by the notion – and perspective. His didactic skill, a keen eye for talent and an unscrupulous business sense led to the founding of a school of painting that in many ways was a formative influence on all Italian Schools of the Quattrocento. Chart IV conveys a distinct impression of this.

Squarcione owned an extensive collection of antiques that served his pupils, notably Andrea Mantegna, as model material. Squarcione had discovered the latter's talent at an early stage, and had probably already adopted him as a ten-year-old. However, when Andrea realized that he was only going to be exploited, he broke with his adoptive father. Together with Nicoletto Pizzolo, an assistant to Fra Filippo, the seventeen-year-old Andrea took on a commission to paint frescoes in the Erimitani Church in Padua (*Overtari Chapel*), which he completed on his own after the violent death of his partner. These frescoes, with scenes from the *Life of St James and Christopher* (largely destroyed in World War II), are regarded as the earliest purely Renaissance work in northern Italy, and made Andrea famous overnight. In his pictures, he combines naive conceptions from Classical antiquity with the plastic realism of Donatello and Uccello's zeal for the correct use of perspective (an extreme example is the *Lamentation of Christ*, Brera, Milan). Severity, an uncompromising attitude and sincerity in Andrea's character are also reflected in his works. He shows a preference for rocky landscapes, in which rugged mountain peaks tower in a steely clear sky, while Classical ruins and meticulously modelled Classical reliefs stand in marked contrast to the alarmingly towering rock formations. His saints look as though they are hewn out of rock, but they are softer and more fluid in outline than those of Castagno, and lack the latter's dramatic movement (*St George*, Accademia, Venice; *Agony in the Garden*, London, N.G.). In his *Madonnas*, however, Mantegna reveals a deep sensitivity that led him to solutions that often move us more than those of Raphael or Titian in their austere truth (*Virgin and Child*, Berlin). The Gonzaga were wise enough to attract him to Mantua, the city to which he owes his reputation, and to which he was to remain faithful for almost fifty years until his death. Of his *frescoes in the Palazzo Ducale*, only the decoration of the *Camera degli sposi* is still well preserved (*Scenes from the Life of Lodovico II Gonzaga*). After the victory of the allies over the French (Fornovo), Andrea painted the *Madonna della Vittoria* (1496) for Francesco II, which, ironically, Napoleon took with him to France, where today it counts among the most precious treasures in the Louvre. Andrea's plastic style was mitigated by the influence of the Bellini, and the occasionally clashing adjacent colours (*Triptych with Adoration of the Child*, *Circumcision of Christ*, and *Ascension*, Uffizi) gave way to a more subdued chromatic harmony (*Parnassus*, Louvre). Already highly regarded and admired in his lifetime, Mantegna has forfeited none of his glory over the centuries. His formative role in Italian painting and his status as one of the greatest masters of the Early Renaissance are undisputed.

Of Squarcione's many pupils and assistants (Vasari mentions 137), most took what they had learned with them into other schools. Other than Mantegna, however, we may clearly number several other Squarcione pupils of above-average ability among the Paduan School. In the case of Marco Zoppo (pl. 60), the influence of the somewhat older Cosmé (Cosimo) Tura (pl. 60), likewise Paduan trained, is unmistakable (cf. *Dead Christ Supported by Saints*, London, N.G.). By contrast with Mantegna, his powerful modelling is more reminiscent of Gothic carving than Classical sculpture. His *Virgin and Child with Angels* (Louvre) moved his interpretation close to that of Crivelli, although he remained inferior to the latter in his picture design and painted detail. Carlo Crivelli, as a pupil of Bartolommeo Vivarini, is often assigned to the Venetian School (see chart II); however, his work is probably more strongly characteristic of his unmistakable Paduan training, expressed in both his meticulous outline and plastic modelling (*Madonna of the Swallow* and *Madonna with SS Francis and Sebastian*, both London, N.G.). Even though Crivelli did not maintain a school of painting in a real sense, his art nevertheless had a considerable influence on the painting of Venice, Umbria and the Marches. In Padua, it was Squarcione's pupil Gregario (Giorgio) Schiavone (pl. 61) in particular who made Crivelli's style of painting his own. Like Crivelli, he showed a preference for flower and fruit garlands, but he never attained the latter's painterly quality (*Virgin and Child*, London, N.G.). He took many ideas from Donatello and his pupils, which, however, was hardly considered reprehensible at the time.

Without Mantegna's genius, neither academic ambition nor Squarcione's mercantile spirit would have been sufficient to raise the status of the Paduan

School above that of the Schools of Lucca or Tolmezzo. Without Squarcione, however, Mantegna probably never would have become a great painter.

V LOMBARDY, PIEDMONT, LIGURIA

What applies to the Roman School of painting effectively applies also to the Milanese School: its truly outstanding representatives were not, in fact, Milanese. Foppa (plates 63, 64) was from Brescia, Bramante from the Marches, Borgogne (pl. 62) from Fossano, and the grand master who was to be a formative influence on Milanese painting from 1485 on – Leonardo da Vinci – was Tuscan. Nevertheless, owing to a remarkable reserve of clever native masters, there was a formation and subsequent development of typical stylistic characteristics throughout the Milanese realm. The sources from which they drew were principally Verona, Padua and Ferrara, until Leonardo's overwhelming influence – which was admittedly not always advantageous – took hold at the beginning of the sixteenth century.

The Milanese School shows a certain preference for grey and brown tones that are often contrasted against a light, turquoise-coloured sky. Especially in early pictures, it is not so much the depth of the picture, as the composition of the space that we seek. We pay great attention to the decoration in stone and material, and richly-structured gold backgrounds are still found in the works of Foppa and Butinone. Under Leonardo's influence, the (Paduan) tendency towards exaggerated plasticity declined, and Bramante's sculptural spirit was superseded by an increased striving towards aesthetic subtlety. Without his genius, Leonardo's successors and imitators remain caught in the representation of what is 'only' charming and 'only' beautiful. This restriction to the 'pretty' (B. Berenson) also becomes a defining characteristic of the later Lombard School.

In the first half of the Cinquecento, northern Italian painting again added a new element to the excessive (although probably heartfelt) aestheticism

of Parmigianino which heralded the arrival of Mannerism.

At the centre of the Lombard School, we find Vincenzo Foppa, who came to Pavia from Brescia in 1456 and did not return to his native home until thirty years later. Together with his ability, a long life, many travels and an extensive œuvre augmented his influence on then-provincial Lombard painting. His style was developed through his contact with Pisanello, Giambellino and Mantegna (compare Mantegna's *Madonna of the Quarries* with Foppa's *Madonna and Child*, both Uffizi). His figures show deportment and vigour, but are inferior to those of Piero della Francesca in their expression. His typical flesh tone, verging on grey, may be a later and unintentional side-effect of his efforts (experiments with colour mixes) to produce new colour effects (*Polyptych: Virgin and Child and the Stigmatization of St Francis*, Brera). Many of Foppa's numerous altarpieces in Milan, Pavia and Genoa are lost. His *decorations in the vestry of S. Maria di Brera* bear witness to his achievements as a frescoist, although time and weathering have been very hard on them. The *Adoration of the Magi* (London, N.G.) falls within the late phase of his œuvre, in which Venetian splendour of colour and meticulous, Paduan-inspired architectural draughtsmanship meet.

Ambrogio da Fossano (called Borgognone) refined the tradition that he adopted from his tutor Foppa, and cultivated the latter's sometimes brash use of colour to produce a silver-toned harmony. His figures are no longer hewn of stone, but are instead modelled by a soft play of light and shadow. His Madonnas are beautiful and have a childlike loveliness; in a later phase, they cannot entirely shake off Leonardo's influence (*Madonna and Sleeping Child*, Brera). All his pictures express a naive piety (*Assumption of the Virgin*, Brera) which, together with an exquisite use of colour and harmonious composition, made him a very endearing painter. Without his loyalty to the tradition of Foppa, the

Lombard School of painting would have become an entirely Leonardo School in the Cinquecento.

Since little of the work of Donato d'Angelo (called Bramante) is still extant, we do not know to what extent he influenced the Lombard School as a painter. His influence on Bernardo Zenale (pl. 65) may have derived from the field of architecture (the latter was also a capable architect), for Bernardo's panel pictures reveal little of Bramante's plastic naturalism. His saints and depictions of the infant Christ often seem somewhat 'sleepy' (*Virgin and Child*, Brera), and the faces of his *Temple Scene* (Brera) are not of very great painterly quality. Consequently, the beautiful panel with the *Madonna and SS Jacob and Phillip with the Donor Family Busti*, also in the Brera, can hardly be ascribed to him.

Bartolommeo Suardi (called Bramantino) is perhaps one of those pupils of Foppa who have lost more than they have gained from Leonardo. In his architectural compositions, he still reveals the influence of his first master, to whom he owes his name, but he has sacrificed expression and form for a lifeless sentimentality in which we seek the true Leonardo in vain, just as in the pictures of Marco d'Oggione. The blurred faces with their rather small eyes, without recognizable signs of hair or beard growth, do not harmonize well with the precise and fluidly painted backgrounds (*Adoration of the Magi*, London, N.G.; *Madonna and Child*, Brera; *Madonna Enthroned with Eight Saints*, Pitti, Florence). Nevertheless, thanks to his excellent light-and-shadow painting and harmonious use of colour, he succeeded in producing such impressive paintings as the Crucifixion in the Brera.

Of Foppa's other pupils, Bernadino de'Conti, Bernadino Butinone (pl. 66; close collaboration with Zenale), Ambrogio Bevilaqua and Macrino d'Alba are especially deserving of mention. Works by Bevilaqua in the Brera include a *Madonna and Child with St Peter, Martyr and King David*. The Virgin's beauty recalls Borgognone, but the assistant figures are weaker; curiously enough, St Peter, with an axe embedded in his split-open skull, looks the most cheerful of all. There is a *Virgin Adoring the Child* by him in Dresden, a picture that would appear very antiquated even without a banner.

The Piedmont line from Macrino d'Alba, via the Scotti, Gaudenzio Ferrari, Girolamo Giovenone and right up to Defendente Ferrari, is remarkable in that it remained largely untouched by Leonardo's influence. Gaudenzio, who probably trained under Stefano Scotti (*Crucifixion with SS Catherine, Francis and Bonaventura*, Brera), and who was more likely an employee than a pupil of Luini, retains the powerful local character, despite being influenced by Perugino and Correggio (*Annunciation*, Berlin), while Defedente reveals Nordic influences that may have reached him via Genoa (*Virgin and Child*, Pitti). Much the same is true of another Piedmont painter, Giovanni Martino Spanzotti, the tutor of Sodoma (pl. 72), who must have been influenced by Burgundian examples via Provence (*SS Sebastian and Catherine*, Brera).

To Leonardo's early circle can be assigned the only slightly younger Giovanni Ambrogio de'Predis and the Milanese Giovanni Battista Boltraffio (pl. 69). If we compare Leonardo's *Lady with an Ermine* (Wawel, Cracow) with Ambrogio's *Girl with Cherries* (Metropolitan Museum, New York), we immediately recognize the dependence of the latter, but also the essential difference between tutor and pupil; the one cultivates sensitivity, combined with alert attentiveness, while the other cultivates coquetry (which for some is less appealing). Leonardo's friend and confidant, Boltraffio, was more refined than Predis, but less inventive. His *Madonnas* are Leonardesque, but more flesh-and-blood than the transfigured beings of his master. Their smiles are suggested; in the case of Leonardo's other imitators, these occasionally become grimaces (*Madonna and Child*, Museum of Fine Arts, Budapest; *Madonna and Child*, London, N.G.). Boltraffio's pictures are always imbued with sweetness and warmth (*Virgin and Child with SS John the Baptist and Sebastian and Two Donors*, Louvre).

Among Leonardo's later pupils, including Cesare da Sesto, Marco d'Oggione, Giampetro, Francesca Melzi and others, Bernardino Luini (pl. 68) stands out in particular. He most of all maintains the Foppa tradition transmitted by Borgognone in his frescoes. The *frescoes of the Chapel of St Joseph in S. Maria della pace*, now in the Brera, give an impression of this. By contrast, he proves to be an unreserved imitator of Leonardo in his panel pictures. He translates Leonardo's depth and mysteriousness into a more accessible pictorial language, something which has never done any harm to an artist's popularity (*Virgin and Sleeping Child*, Louvre; *Virgin and Child of the Rose Garden*, Brera). Luini's grace always borders on mawkishness, but he compensates for this with his feeling for colour and masterful technique. Characteristic of his style is, among others, the *Salome* in the Louvre, which is in no way different from his *Madonnas*; yet we would expect her to commit nothing less than murder.

In the case of the Piedmont artist Antionio Bazzi, to whom angry Florentines gave the unjustified nickname of il Sodoma, we do not know for sure whether he also worked in Leonardo's workshop. There is no doubt, however, that he appropriated stylistic effects from Leonardo. The *sfumato*, the rendering of the hands and probably the peculiarities of the landscape backgrounds, too, all recall the Tuscan master. Despite this, the unconventional Sodoma did not allow himself to be restricted by either Leonardo or Raphael. His talent greatly surpassed that of Bramantino and Luini. Among his better-known pictures are *St Sebastian* (Pitti, pl. 72), *St George Slaying the Dragon* (Washington, N.G.), *Christ on the Mount of Olives* (Pinacoteca Nazionale, Siena), and the *Holy Family* in the Pinakothek in Munich.

Andrea Solario (pl. 70), brother of the great sculptor Christoforo Solario (called il Gobbo) and pupil of Bramantino, also knew how to hold his ground in the face of Leonardo's powerful influence. In his best-known picture, *Madonna of the Green Cushion* (Louvre), the ethereal nature of the Leonardesque Virgins gives way to an immediate freshness and natural movement. His *Madonna of the Carnations* (Brera), too, is quite of this world, and where Leonardo imparts overflowing tenderness, we see in Solario's painting a motherly concern and an idea of the son's fate.

There are some local schools in Lombardy that still need to be mentioned, since they produced various masters who, in individual works, do not suffer in comparison with great names. Boccaccio Boccaccino, born in Ferrara, was a pupil of Domenico Panetti and one of Garofolo's tutors (pl. 87), and hence appears in chart VI. He worked in Genoa, Ferrara, and Venice before settling in Cremona in 1506. His *Road to Calvary* in London is still very reminiscent of Bellini, while the enchanting *Gypsy Girl* in the Uffizi is completely his own. The School of Cremona also gained in importance through his son, Camillo Boccaccino, who was born in Cremona and became one of its most important painters (*Adoration of the Magi*, Nice; *Virgin and Child in Glory with SS Bartholomew, John the Baptist, Albert and Jerome*, Brera). His father's Venetian training is also evident in Camillo's colouring, although his design already anticipated elements of the Baroque. Boccaccio, however, was also the tutor of Pietro Bambo, from the large family of the Bembi, as well as of Galeazzo from the Cremonese painter dynasty of the Campi; there is a beautiful *Madonna and Child with SS Biagio and Anthony Abate* by him in the Brera. Of Galeazzo's sons – here Giulio (*Portrait of his Father*, Galeazzeo, Uffizi), Vicenzo and Cavaliere Antonio, all of whom were gifted painters – Antonio later went to Milan, but also worked in Piancenza, Lodi, Mantua and Brescia. In turn, Boccaccio Boccaccino (the Younger), son of Camillo, completed his apprenticeship with the Campi, which is also an indication of how interwoven the artists' families were amongst themselves, and how stylistic attributes were able to spread and become established over a larger School. Because of his dependence on Romanino, another Cremonese, Altobello Melone, has been included in chart VIII and is dealt with in connection with the School of Brescia.

Lodi, too, produced a number of artists of wider importance. There is a *Madonna and Child with an Angel* by Giovanni Agostino di Lodi in the Brera, a picture that was once ascribed to Bramantino. The impact of the famous painter dynasty of the Piazza (da Lodi) spans a period of more than 170 years, beginning with Bertino in the mid-fifteenth century. This too – since it is by no means a rare occurrence – is an additional aspect that plays a role in the astounding continuity of the Italian Schools. The work of the Piazza led them beyond Lombardy to Venice – where we encounter Paolo, called Fra Cosimo – to Spain and Portugal, where Callisto Piazza achieved fame. There are pictures by Albertino and Martino in the Brera; owing to their poor condition, however, they reveal little of these masters' abilities.

If we exclude Sodoma, whom his native home was unable to hold, it is the painters of the Oldoni family who fundamentally defined the Vercelli School. Bonifazio I Oldoni, originally from Milan, moved to Vercelli at the beginning of the fifteenth century and there founded an artists' dynasty which still featured notable masters towards the end of the sixteenth century. The Oldoni worked both for the Sforza in Milan as well as for the Duke of Savoy in Turin. Hence, they probably also had an opportunity to come into contact with Provençal art.

The School of Pavia is represented by both of the Fasoli, Pier Francesco Sacchi, Cesare Magni, and the Foppa pupil Bernadino de'Conti, among others, all of whom came under Leonardo's spell, and of whom only the last-named rose above mediocrity. In his *Virgin and Child with the Infant St John*, as well as in his *Deposition* (both in the Brera), Bernadino's dependence remains obvious, however. Sacchi later opened a workshop in Genoa and, favoured by the trade connections and political ties of the city, also adopted influences from the north. Genoa and Liguria admittedly did not produce any extraordinary artistic personalities (maybe we do not do justice here to Luca Cambiaso (pl. 76), who last worked in Spain, since we apply other criteria to his contemporaries); nevertheless, they represented a floodgate for external artistic currents that were important for the development of the entire Lombard School. In particular, works of the Flemish School came very early to Genoa, where they also aroused the interest of the Milanese Court in Nordic art. Zanetto Bugato was accepted into the workshop of Rogier van den Weyden after Duchess Bianca Maria Sforza's intercession, an event that is typical of the openness with which foreign artistic traditions were received in Lombardy.

In a geographical and artistic sense, Francesco Mazzola, from Parma, who has gone down in history under the name of Parmigianino (pl. 75), had one foot in the Lombard School and one in the Emilian. Ignoring the political interdependencies of his time, one could have rightly included him only in chart VI since, from a geographic point of view, Parma still belonged to Emilia, and the influence of the Emilian Correggio is unmistakable. However, his place in chart V is also justifiable, since his influence on the Lombard Mannerists may be shown more clearly in this way. There is not a single picture by him in the Brera. In Bologna, by contrast, where he worked for a time, he is represented by several works (e.g., in S. Petronio, with a *St Roche*). Correggio's strong influence, which may be attributable more to collaborative work than to a teaching relationship, did not hinder Parmigianino's development of a completely distinctive style, in which he made a trademark out of the cult of the elegant line. His Madonnas are very fine (by contrast, those of Allegri are often playful in a girlish fashion or slightly uncertain in their expression).

continued on page 65

Colour Plates

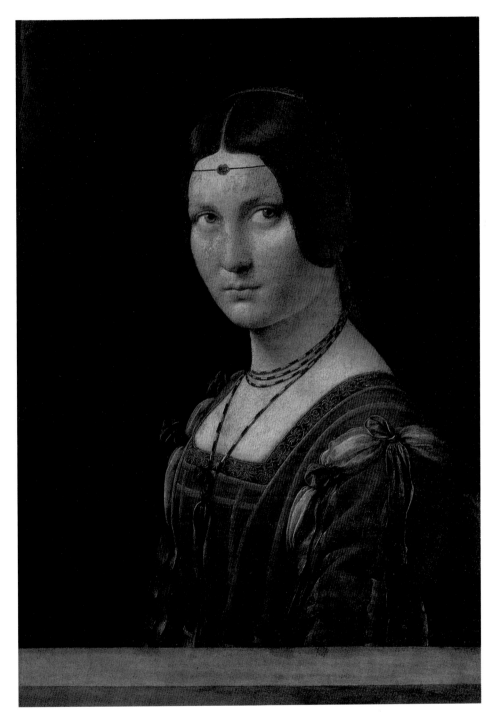

1   Leonardo da Vinci, *Portrait of a Women (La belle Ferronnière)*, 1490–95,
oil on panel, 63 × 45 cm, Louvre, Paris

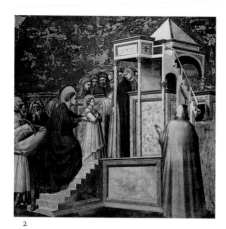

2

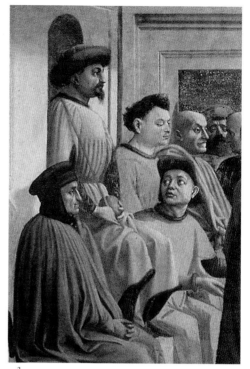

3

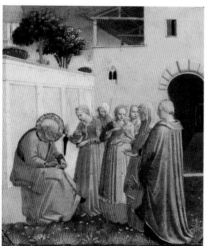

4

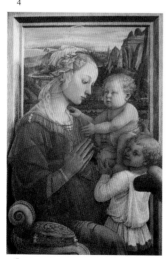

5

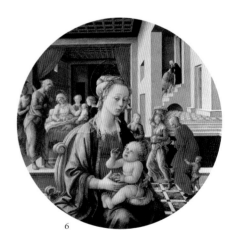

6

2 Giotto, a depiction of the Virgin returning to her parents' house after the wedding, from the fourth scene of the *Life of the Virgin* cycle, 1302–06, fresco, Scrovegni Chapel, Padua

3 Masaccio, *Raising the Son at the Prefect of Antioch* (section), 1425–27, fresco, 232 × 597 cm, Santa Maria del Carmine, Brancacci-Chapele, Florence

4 Beato Angelico, *Naming of St John the Baptist*, before 1435, tempera on panel, 26 × 24 cm, San Marco Museum, Venice

5 Filippo Lippi, *Madonna and Child with Two Angels*, around 1453, tempera on panel, 95 × 62 cm, Uffizi, Florence

6 Filippo Lippi, *Virgin and Child with Scenes from the Life of the Virgin*, 1452 (not completed), tempera on panel, ⌀135 cm, Palazzo Pitti, Galleria Palatina, Florence

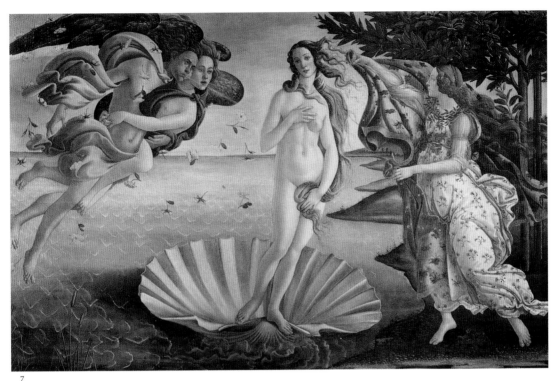

7

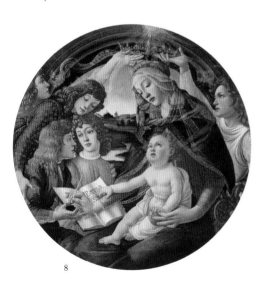

8

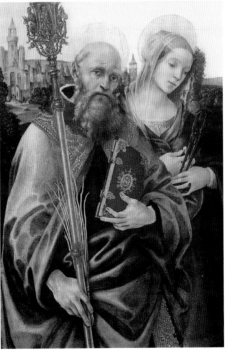

9

7   Sandro Botticelli, *Birth of Venus*, 1484, tempera on canvas, 172.5 × 278.5 cm, Uffizi, Florence

8   Sandro Botticelli, *Madonna of the Magnificat (Virgin and Child with Five Angels)*, between 1481 and 1485, tempera on panel, ⌀ 118 cm, Uffizi, Florence

9   Filippino Lippi, *SS Bernard and Appolonia*, 1483, tempera on panel, 157.5 × 60 cm, Norton Simon Foundation, Pasadena (California)

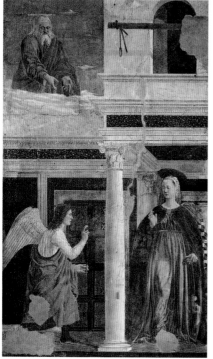

10

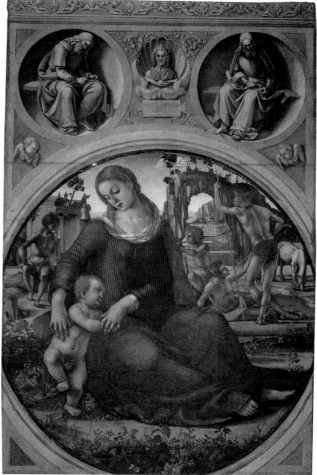

10 Piero della Francesca, *Annunciation,* around 1455, fresco, 329 × 193 cm, San Francesco, Arezzo

11 Luca Signorelli, *Virgin and Child (Medici Tondo),* around 1490, oil on panel, 170 × 117.5 cm, Uffizi, Florence

12 Leonardo da Vinci, *Annunciation,* between 1472 and 1475, oil on panel, 98 × 217 cm, Uffizi, Florence

11

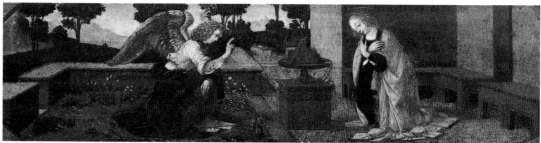

12

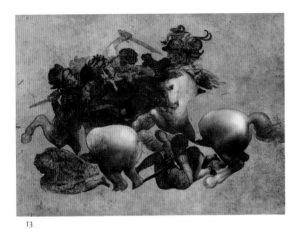

13

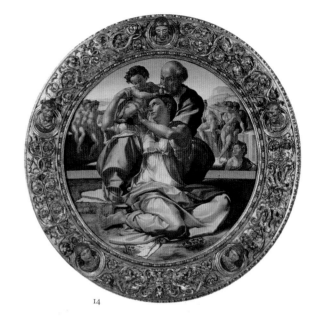

14

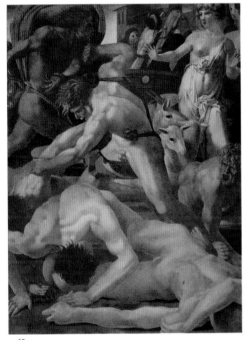

15

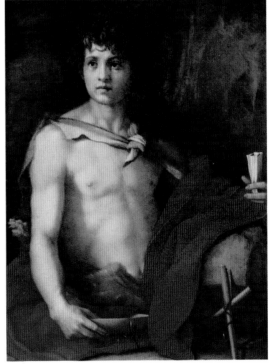

16

13 Leonardo da Vinci, *Tavolo Doria (group of horses for the 'Battle of Anghiari')*, around 1503–04, oil on poplar wood, 85 × 115 cm, Historisches Museum der Pfalz, Speyer

14 Michelangelo Buonarroti, *Doni Tondo*, 1504, oil on panel, ⌀ 120 cm (without frame), Uffizi, Florence

15 Rosso Fiorentino, *Moses Defending the Daughters of Jethro*, before 1530, oil on canvas, 160 × 117 cm, Uffizi, Florence

16 Andrea del Sarto, *Young St John the Baptist*, 1523, oil on panel, 94 × 68 cm, Palazzo Pitti, Galleria Palatina, Florence

17 Mariotto Albertinelli,
The Visitation, 1503,
oil on panel, 232 × 146 cm,
Uffizi, Florence

18 Pontormo, *Supper at
Emmaus,* 1525, oil on canvas,
230 × 173 cm, Uffizi, Florence

19 Bronzino, *Eleonora of
Toledo and her Son Giovanni,*
around 1545, oil on panel,
115 × 96 cm, Uffizi, Florence

20 Cristofano Allori, *Judith
with the Head of Holofernes,*
around 1619–20, oil on
canvas, 139 × 116 cm, Palazzo
Pitti, Galleria Palatina,
Florence

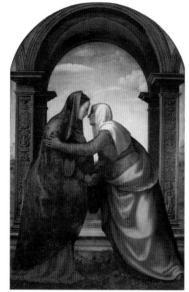

17

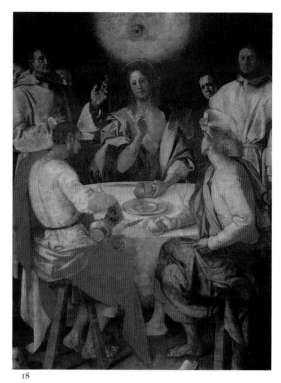

18

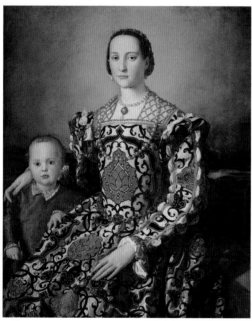

19

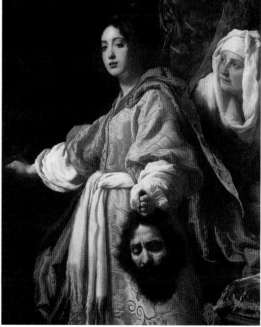

20

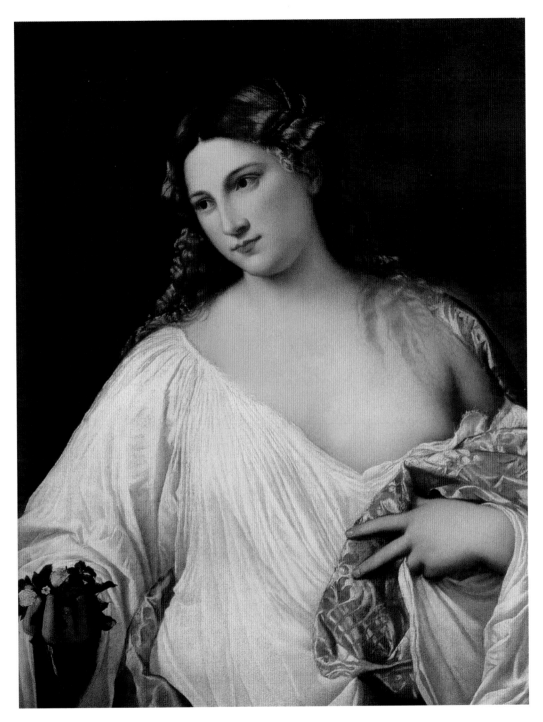

21   Titian, actually Tiziano Veccellio, *Flora*, around 1514, oil on canvas, 80 × 63.5 cm, Uffizi, Florence

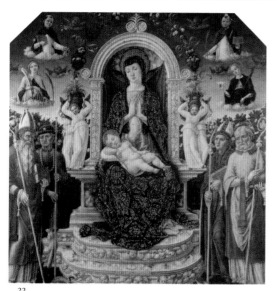

22

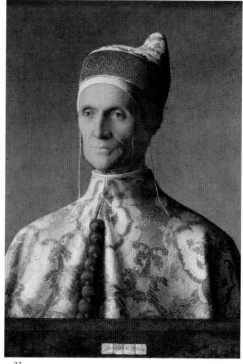

23

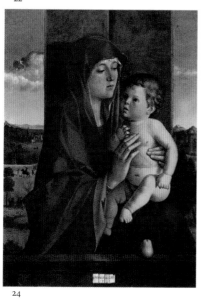

24

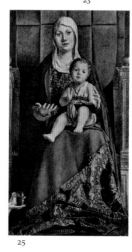

25

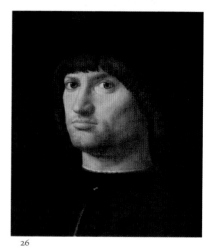

26

22   Bartolomeo Vivarini, *Sacra Conversazione*, 1465, Museo di Capodimonte, Naples

23   Giovanni Bellini, *Doge Leonardo Loredan*, before 1507, National Gallery, London

24   Giovanni Bellini, *Virgin and Child*, between 1501 and 1504, oil on poplar wood, 61.6 × 45.1 cm,
Accademia Carrara, Bergamo

25   Antonello da Messina, *Virgin and Child*, completed in 1476, fragment from the central part of the
'Pala di San Cassiano', altarpiece, oil on panel, 115 × 63 cm, Kunsthistorisches Museum, Vienna

26   Antonello da Messina, *Portrait of a Man Known as The Condottiere*, 1475, oil on panel, 36 × 30 cm, Louvre, Paris

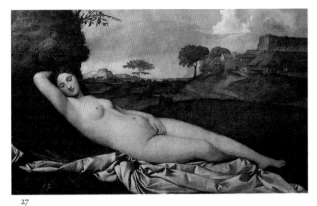

27

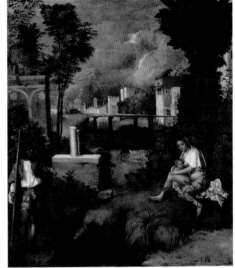

28

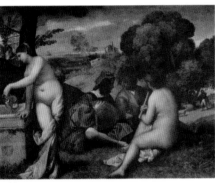

29

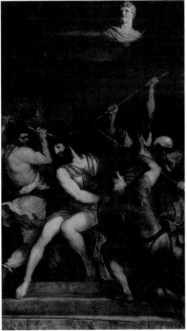

31

30

27 Giorgione, *Sleeping Venus,* around 1510, oil on canvas, 108 × 175 cm, Staatliche Kunstsammlungen, Dresden

28 Giorgione, *Tempest (La Tempesta),* shortly after 1505, oil on canvas, 82 × 73 cm, Galleria dell'Accademia, Venice

29 Titian, actually Tiziano Veccellio, *Concert Champêtre,* 1510/11, canvas, 105 × 137 cm, Louvre, Paris

30 Jacopo Negretti, actually Palma Vecchio, *Sacra Conversazione,* around 1528, oil on canvas, 127 × 195 cm, Galleria dell'Accademia, Venice

31 Titian, actually Tiziano Vecellio, *Christ Crowned with Thorns,* around 1543, panel, 303 × 180 cm, Louvre, Paris

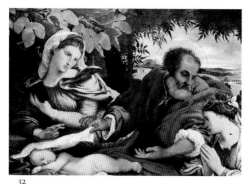

32

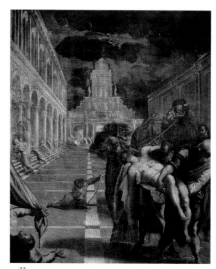

33

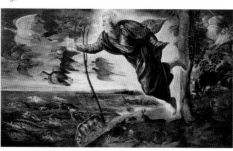

34

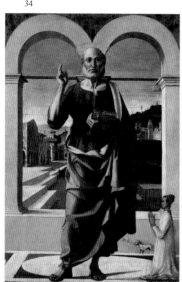

35

32   Lorenzo Lotto, *Holy Family with St Catherine of Alexandria,* 1533, canvas, 81 × 115 cm, Accademia Carrara, Bergamo

33   Jacopo Robusti, called Tintoretto, *Removal of the Body of St Mark,* 1562–66, oil on canvas, 398 × 315 cm, Galleria dell'Accademia, Venice

34   Jacopo Robusti, called Tintoretto, *The Creation of the Animals,* around 1550, oil on canvas, 151 × 258 cm, Galleria dell'Accademia, Venice

35   Bartolomeo Cincani, called Montagna, *St Peter,* between 1504 and 1506, panel, 60 × 39 cm, Galleria dell'Accademia, Venice

36   Cima da Conegliano, actually Giovanni Battista Cima, *Maria with Child between John the Baptist and St Mary Magdalene,* panel, 167 × 110 cm, Louvre, Paris

37   Carlo Crivelli, *Annunciation,* 1486, (transferred to canvas), 207 × 146.7 cm, National Gallery, London

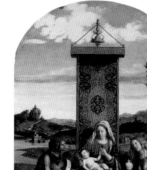

36

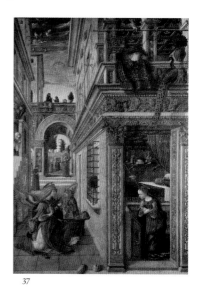

37

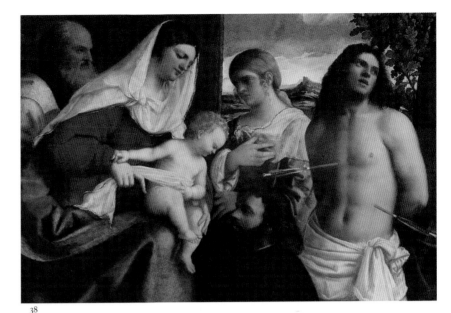

38   Sebastiano del Piombo, actually
Sebastiano Luciani (around 1485–1547),
Sacra Conversazione, oil on panel,
95 × 136 cm, Louvre, Paris

39   Jacopo Bassano (1515–92), *Entomb-
ment,* Santa Maria in Vanzo, Padua

40   Paris Bordone, *Presentation of
the Ring to the Doge,* around 1545,
oil on canvas, transferred to canvas,
370 × 300 cm, Galleria dell'Accademia,
Venice

38

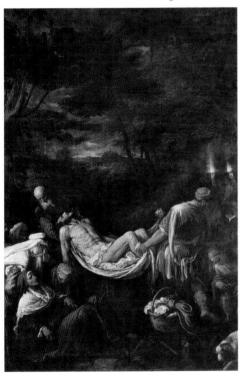

39

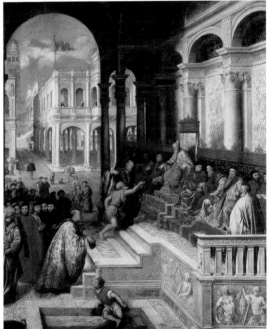

40

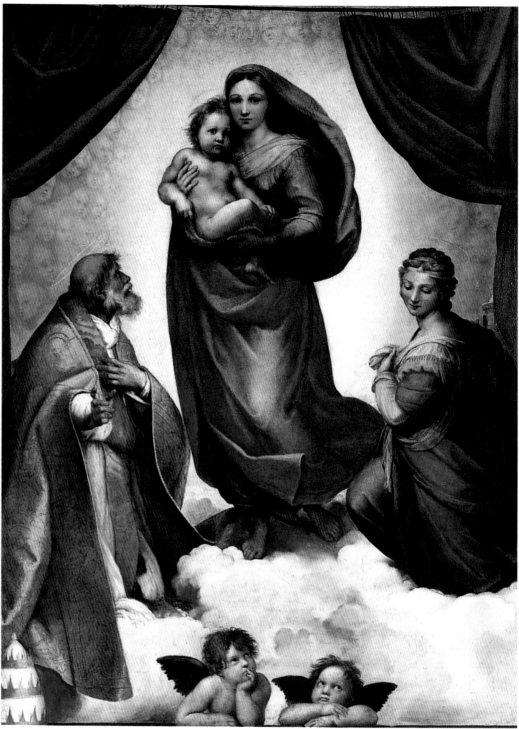

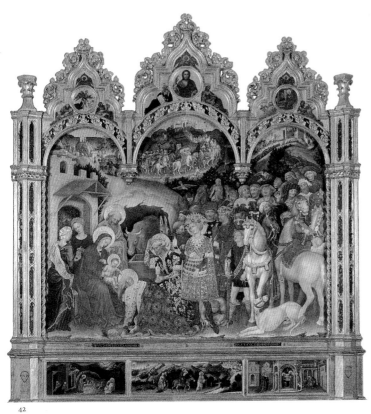

42

41 Raphael, *Sistine Madonna*, 1512/13, oil on canvas, 269.5 × 201 cm, Gemäldegalerie Dresden, Dresden

42 Gentile da Fabriano, *Adoration of the Magi*, gable with Christ giving blessing, annunciation, prophets and cherub; pedrella panel: *Nativity, Flight into Egypt, Presentation in the Temple,* 1423, tempera on panel, 173 × 220 cm, Uffizi, Florence

43 Benozzo Gozzoli, *Medici Family as the Magi*, begun in 1459, fresco, Chapel of the Palazzo Medici-Riccardi, Florence

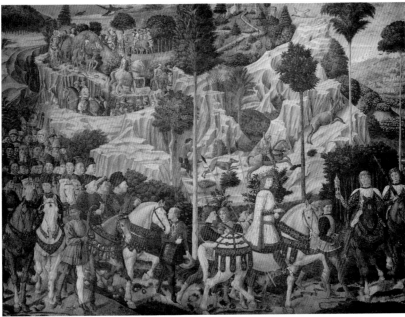

43

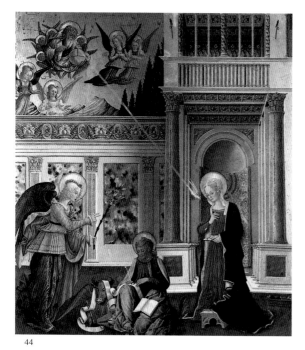

44

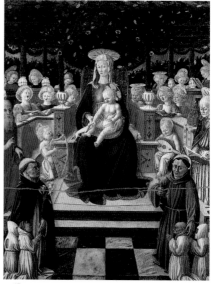

45

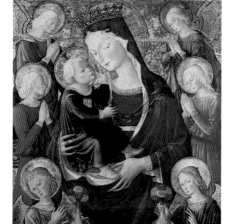

46

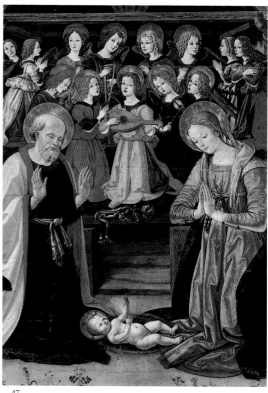

44 Benedetto Bonfigli, *Annunciation*, between 1455 and 1460, tempera on panel, 227 × 200 cm, Galleria Nazionale dell' Umbria, Perugia

45 Giovanni Boccati, *Madonna del pergolata (Virgin and Child with Saints)*, 1447, tempera on panel, 186.5 × 248 cm, Perugia (as above)

46 Bartolomeo Caporali, *Virgin and Child with Angels*, between 1477 and 1479, tempera on panel, 108 × 94 cm, Perugia (as above)

47 Fiorenzo di Lorenzo, *The Adoration of the Magi* (section), c. 1490, tempera on panel, 151 × 209 cm, Perugia (as above)

47

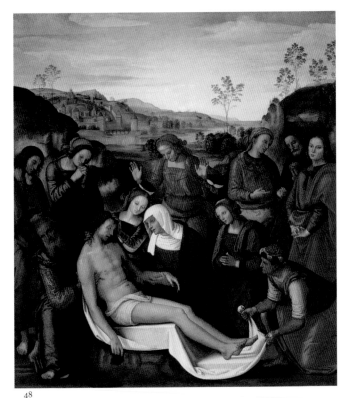

48

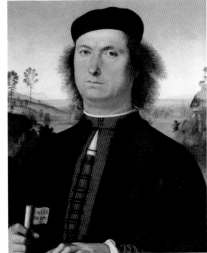

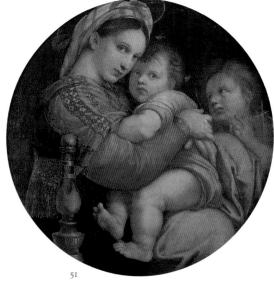

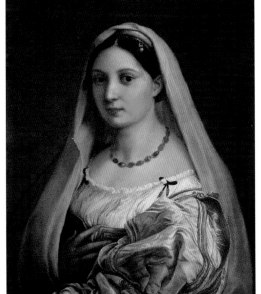

50

48 Perugino, actually Pietro di Cristoforo Vannucci, *Lamentation*, 1495, oil on panel, 214 × 195 cm, Palazzo Pitti, Galleria Palatina, Florence

49 Perugino, actually Pietro di Cristoforo Vannucci, *Portrait of Francesco delle Opere*, 1494, oil on panel, 52 × 44 cm, Uffizi, Florence

50 Raphael, *Donna Velata*, between 1512 and 1516, oil on canvas, 82 × 60.5 cm, Palazzo Pitti, Galleria Palatina, Florence

51 Raphael, *Madonna della seggiola*, 1513, oil on panel, ⌀ 71 cm, Palazzo Pitti, Galleria Palatina, Florence

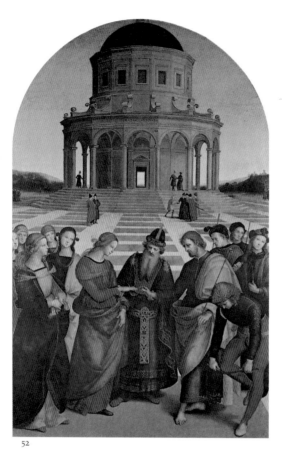

52

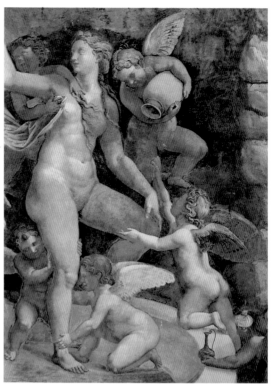

53

52   Raphael, *Betrothal of the Virgin*, 1504,
oil on panel, 170 × 117 cm, Brera, Milan

53   Giulio Romano, *Mars and Venus* (section),
around 1526–28, fresco, Palazzo Te, Mantua

54   Federico Barocci, *Portrait of Francesco Maria II
della Rovere*, after 1572, oil on canvas, 113 × 93 cm,
Uffizi, Florence

55   Andrea Mantegna, *Madonna and Child*,
around 1460, Museo Poldi Pezzoli, Milan

54

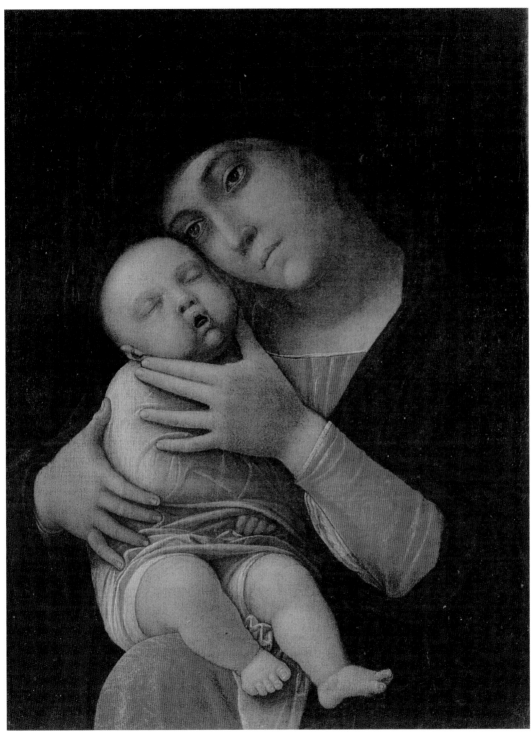

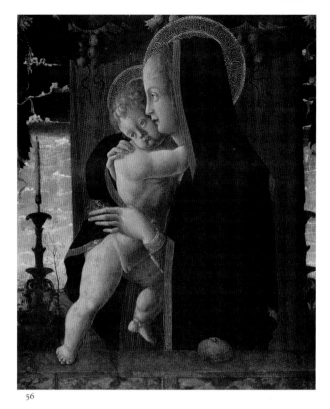

56

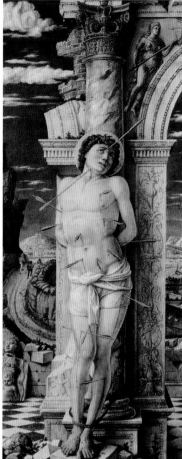

57

56   Francesco Squarcione, *Virgin and Child (Madonna De Lazara)*, around 1460, poplar wood, 82 × 70 cm, Gemäldegalerie, Berlin

57   Andrea Mantegna, *St Sebastian*, 1459, poplar wood, 68 × 30 cm, Kunsthistorisches Museum, Vienna

58   Andrea Mantegna, *Martyrdom of St Christopher* (section), 1451–55, (largely destroyed during World War II), fresco, Emeritani Church, Ovetari Chapel, Padua

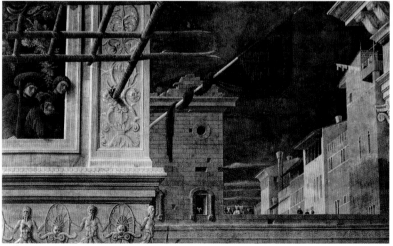

58

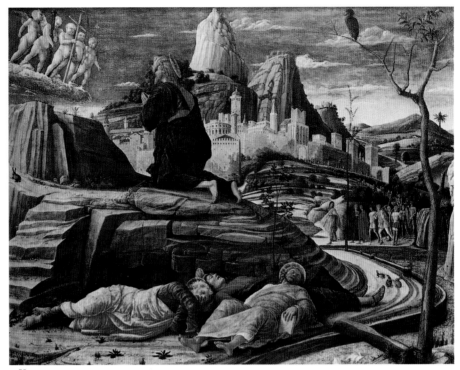

59

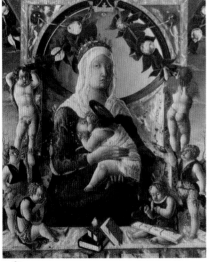

60

61

59 Andrea Mantegna, *Agony in the Garden*, around 1460, tempera on panel, 62.9 × 80 cm, National Gallery, London

60 Marco Zoppo, *Virgin and Child ('Madonna del latte')*, 1455, transferred from panel to canvas, 89 × 72 cm, Louvre, Paris

61 Giorgio Chiulinovich, called Schiavone (1436–1504), *Virgin and Child with Angels*, 1484, Walters Art Gallery, Baltimore

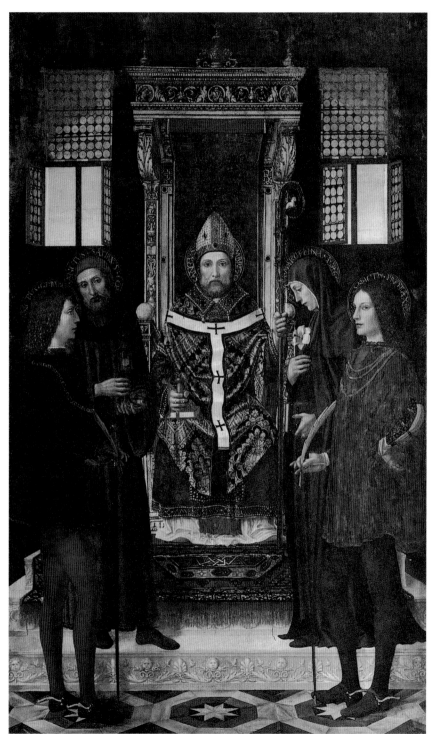

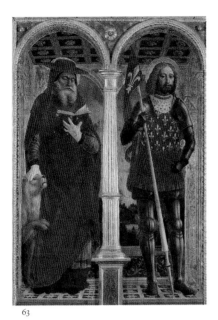

63

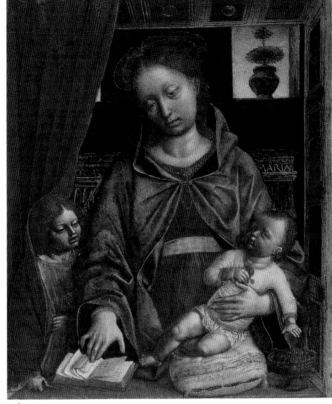

64

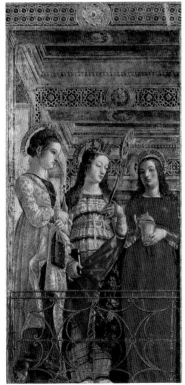

65

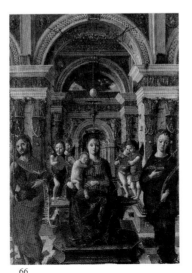

66

62 Ambrogio Borgognone, (around 1453–1523), *SS Jerome and Alexander, St Ambrose with Saints*, Certosa, Pavia

63 Vincenzo Foppa (after 1425–1516), 137 × 39 cm, altarpiece from Santa Maria delle Grazie in Bergamo, Brera, Milan

64 Vincenzo Foppa, *Madonna and Child with an Angel*, completed in 1480, tempera on panel, 41 × 32.5 cm, Uffizi, Florence

65 Bernardo Zenale (around 1450–1526), *SS Lucy, Catharine and Magdalene*, altarpiece, Parish Church, Treviglio (Bergamo)

66 Bernardino Butinone (1436–1507), *Virgin and Child with Saints*, Isola Bella, Borromeo Collection

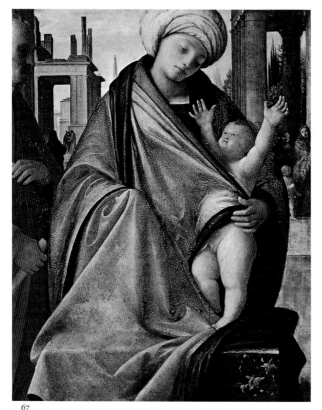

67

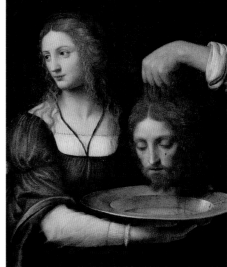

68

67   Bramantino, actually Bartolomeo Suardi, *Madonna and Child*, around 1512, panel, 61 × 47 cm, Brera, Milan

68   Bernardino Luini (around 1475–1532), *Salome with the Head of the Baptist*, canvas, 63 × 55 cm, Louvre, Paris

69   Giovanni Antonio Boltraffio (1467–1516), *Virgin and Child with SS John the Baptist and Sebastian and Two Donors*, panel, 186 × 184 cm, Louvre, Paris

70   Andrea Solario, actually Andrea di Bartolo, *Madonna of the Green Cushion*, 1507/10, panel, 60 × 48 cm, Louvre, Paris

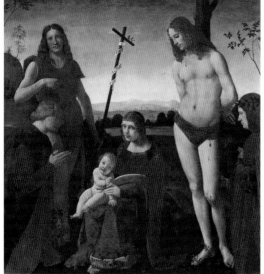

69

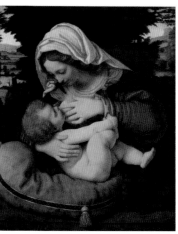

70

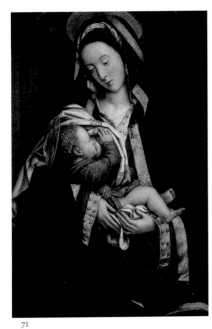

71

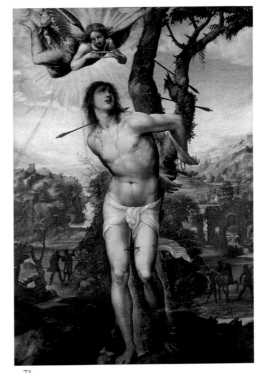

72

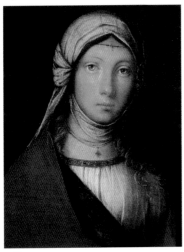

73

74

71 Defendente Ferrari, *Madonna and Child*, between 1509 and 1535, oil on panel, Palazzo Pitti, Florence

72 Sodoma, actually Giovanni Antonio Bazzi, *St Sebastian*, between 1525 and 1531, oil on canvas, 204 × 145 cm, Palazzo Pitti, Galleria Palatina, Florence

73 Boccaccio Boccaccino, *Gypsy Girl*, around 1505, oil on panel, 24 × 19 cm, Uffizi, Florence

74 Parmigianino, *Madonna of the Long Neck*, after 1534, oil on panel, 219 × 135 cm, Uffizi, Florence

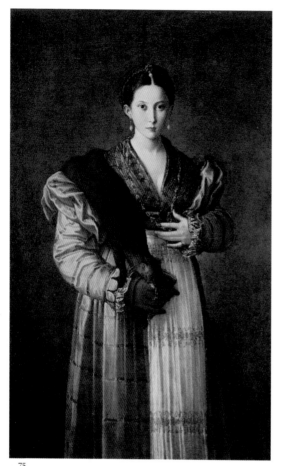

75

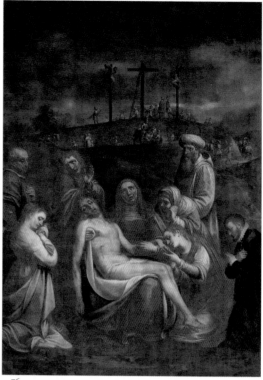

76

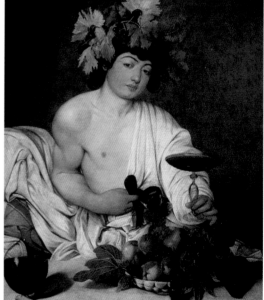

77

75   Parmigianino, *Antea*, between 1530 and 1535,
oil on canvas, 136 × 86 cm, Capodimonte, Naples

76   Luca Cambiaso, *Pietà*, Basilica di Nostra
Signora Assunta in Carignano, Genoa

77   Caravaggio, *Bacchus*, around 1596/97,
oil on canvas, 95 × 85 cm, Uffizi, Florence

78   Correggio (1489–1534), *Noli me tangere*,
panel transferred to canvas, 130 × 103 cm,
Prado, Madrid

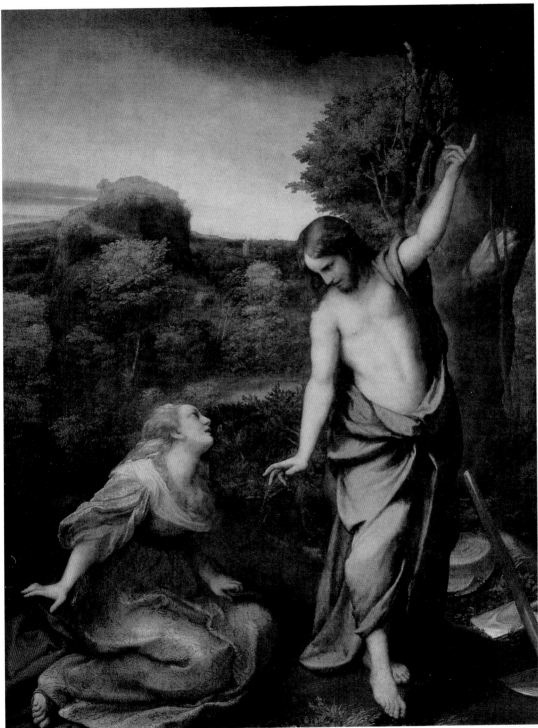

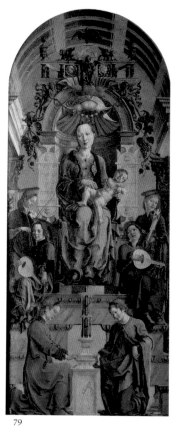

79

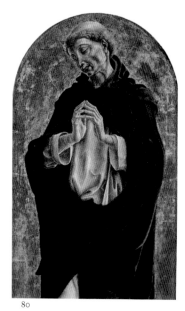

80

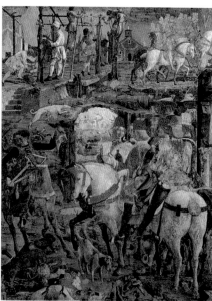

81

79　Cosmè (Cosimo) Tura, *Virgin and Child with Music-making Angels ('Madonna del Roverella')*, around 1475, tempera, 239 × 101.6 cm, National Gallery, London

80　Cosmè (Cosimo) Tura, *St Dominic*, after 1485, tempera on panel, 51 × 32 cm, Uffizi, Florence

81　Francesco del Cossa, *The Month of March*, from the fresco cycle in the Hall of the Months (a total painted area of 540 m²), begun in 1470, Palazzo Schifanoia, Ferrara

82　Ercole de' Roberti, *Pietà*, between 1480 and 1496, panel, Walker Art Gallery, Liverpool

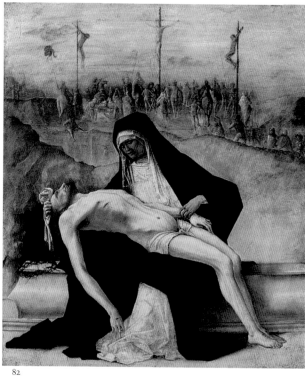

82

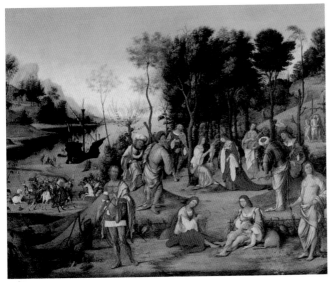

83

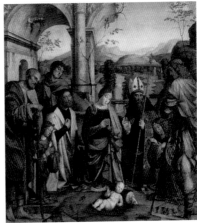

84

83 Lorenzo Costa, *Allegory for the Court of Isabella d'Este*, after 1510, canvas, 165 × 198 cm, Louvre, Paris

84 Francesco Francia, *Adoration of the Child*, around 1500, Pinacoteca Nazionale, Bologna

85 Melozzo da Forlì, *Sixtus IV Founding the Vatican Library*, 1480–81, fresco, transferred to canvas, 370 × 315 cm, Pinacoteca Vaticana, Rome

86 Dosso Dossi, actually Giovanni Luteri, *Rest on the Flight into Egypt*, around 1520, tempera on panel, 52 × 42.5 cm, Uffizi, Florence

87 Garofalo, actually Benvenuto Tisi, *Annunciation*, around 1550, oil on panel, 55 × 76 cm, Uffizi, Florence

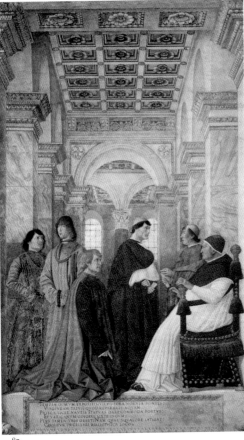

85

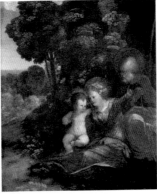

86

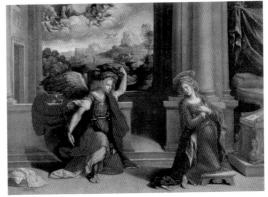

87

88 Correggio, *Virgin of St George*,
1530–32, oil on poplar wood, 285 × 190 cm,
Staatliche Kunstsammlungen, Dresden

89 Correggio, *Adoration of the Child*,
around 1530–35, oil on panel, 81 × 77 cm,
Uffizi, Florence

90 Bartolommeo Passarotti, *Portrait of
a Nobleman with Two Dogs*, around 1575,
oil on canvas, 103 × 84 cm, Palazzo Pitti,
Galleria Palatina, Florence

91 Nicolò dell'Abate (1509–71), *The
Concert*, fresco, Palazzo Poggi, Bologna

92 Ludovico Carracci (1555–1619),
Galatea, 1484, Galleria Estense, Modena
Galleria Estense, Modena

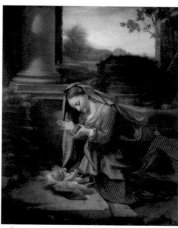

89

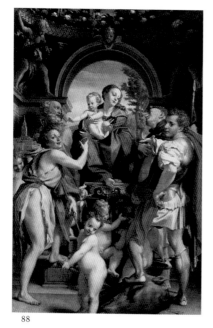

88

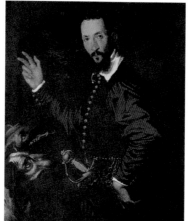

90

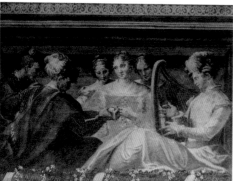

91

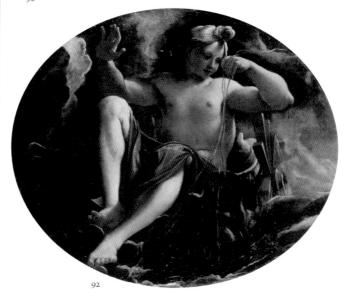

92

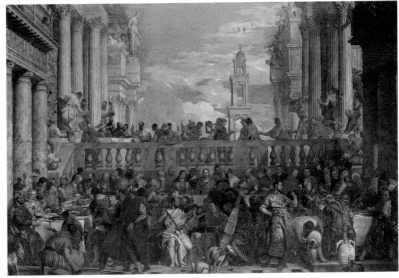

93

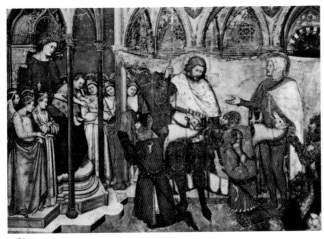

94

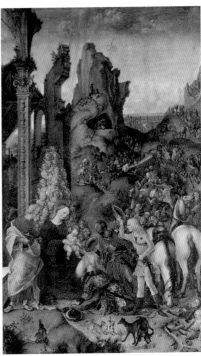

96

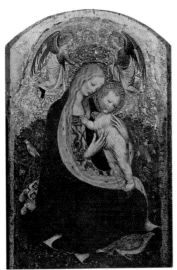

95

93   Veronese, actually Paolo Caliari,
Marriage at Cana, 1562/63, canvas,
666 × 990 cm, Louvre, Paris

94   Altichiero, *Cavalli Family Adoring
the Virgin and Child*, around 1390, votive
fresco, S. Anastasia, Capella Cavalli,
Verona

95   Pisanello, *Virgin and Child with
a Quail*, Castelvecchio, Verona

96   Liberale da Verona (around
1445–1526/29), *Adoration of the Magi*,
Cathedral, Verona

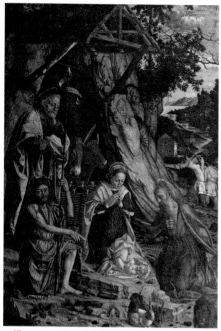

97

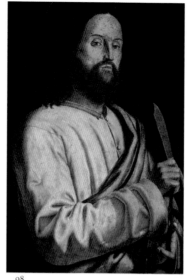

98

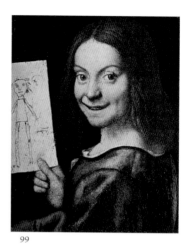

99

97 Gerolamo dai Libri (1474–1556), *Adoration of SS Jerome and John the Baptist*, 219 × 152 cm, Museo Castelvecchio, Verona

98 Francesco Morone (1471–1529), *St Bartholomew*, 59 × 39 cm, Castelvecchio, Verona

99 Giovanni Caroto (1488–1562), *Red-headed Youth Holding a Drawing*, wood, 37 × 29 cm, Castelvecchio, Verona

100 Brusasorci, actually Domenico Ricco, *Bathseba Bathing*, 1525, oil on canvas, 91 × 98 cm, Uffizi, Florence

101 Paolo Veronese, actually Paolo Caliari (1528–88), *Lamentation*, 76 × 117 cm, Museo Castelvecchio, Verona

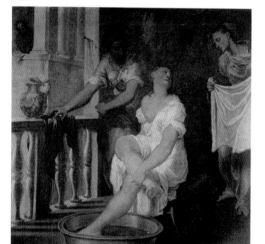

100

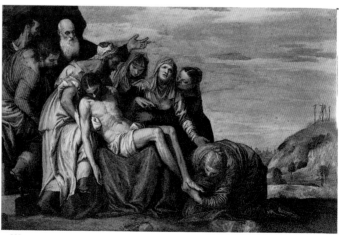

101

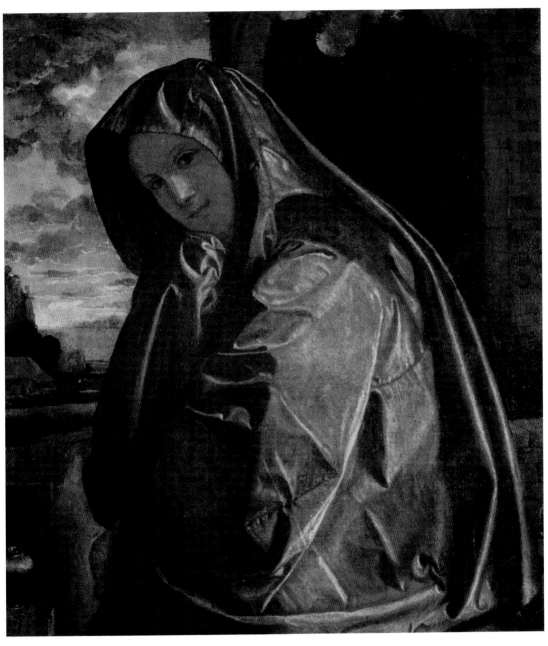

102   Giovanni Girolamo Savoldo, *St Mary Magdalene*, between 1530 and 1540, oil on canvas, 85 × 79 cm, Palazzo Pitti, Meridiana (provisional location), Florence

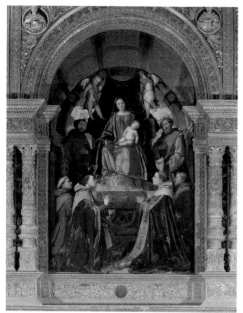

103

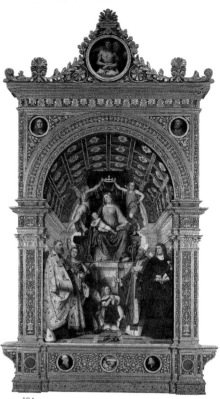

104

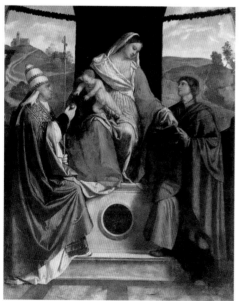

105

103   Girolamo Romanino, *Virgin and Child Enthroned with Saints*, around 1532, San Francesco, Brescia

104   Girolamo Romanino, *Altar for S. Giustina*, 1514, Eremitani Museum, Padua

105   Moretto da Brescia (around 1490–1554), *Coronation of the Virgin with Saints*, Parish Church, San Gregorio nelle Alpi

106   Giovanni Battista Moroni, *Portrait of a Lady*, around 1558, oil on canvas, 53 × 45.6 cm, Palazzo Pitti, Galleria Palatina, Florence

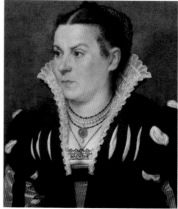

106

However, Correggio's mythological figures still assume a trace of that erotic aura (*Virgin of the Rose*, Gemäldegalerie Dresden; *Madonna of the Long Neck*, Uffizi; *Virgin and Child with SS John the Baptist and Jerome*, London, N.G.). Parmigianino's Mannerist traits are unmistakable, as is his indirect influence on the School of Fontainebleau (cf. *Mystic Marriage of St Catherine*, London, N.G.). In his portraits, he is on a par with the greatest Italian portraitists (*The Antiquarian*, London, N.G.); the *Antea* in Naples (Capodimonte) is certainly one of the most beautiful portraits of a woman in all Italian painting. B. Berenson describes Parmagianino as the "last true Renaissance artist in northern Italy".

Ercole Procaccini came from the Bolognese School. He had also collaborated in Rome with Prospero Fontana before finally settling in Milan. He is still predominantly Classicist-orientated, and in stylistic terms he developed from Girolamo da Carpi and Innocenzo da Imola. The organ doors in the Cathedral of Parma with *St Cecilia and David* are indicative of Parmagianino's influence. His son, Camillo Procaccini, already counts as one of the Late Mannerists, as does the gifted Giovanni Battista Crespi who appropriated certain elements from Gaudenzio Ferrari and later maintained contact with Camillo. Quite alone at the bottom of the chart is one of the most famous Lombards, Caravaggio (actually Michelangelo Merisi), whom we can no longer classify among the Renaissance masters, and of whose artistic origins we know nothing. A speculative interpretation, but one that would sound pleasing to a Lombard, would be that of his art as the inevitable apogee of a painterly tradition whose eclectic tendencies were time and again surpassed by its integrative power.

VI EMILIA-ROMAGNA

There was no prelude to the Renaissance of any note in Ferrara. It was initiated by Cosimo Tura's return from Padua (circa 1450), where he had become acquainted with Donatello's œuvre in Squarcione's workshop. He remained faithful to what he learned there – probably also from Mantegna – for the rest of his life. The impressions that he gained from Piero della Francesca's stay in Ferrara did not lead to any fundamental change of direction in his art. For him, painting meant to chisel using a brush. In an uncompromising manner, he fashioned people, materials and bare, rocky landscapes to colourful reliefs, against which naked bodies and limbs stand out like light-coloured marble. Without exception, his saints are solemn ascetics with sinewy necks, bony fingers and hollow cheeks. Tura does not seek beauty, not even in his *Madonnas*, which are thus distinguished in an unbecoming manner from the Bellinesque Virgins of Mantegna, and when he does give them a smile it does not make them any more endearing (*Virgin and Child*, Accademia, Venice; *Virgin and Child with Music-making Angels*, London, N.G.). However, by these means, Tura created works of shocking forcefulness, making him a great painter (*St Jerome*, London, N.G.; *Pietà*, Louvre; *Crucified Christ*, Brera; *The Body of Christ Held by Two Angels*, Vienna). Concurrent interpretations or lasting influences from Florence and Venice were largely absent in Ferrara during the second half of the Quattrocento, which meant that Cosimo could pursue his artistic course without distraction and had a formative stylistic influence on all painting in Emilia-Romagna during the Cinquecento.

In Francesca Cossa's œuvre (pl. 81), we find his tutor's style of painting in a milder form. Piero della Francesca must have made a profound impression on him. This is evident in the *frescoes in the Palazzo Schifanoia* (Ferrara) and the so-called *Allegory of Autumn* in Berlin, which, stylistically and thematically, are very close to the Schifanoia decorations. Movement is more important to him, but his landscapes are no less barren or rocky than those of Tura. His *Madonnas* and depictions of the infant Christ look less bizarre (*Madonna della Mercanzia*, Pinacoteca

Nazionale, Bologna), and his saints have more of Piero's dignity than they do of Tura's obsessiveness. Nevertheless, upon closer inspection of the *Children of Apollo* of the *Schifanoia frescoes*, we have more of an impression of a collection of Mongoloid dwarfs than of the descendants of the God of Beauty. Oddly enough, the *Annunciation* in Berlin has little of Tura in the Virgin and angel, and much of Mantegna in the rich architecture, although this is a very early work of Cossa's.

With Cossa's move to Bologna (around 1470), the Ferrarese tradition branched out into the lines of Cossa-G. Galassa-L. Costa-Francia and that of Tura-Panetti-Roberti-Garofalo, the latter line remaining in Ferrara. Domenico Panetti was a pupil of Bono da Ferrara and of Tura, to whom he is most indebted stylistically (*Virgin with Saints*, London, N.G.; *St Hieronymus*, Herron Art Institute, Indianapolis). He is considered to have been the actual tutor of Garofalo (actually Benvenuto Tisi), who is well-represented in the Dresdner Galerie with *Poseidon and Athena* and also *Mars and Venus by Troy*. In Rome, Garofalo bowed to Raphael's influence, but remained a true Ferrarese until the end. The National Gallery in London has a series of exquisite works by him, of which the *Vision of St Augustine* and the *Holy Family with SS John the Baptist, Elisabeth, Zacharias and Francis* in particular bear witness to Raphael's influence. Unlike his co-pupil Lorenzo Costa (pl. 83), Ercole de'Roberti (pl. 82) occasionally took the style of his master Tura to extremes. His parched *St John the Baptist* stands in a lifeless rocky desert, next to which a landscape by Cossa seems like a garden of paradise (Berlin). He attains movement from carefully observed and drawn outline, which has to replace muscle play and plasticity in his work (*The Agony in the Garden and the Betrayal of Christ* and *Road to Calvary* in Dresden). He has a preference for brownish tones which he often sets against a luminous ruby red (the panels *St Michael* and *St Appolonia*, Louvre; *Christ Blessing the Host*, London, N.G.).

Ercole is a peculiar painter, but was highly regarded at the Este Court and is justifiably regarded as one of the great masters of the Ferrarese School.

The other great Tura pupil, Lorenzo Costa, had settled in Bologna and set up a painting workshop in the house of the goldsmith Francesco Raibolini – called Francia (pl. 84) – it is often suggested that he, as the younger, was the pupil of Francia, but the opposite is probably true, for there is much to indicate that the latter was ultimately converted to painting under the influence of his friend Lorenzo. Moreover, Lorenzo's friend Francesco Bianchi (*Madonna and Child Enthroned with SS Hieronymus and Sebastian*, S. Pietro, Modena), who had long been in contact with Francia, may have acted as mediator here. Costa was the first Ferrarese to discover that a landscape consists of more than just desert and rock (*Allegory for the Court of Isabella d'Este*, Louvre). From Roberti, he took his narrative, but not dramatic, depth (cf. the *frescoes in the Oratorio di Sta. Cecilia*, Bologna). Of his altarpieces, the *Virgin and Child Enthroned with SS Sebastian, James, Jerome and George* in S. Petronio in Bologna is the most important. Here, for once, he eschews an expression of sympathy in which he merely tilts the head alone, a characteristic which he shares with Francia and Perugino, and which occasionally give his pictures a naive quality. His *Concert* (London, N.G.) is refreshingly natural, with carefully co-ordinated colours, and depicts a singing trio with a mandolin. Costa, who unlike Roberti lived to a great age, ended his career at the Court at Mantua.

Like many who paint 'agreeably', Francesco Francia has a mixed reputation in the art world. Some call him noble (I. Lermolieff), others are bored by him, and F. Knapp finds him "feeble and sullen in expression". Beauty makes it easier for us to overlook a flawed character than do intellect and soul a cleft palate. The same applies to art, and hence Francia, with his sense of beauty, became a famous painter; he cannot, however, be numbered among the greats. His pictures have much in common with those of Perugino, although not in terms of spatial depth. His figures seem somewhat stiff and bored (*Adoration of the Shepherds*, Bologna; *Virgin and Child with Two Angels*, Pinakothek, Munich). His female figures and angels have the same, somewhat pert, small mouth with a crescent-shaped lower lip that we also find in the works of Costa and the young Raphael. Meanwhile, Francesco Cossa's influence is plain in Francia's picture *Christ Held by Two Angels* (Pinacoteca Nazionale, Bologna). His portraits of *Evangelista Scappi* (Uffizi) and of *Bartolomeo Bianchini* (London, N.G.) reveal him to be highly gifted portraitist. From his atmospheric landscapes, we may conclude that his sensitivity was not merely an attitude; in these, he often surpasses his alleged mentor, Perugino. His *Madonna of the Rose-hedge* (Pinakothek, Munich), too, perhaps Francia's best-known picture, is something that we can hardly imagine as being from Perugino's hand.

We should also mention Timoteo Vitti, who also appears in chart III. He played an important role as a mediator between his tutor, Costa, and his pupil Raphael. Anyone who views his *Mary Magdalene* in the Bologna Pinacoteca cannot help but acknowledge that the young Raphael by no means learned everything he knew from Perugino.

Marco Zoppo, born in Cento between Ferrara and Bologna, is counted as one of the Bolognese, although he is stylistically more dependent on Padua (see also chart IV). He came from the Squarcione School and later digested Venetian influences, possibly in collaboration with the Bellini (*St Hieronymus*, Pinacoteca, Bologna). His *Dead Christ Supported by Two Saints* (London, N.G.) is evidence of his affinity with Mantegna. Il Zoppo spent almost his entire life in Venice, which is why there is little to support the assumption that Francesco Francia trained under him. More important than Zoppo is Melozzo da Forlì, but, unfortunately, there are only a few extant works that are verifiably by him. His *frescoes in the Vatican* support the hypothesis that that Piero della Francesca was one of his tutors. What in the case of Piero seems static and formal, Melozzo transforms into gestures and movement. His most famous work is the Vatican fresco *Sixtus IV Founding the Vatican Library*, in which the magnificent Renaissance architecture makes an appropriate setting for the dignified and meticulously characterized group of people. The *Music-making Angel* of SS Apostoli (Rome), now in the Vatican museums, makes us deplore that only fragments remain of these splendid frescoes. Typical of Melozzo is his generously used perspective from below, which is also the distinguishing characteristic of his pictures of the *Sciences at the Court at Urbino* (London and Berlin). His pupil, Marco Palmezzano, devoted himself entirely to his master's style, but remained inferior to him in his execution (frescoes in San Biagio, Forlì). Some of Marco's best works were long ascribed to Melozzo.

Dosso Dossi (actually Giovanni di Luteri, pl. 86), of Ferrara, drew little from, or kept little of, his native tradition. After several years in Venice, he became totally Venetian in style. Weak in his draughtsmanship and in his conveyance of physicality, he revels instead in powerfully painted landscapes. He loves to place his richly and colourfully-robed figures in front of shadowy backgrounds, where they are illuminated by a mild, warm light (*Melissa*, Pal. Borghese, Rome). Some of his most beautiful paintings, in part completed by his brother Battista, are today in the Gemäldegalerie in Dresden, e.g., the *St George and the Dragon* (a freely-interpreted copy of Raphael's picture in Washington) and the *Allegory of Peace*. The *Circe with Lovers* (Washington, N.G.), a painting which shows Dosso to be a meticulous painter of animals, is completely Giorgionesque. He was a close friend of Garofolo, with whom he collaborated on commissions.

Among Cossa's successors (an apprenticeship with him is not documented), Ercole Grandi, friend and employee of Lorenzo Costa, also deserves mention. He was occasionally confused with Roberto dei Grandi, to whom he was probably related. The eclecticist Amico Aspertini drew from many styles, but, owing to his unconventional compositions and strange inspirations, he managed to avoid becoming an imitator (*Pietà*, S. Petronio; *Pala del 'tirocinio'*, Pinacoteca, Bologna). It is easier to describe in such terms his employee, Ramenghi di Bagnacavallo, who took much from Dosso and later from Raphael (*Betrayal of Christ*, S. Michele in Bosco, Bologna). He was, however, a better painter than Aspertini (cf. also *Precious Blood of Christ*, S. Michele Arcangelo, and Virgin and Child in Glory with Saints, S. Donnino, Bologna), and, as a tutor of Primaticcio and Nicolò del'Abate (pl. 91), he also influenced the development of Mannerism.

From Dosso, we are led to Antonio Allegri of Correggio and to Girolamo da Carpi. Through his surname, Antonio helped his native city to attain world-wide acclaim. Girolamo was not quite so successful in this; nevertheless, some very impressive portraits by him are to be found in the great galleries of the world (*Alphonse II as a Boy*, Capodimonte, Naples; *Cardinal Ippolito de'Medici and Monsignor Mario*, London, N.G.). As the principal master of the Emilian School, Correggio, who calls to mind Tura's pupils Bianchi and Costa, is far removed from the Ferrarese tradition. In order to be able to discover traces of Costa in his work, we must to go back to the first decade of the Cinquecento and examine the small panel with the *Virgin in Glory* in the Uffizi. However, the Dresden altarpiece *Virgin of St Francis* (1514–15) already shows the influence of Raphael and Leonardo (quite plain in John, who is pointing to the Virgin). The *Rest on the Flight into Egypt* (Uffizi), painted shortly afterwards and composed in a diagonal running from upper left to lower right, shows Correggio as already a perfect synthesis

between the Leonardesque *sfumato* and the Umbrian's colour composition (cf. also *Noli me tangere* from 1519, Prado). An achievement that is entirely his own is the further development of the *sfumato* into 'light-dark painting', with imaginary or concealed sources of light (*Holy Night*, Gemäldegalerie, Dresden; *Adoration of the Child*, Uffizi). Using finer means than Luini, he, too, pursued the reproduction of loveliness, and in so doing painted himself into the hearts of believers and unbelievers alike. He has been reproached for his sentimentality (*Virgin of the Basket*, London, N.G.), but not, however, for the sensuous aura that emanates from his Christian and Gentile saints. We do not disapprove of this, because we sense that this was not his aim but rather a natural consequence of his artistic will (*Ganymede*, Kunsthistorisches Museum, Vienna; *Jupiter and Antiope*, Louvre; *'School of Love'*, London, N.G.). This distinguishes him from the Mannerists, who nevertheless are greatly indebted to him stylistically. In some respects, he was even ahead of them, and many of his works would not seem at all out of place in a Baroque gallery (cf. also the *cupola fresco* in the Cathedral of Parma).

When we speak of the Bolognese, we mean especially the Mannerists Primaticcio (the later head of the School of Fontainebleau), Nicolò dell'Abate, Bartolommeo Passerotti (pl. 90), Prospero, Lavinia Fontana and also the three Carracci. The last of these, however, had already turned their backs on the goals of Fontainebleau. We no longer find Prospero's portrait art convincing today, while his religious depictions betray something of the spirit that was to influence artists following the Council of Trent (*Baptism of Christ*, S. Giacomo, Capella Poggi; *Deposition*, Pinacoteca, Bologna). Even the portraits by his daughter Lavinia (much in demand at the time), in which precious jewellery and splendid robes play a slightly too overwhelming role, are less appealing to us today. A comparison of her *Minerva* in the Borghese Gallery in Rome with the lively female figures of Carracci clearly shows the contrast between the delicious and intellectual Mannerism of the Bolognese and a new style that already proclaims the Baroque. In their contrivance and atmospheric coldness, the landscapes of Nicolò dell'Abate represent something of a step back compared with those of Dosso and Correggio (*Deer Hunt*, Borghese, Rome). While the Bagnacavallo pupil Pellegrino Tibaldi digested influences from Michelangelo in his frescoes in the Palazzo Poggi (*The Odyssey*) and in S. Giacomo (*Concezione del Battista*), Bartolommeo Cesi largely subjugated himself to the demands of the Council of Trent, aiding the general comprehension of his pictorial themes by making his protagonists act with their eyes and hands as if they were communicating in deaf-and-dumb language (*Madonna and Child in Glory and Three Saints*, Pinacoteca, Bologna; *Madonna and Child in Glory with SS Benedict, Francis and John the Baptist*, S. Giacomo, Bologna).

With their reflection on Classical traditions, the cousins Ludovico and Annibale Carracci bridged the gap between Renaissance and Baroque more closely than did the School of Fontainebleau. Annibale's *Lamentation of Christ* and Ludovico's *Betrothal of the Virgin* (both in London) are examples of this. Annibale in particular was successful in fusing Venetian colour with Tuscan sense of form (*Crucifixion with Saints*, S. Carità, Bologna). The *Lamentation* in the Eremitage in St Petersburg has a touching sense of drama and truth – despite the Mannerist gestures of St John – not least in the form of the dead Christ. Whoever searches for the missing links between Correggio and Rubens will find them in the works of the Carracci (*Bacchante*, Uffizi). Their Classicism had, however, also inspired Poussin. The Carracci Academy produced Francesco Albani, Guido Reni and Guercino (influenced by Caravaggio), all highly regarded in their time. We no longer find anything of Cosimo Tura in their art.

In the Veronese School of painting, it is possible to demonstrate a continuous stylistic development between the thirteenth and seventeenth centuries. Even in the constant exchange with the powerful Venetian School, and – in the second half of the fifteenth century – an openness to strong Paduan influences, the Veronese School lost little of its independence and, in particular, its predominantly endearing character. Veronese *joie de vivre* willingly absorbed Venetian colourfulness, despite the all-too academic tendencies of Paduan art, from which it filtered out the Classical and realistic elements, fusing what remained with its own, Nordic-influenced tradition.

The father of the Veronese School is considered to have been the great Altichiero da Zevio (pl. 94), whose *frescoes* in the Basilica di Sant'Antonio in Padua (*Crucifixion* and *Life of St Jacob*) and in S. Anastasia in Verona today bear witness to the upheaval that they caused in the northern Italian painting of the Trecento. At first glance still Gothic in style, his pictures already contain those elements that would become typical of the new painting: physiognomic differentiation, dramatic movement (cf. *Martyrdom of St Catherine*, S. Giorgio, Padua), spatial depth and a striving for plasticity. Giotto's example is unmistakable, his noble formality however displaced by more humanity and down-to-earthness in Altichiero's work (*Cavalli frescoes*, S. Anastasia). The majority of the *frescoes in S. Giorgio* in Padua are probably by his employee Giacomo Avanzi; seven paintings are certainly by the great master's hand, however. Turone of Lombardy, from whom the Castelvecchio in Verona has the no longer complete but otherwise well-preserved *Trinity Polyptych*, also took cues from Giotto and achieved a spatial effect by means of carefully employed perspective.

Strong Nordic influences came to Verona through Stefano da Zevio, painter at the Court of

Philip I of Burgundy. The panel of the *Madonna of the Rose Garden* (Castelvecchio), which in both its structure and detailed reproduction of flowers and birds almost gives the impression of a Persian miniature, is completely non-Italian. Nevertheless, it prepares us for the painting of Antonio di Puccio Pisano (called Pisanello, pl. 95), who must be acknowledged as central to the Veronese art of the Quattrocento. His glory is based not least on his achievements as a medallist, and not merely because he received more honours for these than for his mastery as a painter. His painterly œuvre, profoundly influenced by both Stefano da Zevio and also Gentile da Fabriano, with whom he had collaborated in the Doge's Palace in Venice, is still very puzzling today. Diverse influences, contact with totally divergent traditions (Burgundy, Venice, Florence), combined with a versatile talent as a miniaturist, frescoist and medallist, resulted in an œuvre that is not without its contradictions, this due the fact that it is, in part, a hundred years ahead of its time. Only in this way is it possible to explain why some of his pictures were even attributed to Dürer and Leonardo. Few have survived the intervening years, however. Fires left nothing remaining of his decoration of the Doge's Palace, on which – with interruptions – he spent a total of seventeen years. The small panel *Madonna of the Quail* (Castelvecchio) cannot be ascribed to him with absolute certainty; lack of assurance in the draughtsmanship tends to point against this. However, the *Vision of St Eustace* and the *Virgin with SS George and Anthony Abate* (both London, N.G.) are considered to be verifiably by him. The *Eustace* in particular, with its lovingly painted animals and splendid rider, shining forth from the fabulous dark of the forest like precious stones, gives an impression of Pisanello's unique art.

Liberale da Verona (pl. 96) is more closely bound to the Gothic than his mentor Pisanello, fifty years older than he. Even the influences of Mantegna and Antonello were insufficient to win over the Late Gothic-influenced miniaturist, born in Tuscany, to the new style without reservation (*Missale Romanum*, Biblioteca Communale, Siena). This inner conflict may explain the highly variable quality of his painting (*Adoration of the Child with St Hieronymus*, Castelvecchio). For this reason, too, we cannot expect too much from some of his works, since as chest decorations (so-called *cassone* panels) they should be appraised differently (*Rape of Europe*, Louvre). Also from a chest, but nevertheless of greater artistic importance, is the London panel with the *Suicide of Dido*. This clearly reflects Mantegna's influence, as does the touching *Lamentation* in the Alte Pinakothek in Munich. The *Virgin and Child with Two Angels* (London, N.G.) implies Venetian influences.

Francesco Bonsignori reveals himself to be influenced by Liberale and Mantegna in equal measure. He was summoned to the Court at Mantua, where he painted mainly historical themes and portraits (*Portrait of a Senator*, London, N.G.). His *Madonna with Saints* in the Castelvecchio, Verona, recalls the School of Murano (cf. St Hieronymus in particular), while the *Virgin Adoring the Child* (Castelvecchio) shows strong Mannerist features in his striving for spatial depth and plasticity.

Of Liberale's pupils, Giovanni Francesco Caroto (pl. 99) was "the best . . . and most capable Veronese painter of his generation" (B. Berenson). His early works (*Flight into Egypt* and *Infanticide in Bethlehem*, both in the Uffizi) reveal him to have been already a master of design and dramatic gesture. An encounter with Mantegna influenced him more profoundly than it did Nicolò Giolfino, who, despite his friendship with Andrea, remained more faithful to Liberale's way of seeing. Caroto's *Pietà* (Castelvecchio) is imbued with sensitivity and realism, but remains conservative in its design. His female saints are often reminiscent of Classical goddesses (*St Ursula*, S. Giorgio in Braida, Verona), and cannot deny their Raphaelesque origins. The *Sofonisba* seems to us to be of almost Davidesque Classicism; the same cannot be said for what is probably Caroto's most famous picture, the *Red-headed Youth Holding a Drawing*, in which the boy smiles at us as if he were in a snapshot (both in the Castelvecchio, Verona).

Via the essentially Venice-influenced Domenico Brusasorci (pl. 100), the tradition of Caroto leads us to Paolo Farinati and Paolo Caliari (pl. 101) – who, under the name of Veronese was to become one of the great names of the Italian School of painting – and on to Giambattista Zelotti and Giovanni Antonio Fasolo. Brusasorci discovered the use of colour as a means of design, and, by rejecting strict Paduan outline and turning towards pure painterly design, gave the School of Verona great importance (*Portrait of a Lady*, Providence, Museum of Art). The influence of Giulio Romano is demonstrated, amongst other things, in his later *decorations in the Palazzo Iseppo da Porto* (Mantua) and in his *Martyrdom of St Barbara* (S. Barbara, Mantua).

Domenico Morone, who trained in Padua, was later subject to the influence of Carpaccio, as shown most convincingly in the *Expulsion of the Bonacolsi from Mantua* (Mantua) and the *Trumpet Banner with the Rape of the Sabine Women* (London, N.G.). We find recollections of Schiavone in the physiognomy and flesh tones of the *Virgin and Child* in the Castelvecchio, Verona, a picture that, in its touching composition and realistic warmth, can be regarded as an outstanding example of Veronese painting in the Cinquecento. More works are preserved by Domenico than by his son and pupil, Francesco Morone (pl. 98), whose well co-ordinated, luminous colour dilutes his Paduan heritage (*St Bartholomew*, Castelvecchio; *Virgin and Child*, London, N.G.). He painted numerous *frescoes and panel pictures* for monasteries and churches in Verona and environs (e.g., in Santa Maria in Organo), resulting from close collaboration with Girolamo dai Libri (pl. 97). Girolamo's endearing paintings reveal the tradition of the book illuminator in their faithful reproduction of detail and in their meticulously executed landscape backgrounds (*Adoration with SS Hieronymus and John the Baptist*; *Virgin and Child with SS Peter and Andrew*, both in the Castelvecchio, Verona).

With Francesco Marco Torbido, Giorgione 'gained his entry' into Veronese painting (*Portrait of a Man*, Brera, Milan). However, Torbido's masterpieces also include the *frescoes in the Cathedral of Verona*, with scenes from the *Life of the Virgin and the Prophets*, which are based on cartoons by Giulio Romano. The altarpiece with the *Trinity, Madonna and Saints* in S. Fermo, Verona, is marvellous, and typical of his art. Via Antonio (Giovanni Antonio) Badile, the grandson of Giovanni Badile, his Giorgionesque achievements and also his preference for large-scale, sculptured compositions were transmitted at an early stage to the most famous painter of this School, Paolo Veronese (pl. 93). However, Veronese also unifies the influences of Caroto and Domenico Brusasorci. B. Berenson calls him the "first pure artist-as-painter in Italy". Veronese soon felt too restricted in his native city. After works on the Cathedral of Mantua, he became attracted to Venice, where he quickly gained recognition and, with his works in the Doge's Palace (*Triumph of Venice* in the Sala del Gran Consiglio), attained new citizenship. Despite the powerful artistic personalities in whose circles he moved, and from whom he appropriated certain elements (especially from Tintoretto), his genius was never in danger of losing its individuality and inventive spirit. He combined his enthusiasm for colour – which had hindered him from becoming a sculptor early on – with an intuitive talent for design and composition, which ensures that even his large-format paintings never lose their inner coherence and concentration on the central theme (*Marriage at Cana*, Louvre; *Feast in the House of the Levi*, Accademia, Venice), despite the interplay of colours, the many figures and an abundance of splendid details. However, he never forgot what he acquired in Verona: he almost always used Pseudo-Classical architectures for his design of space, the colourful groups of people standing out against the light facades in such a graphic fashion that it is as if they are seen through a stereoscope (*Family of Darius by Alexandria*, London, N.G.). Even in the *Adoration of the Magi* (also London), the stable of Bethlehem is shown leaning against the ruins of a giant Roman arch. However, it is this painting in particular that reveals the strongest leanings towards the neighbouring School of Bassano in its interpretation and subdued colouring. Veronese, the most important Italian painter in the span between the Renaissance and modern times, is in some respects one of the greatest painting geniuses that the world has produced. We can speculate as to whether it is his lack of depth and his undimmed world view, for which he has been reproached, that set free in him those powers that were essential for his apparently playful mastery of great painterly challenges. His painting, which showed the way for the great Giovanni Battista Tiepolo, is thus completely imbued with Venice's *joie de vivre*, and yet Paolo Caliari is still justified in bearing the surname of Veronese.

Of the late Veronese artists, who took the path towards Mannerism much earlier than their Venetian counterparts, there is another artist who is deserving of mention in addition to Paolo Caliari above. Paolo Farinati was a brilliant draughtsman, and hence had much with which to counteract the painterly influences of his tutor Brusasorci. His pictures display convincing realism and, in their structure, reveal the example of Veronese (*Ecce homo*, Castelvecchio). During his long life, he produced an extensive œuvre that reflects many influences, although with much repetition. Other pupils of Brusasorci, such as his son Felice, Giambattista Zelotti (the nephew of Paolo Farinati), and Bernadino India, remained faithful to their tutor's painting style. They occasionally produced works

which, in their painterly interpretation, anticipate the late works of Titian and Tintoretto (cf. *Flagellation of Christ* by Felice Brusasorci in the Madonna di Campagna church of Verona). While Claudia Ridolfi assumed Mannerist traits perhaps even more so than his contemporaries (*Angel of the Annunciation*, Castelvecchio), the much younger Marcantonio Bassetti was able to assert his own position, despite being undisputedly Baroque. In his portraits (e.g., in the Castelvecchio), which, owing to their concentration on the face and their psychological depth, bear comparison with Rembrandt's portraits, we already find the realism of the end of the seventeenth century represented in exemplary fashion. Here, the Venetian School has nothing comparable to offer.

VIII BRESCIA

Despite an unmistakable Venetian influence, the Brescian School formed and maintained its own character. It owes this not least to Vincenzo Foppa, born in Brescia but active in Milan and Pavia, whose artistic legacy was transmitted further in his native home by his pupils Vincenzo Civerchio (*Birth of Christ with St Catherine*, Brera) and Floriano Ferramola (*Virgin and Child, John the Baptist and a Pope*, Pinacoteca, Brescia). Foppa's great form and Venetian use of colour are combined in the œuvre of Girolamo Romani (called Romanino, plates 103, 104). In his colour co-ordination, he never attains the level of his mentor, Giorgione, but compensates for this with simple, harmonious design (*Virgin and Child Enthroned with Saints*, Museo Civico, Padua; *Adoration of the Child*, Erimitage, St Petersburg; *Dinner at Emmaus*, Brescia). His co-pupil while under Ferramola, Moretto da Brescia (actually Alessandro Bonvicino, pl. 105), is perhaps the most important pupil of this School. His colouring is more subdued than that of the Venetians, but is exquisite and rich in nuances. His saints have a Classical dignity, e.g. the *Justina* in Vienna, whose sad, knowing look puts us in mind of Titian's *Coin* in Dresden. An example of his imaginative composition is the Elias and the Angel (S. Giovanni, Brescia). He cannot compete with the great Venetians in his landscapes, but he certainly can in his portrait art. Through his astute psychological depth and a design that leaves nothing to chance, he was able to produce portraits that can stand alongside any of Titian's (including *Portrait of a Young Man*, London, N.G.; *Portrait of a Cleric*, Alte Pinakothek, Munich).

His pupil, Giovanni Battista Moroni (pl. 106), owes his past and present reputation exclusively to his portraits. His altarpieces (including *Last Judgement*, Parish Church in Goriago; *Coronation of the Virgin*, S. Trinità, Bergamo) are of lesser importance. Of his portraits, which in their structure and painterly quality are on a par with those of his tutor (and, indeed, are occasionally superior) but which do not reveal the interpretation of personality that distinguishes Moretto, *'The Tailor'* in London (N.G.) is the best known, and perhaps also the best. His splendid painting technique is also evident in the *Portrait of a Noblewoman*, also in London.

Giovanni Girolamo Salvoldo (pl. 102) is often unjustifiably counted among the Venetians. His restraint, his preference for twilight and the mysterious, as well as his fine silver tone, which he shares with some of the Lombard masters, must be attributed to the heritage of his native home, Brescia, and is hardly a result of his Venetian training. In Florence, he remained faithful to Fra Bartolommeo, and Venice to Giorgione and Titian. What he took from them, however, he transformed into pictures that are absolutely his own. Moretto has some of his elements, but it is impossible to be sure whether this is due to a common heritage or to influence. A typical example of Salvoldo's individuality is his *Maria Magdalene* (Pitti and London, N.G.): the head and upper body are enveloped in cloth, illuminated by a golden evening light, while the saint gazes thoughtfully at the viewer – an extremely atmospheric and enigmatic picture. The Louvre has his *Portrait of an Artist*, which attracts attention if only by way of its unusual composition and the two mirrors standing at right angles to one another. The *Transfiguration* (Uffizi) is from the master's later years: the boys arranged in shadow at Christ's feet, with their faces and robes lit up by a warm, reddish light, may have served Georges de la Tour as an example a hundred years later.

The Cremonese Altobello Meloni also deserves mention. Especially in his early pictures, he is an example of the appropriation of the Romanino style by the Lombard School (*Deposition*, Brera).

Index of Artists

with references to the different schools
and the importance of each artist
(see also the charts pp. 193 ff.)

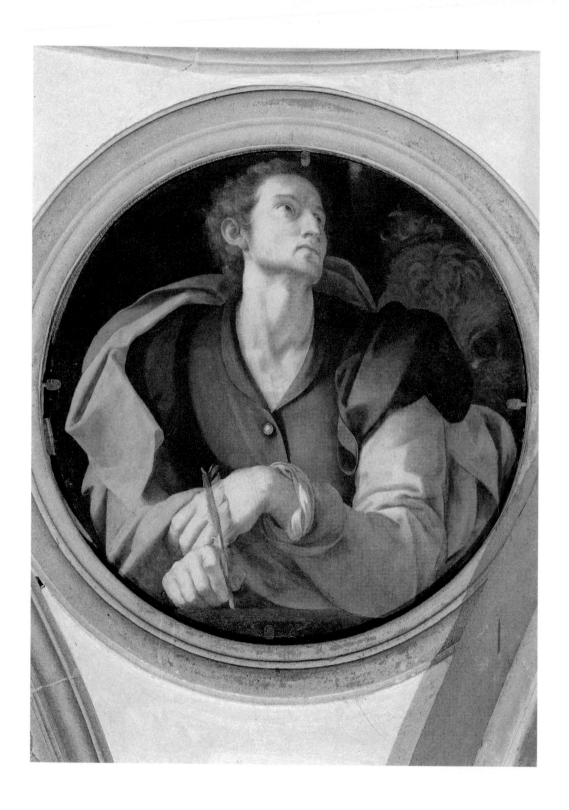

Name	Years of birth, death	School	Comments / References
Abbate, Nicolò dell' Niccolino, Messer Niccolò *pl. 91*	* Modena, after 1509 † France 1571	Fontainebleau VI Emilia-Romagna (C4)	Pupil of his father, Giovanni dell' Abbate; there-after apprenticeship under the sculptor Antonio Begarelli. Trained in accordance with Bagnacavallo and P. Fontana. Studied Flemish landscape painting. Influences from Parmigianino and Correggio. In 1552, he followed Primaticcio to France, where he became one of the founders of the Fontainebleau School.
Adrechi, Stefano	* Nice 1495/1500 doc. until 1541	Liguria V Lombardy (C2)	Painter from Nice in stylistic affinity to L. Brea. Nordic influences. Collaboration with Agostino Casanova is documented from 1523. Active in Genoa and elsewhere in Liguria.
Agabiti, Pietro Paolo	* Sassoferrato, around 1485 † Cupramonte, after 1540	Venice II Venice (C4)	Possibly a pupil of L. Lotto, whose style he at least appropriates. Also influenced by M. Palmezzano. There are a number of paintings by him in the churches of Sassoferrato. Also active as a sculptor and architect.
Agostino da Casanova	active in Liguria btw. 1523 and 1556	Liguria V Lombardy (B6)	Collaboration with Stefano Adrechi of Nice. Influenced by Giovanni Cambiaso.
Agresti , Livio in Vasari erroneously "Livio da Forlì"	* Forlì, active in Rome around 1550 † Rome 1579	III Umbria/Marches (AB4)	Pupil of Perino del Vaga; stylistically, a successor to Raphael.
Alba, Macrino d' Giangiacomo del Alladio	* Piedmont, before 1470 † before 1528	Piedmont V Lombardy (B3)	Training in Vercelli and Milan. Probably spent a period in the Foppa workshop.
Albani, Francesco	* Bologna 1578 † Bologna 1660	Bologna VI Emilia-Romagna (A4)	Came at a very young age into Calvaert's workshop; there, came into contact with Reni. Then adopted commissions for the Carracci. One of the great masters of the Bolognese School; had a crucial influence on Baroque painting owing to his many pupils (incl. Cignani, G.B. Mola, A. Sacchi, and others).
Alberegno, Jacobello	† Venice 1397	Venice II Venice (BC1)	Circle of Paolo Veneziano.
Alberti, Michele	* Florence (?) doc. btw. 1535 and 1582	Florence V Lombardy (A4)	According to Vasari, from Florence. In Rome, he worked for Daniele da Volterra.
Albertinelli, Mariotto *pl. 17*	* Florence 1474 † Florence 1515	Florence I Tuscany (A5)	Pupil of Cosimo Roselli, where he made the acquaintance of Fra Bartolommeo. They later maintained a common studio, until they quarrelled in 1512. It is often difficult to distinguish between their respective works.
Alemagna also Alamagna, see Giovanni d'Alemagna			
Alemanno, Pietro also Alemanni	doc. in the Marches 1475–97 † after 1497	Marches III Umbria/Marches (B2)	Pupil and possibly employee of C. Crivelli. Distinct Paduan influence. Mainly active in the Marches (incl. Ascoli Piceno, Monterubbiano, and Castel Folignano).

Aleni, Tommaso Alenis, called Il Fadino	active in Cremona 1500–26	Cremona V Lombardy (C3)	Painting style is reminiscent of Mazzola and the Venetians of the late Quattrocento. There is much to indicate closer contacts with Galeazzo Campi.
Alfani, Domenico Domenico di Peride	* Perugia, around 1480 † Perugia, after 1553	Perugia III Umbria/Marches (B3)	Raphael was a crucial formative influence. Detectable influences from Fra Bartolommeo.
Alfani, Orazio	* Perugia, around 1510 † Rome 1583	Perugia III Umbria/Marches (B4)	Founding member and later director of the Accademia da Perugia. Employee of his father, Domenico A.
Alibrando, Girolamo Il Raffaelo di Messina	* Messina, around 1470 † 1524	Sicily V Lombardy (B4)	Alibrando's training has not yet been elucidated. A period in Naples was evidently followed by contact with the Lombard School (Bramantino?).
Aliense see Vassilacchi			
Allegri, Antonio see Correggio			
Allegri, Lorenzo	† Correggio 1527	Emilia VI Emilia-Romagna (B3)	Correggio's uncle.
Allegri, Pomponio	* Correggio 1521 † Correggio, after 1593	Emilia VI Emilia-Romagna (BC3)	Son of Correggio, who may however have instructed him in the rudiments of art. Probably a pupil of F.M. Rondani. Later approached the style of the second generation of Parmesan Mannerists (Bertoja and others).
Allori, Alessandro Alessandro Bronzino	* Florence 1535 † Florence 1607	Florence I Tuscany (B7)	Close friend of Bronzino. Became independent in early years. He produced his early works under the impression that Michelangelo made on him. Later, he combined the meticulous Florentine draughtsmanship with the Venetian *chiaroscuro*. His paintings impress by their outstanding technique, although they seem somewhat cold and calculated. Alessandro, together with his (gifted) son, is nevertheless one of the great Florentine Mannerists.
Allori, Cristofano occasionally Bronzino *pl. 20*	* Florence 1577 † Florence 1627	Florence I Tuscany (B7)	Son and pupil of Alessandro. Important representative of the Ital. Late Renaissance with repercussions for the subsequent artistic epoch.
Altichiero da Zevio Alighieri da Zevio *pl. 94*	* Zevio, around 1320 † around 1395	Verona VII Verona (AB1)	The Veronese School took him as a point of departure. Worked in Verona and Padua. Approaches to overcome Gothic rigidity are clearly recognizable in his work. Giotto was a formative influence.
Altobello Melone Altobello dei Meloni	* Cremona (?), around 1485 † before 1543	Cremona VIII Brescia (A2)	Romanino School. Mainly worked in Cremona, however.
Alunno see Niccolò da Foligno			
Amadeo da Pistoia see Maestro Esiguo			
Amalteo, Pomponio	* Motta da Livenza 1505 † San Vito al Taglia- mento 1588	Friuli II Venice (C5)	Training in Porderone's workshop (from *c.* 1515). He carried on the master's work after the latter's death. Remained in the Friulian tradition.
Amatrice, Cola dell see Cola			

Amatrice, Cola dell'
see Cola

Ambrogio da Asti	active in the 1st half of the 16th c.	Pisa I Tuscany (A6)	Could not yet be clearly identified. A panel in Pisa. Influence of D. Ghirlandaio (?).

Ambrogio da Fossano
see Borgognone

Amico di Sandro	15th c.	Florence I Tuscany (A5)	A fictitious name invented by Berenson for an imaginary artist, to whom he ascribed some forty paintings. Berenson himself later abandoned this notion.
Andrea da Assisi l' Ingegno	doc. btw. 1480 and 1521	Umbria III Umbria/Marches (B2)	Vasari describes him as one of Perugino's best assistants.
Andrea da Bologna	active 2nd half of the 14th c.	Bologna	Possibly identical to the miniaturist Andrea di Guido. A *polyptych* (1369), in the museum of Fermo, together with the *Madonna of Humility* (1372), in Pansola, are attributed to him.

Andrea da Como
see Andrea de' Passeri

Andrea da Firenze Andrea Buonaiuto	active in Florence and Pisa, 1346–77	Florence I Tuscany (A1)	In the tradition of Simone Martini.
Andrea da Murano	doc. in Venice from 1463 † Castelfranco 1512	Murano II Venice (A1)	Son of Giovanni da Murano and brother of Girolamo. Works documented from 1462 on. Assistant in the Vivarini workshop. Also worked in Treviso. Last recorded in 1505.

Andrea da Salerno
see Sabatini

Andrea de' Passeri Andrea da Como (?)	doc. in Como 1487–1513/17	Como V Lombardy (A2)	Painter and sculptor in Como. From 1588, active for the Cathedral in Como. Took ideas from Montorfano, Bramante, and Zenale.
Andrea del Brescianino Andrea Piccinelli	* Brescia, around 1485 † Florence, around 1545	Florence I Tuscany (C5)	Documented in Siena, 1507–24. Thereafter, back in Florence.
Andrea di Bartolo *pl. 70*	active 1389–1428 † Siena 1428	Siena I Tuscany (B3)	Son of Bartolo di Fredi. Worked mainly for the Cathedral of Siena. Many preserved works. Probably the father of Giorgio d'Andrea Bartoli.
Andrea di Giusto Manzini	doc. in Florence from 1423 † Florence 1450	Florence I Tuscany (A3)	Successor to Fra Angelico and Masaccio. Assistant to Bicci di Lorenzo.
Andrea di Niccolò di Giacomo	* Siena, around 1440 doc. until 1514	Siena I Tuscany (B4)	Pupil of Matteo di Giovanni Bartoli. In 1470, collaboration with Giovanni di Paolo in Siena.
Andrea di Vanni d'Andrea	* Siena, around 1332 † around 1455	Siena I Tuscany (A2)	In the tradition of Simone Martini and Lippo Memmi. Pupil of Barna (?). Periods in Naples and Sicily.
Andreasi, Ippolito	* Mantua 1548 † Mantua 1608	Mantua V Lombardy (B6)	A typical representative of Mantovanian Mannerism. Parmesan and Roman influences.

Angelico, Fra Giovanni da Fiesole, Fra Beato; actually Guido di Pietro *pl. 4*	* Vicchio 1387 † Rome 1455	Florence I Tuscany (BC2)	One of the grand masters of the Florentine Early Renaissance. Had a great influence on the subsequent generation (Fra Filippo, Dom. Veneziano, Piero della Francesca). Initially still bound to the Gothic style, his painting became ever more assured in its draughtsmanship and richer in colour. In Rome, confronted with the new spirit, he lost much of his intimacy and became grander and more monumental in his frescoes. Angelico was honoured very early on in Florence and Fiesole (qualified in 1634, and officially confirmed in 1940). Like St Luke, he is considered an artists' patron.
Angelo di Baldassare	active mid-15th c.	Umbria III Umbria/Marches (AB2)	In the sphere of influence of Nicolò da Foligno.
Angelo di Bartolommeo called Zotto	doc. in Padua 1469–86	Padua IV Padua (A1)	Son of Bartolommeo Fiumicello. Influenced by Mantegna and the Murano School. Contacts with Jacopo Montagnana.
Angelo di Silvestro	doc. in Padua 1464–1509	Padua IV Padua (AB2)	Came into the Squarcione workshop in 1465.
Anselmi, Michelangelo Michelangelo da Lucca	* Lucca 1491 † Parma 1554	Parma V Lombardy (AB4)	Nothing definite is known about his early training. All indications point to Sodoma and Beccafumi, from whose style he never fully broke away. His later works reveal an orientation towards Parmigianino and Correggio.
Ansuino da Forlì	* Forlì active in the 15th c. in Padua and elsewhere	Forlì VI Emilia-Romagna (C1)	Doc. in Padua, 1451. Pupil of Mantegna; later, crucial Florentine influences.
Antonello da Messina Antonello di Giovanni degli Antoni *plates 25, 26*	* Messina, around 1430 † Messina 1479	Sicily II Venice (C1)	Although his stay in Venice was only brief, his encounters with local artists (Bellini, Vivarini, Jacopo de Barberi, Pennachi, and others) had a lasting impact. His merit lay in transmitting Dutch-Flemish detail, with which he had been confronted with in Sicily and in Naples, to the Venetian School. Claims that he taught oil painting to Giambellini (Vasari) are certainly unsubstantiated. His son, Jacobello di Antonello, copied his style.
Antonello da Serravalle	doc. btw. 1482 and 1507	Venice II Venice (C2)	Active in Sacile and Vittorio Veneto. From the Giambellini circle.
Antoniazzo Romano Antonio Aquilio	* around 1430 † 1508/12	Umbria III Umbria/Marches (B2)	Pupil of B. Gozzoli. Mainly active in Rome. His work reveals influences from Perugino, Melozzo da Forlì, D. Ghirlandaio, and Angelico, with whom he collaborated in 1446–49 and in 1453–55. Important in 15th-c. Roman painting.
Antonio da Crevalcore Antonio Leonelli da C. or Leonello da Crevalcore	active in Bologna from 1478 † Bologna, btw. 1513 and 1525	Bologna VI Emilia-Romagna (C2)	Probably trained in Ferrara. Preference for painting flowers, fruits, and still-lifes.
Antonio da Fabriano Antonio di Agostino di Ser Giovanni da Fabriano	active btw. 1450 and 1490 in Fabriano and Sassoferrato	Fabriano III Umbria/Marches (A1)	Circle of Alegretto Nuzi.
Antonio da Ferrara	active in the 15th c., in Ferrara	Ferrara	Father-in-law of Timoteo Viti. No preserved works.

Antonio da Firenze I	doc. in Udine from 1484 † Udine 1506	Friuli II Venice (BC2)	Workshop in Udine, of which Pellegrino da San Daniele was also a member in 1488.
Antonio da Firenze II Antonio di Jacopo	active in Florence, 1st half of the 15th c.	Florence I Tuscany (A4)	Influenced by Castagno and Fra Angelico.
Antonio da Mel see Giovanni da Mel			
Antonio da Murano	2nd half of the15th c.	Murano II Venice (C1)	Preceded Antonio Vivarini, and not to be confused with him.
Antonio da Negroponte	active in the 15th c.	Venice IV Padua (A2)	Pupil of Marco Zoppo.
Antonio da Padova	active in the 14th c., in Padua	Padua IV Padua (B1)	From the school of Giusto de' Menabuoi.
Antonio da Tisoi	active in Belluno, c. 1490–1520	Belluno II Venice (A2)	Son of the painter Dioneo da Tisoi. Influences from Jacopo Montagnana (from his frescoes in Belluno) and Carpaccio. He later approached the style of Alvise Vivarini.
Antonio da Viterbo	* Viterbo 1400/10 † after 1480	Umbria III Umbria/Marches (A2)	Presumably the father of Francesco di Antonio (il Balletta) and long confused with Antonio del Massaro (il Pastura). Stylistically allied to Benozzo Gozzoli; Sienese influences also probable, however. Mainly worked in Rome.
Antonio del Cerajuolo also Ceraiolo	1st half of the 16th c., in Florence	Florence I Tuscany (B6)	Pupil of Credi, then under Ridolfo Ghirlandaio.
Antonio Monregalese	active in Liguria, first half of the 15th c.	Liguria V Lombardy (BC1)	Verifiably in Piedmont and in western Liguria. Still Late Gothic.
Antonio Veneziano Antonio di Francesco da Venezia	active 1369–1435, in Tuscany	Venice I Tuscany (A2)	Doc. in Siena, Florence, and Pisa.
Appolonio di Giovanni	* Florence 1415 or 1417 † Florence 1465	Florence I Tuscany (C34)	His workshop specialized in chests (cassone). His companion was Marco del Buono Giamberti. Stylistically allied to Pesellino.
Aragonese, Sebastiano di Ghedi	* Chiedi 1523 † after 1567	Brescia VIII Brescia (B2)	Son of the Spanish painter Alessandro Aragonese. Worked under G. Romanino, whose style he appropriated.
Araldi, Alessandro	* Parma, around 1460 † 1530	Parma V Lombardy (C3)	Assistant to Cristoforo Caselli, and in the Mazzola workshop. Influences from Francia and Costa. Borrowed from the moderate Bolognese Classicism.
Arcangelo di Cola da Camerino	doc. 1416–29	Camerino III Umbria/Marches (A1)	Formative influences from contemporary Florentines (incl. Ghiberti) and G. da Fabriano. Mainly active in the Marches (Ancona, Osimo, Camerino).
Arcimboldo, Biagio	1st half of the 16th c.	Milan V Lombardy (A5)	Father and first tutor of Giuseppe A.
Arcimboldo, Giuseppe	* Milan 1527 † Milan 1593	Milan V Lombardy (A5)	Son of Biagio A. Famous for his curious portraits of assembled fruits and plants; also devoted himself to religious themes, however. In 1562, appointed to the Emperor's Court at Prague, where he completed *Four Seasons* and the *Elements*. A period in Vienna. Served under three emperors and – being in any case of noble background – was made a Count Palatinate.

Aretino, Spinello see Spinello, Luca			
Aretino, Valerio Olivieri, Valerio di Agostino d'	* Arezzo 1549 † Perugia 1619	Perugia III Umbria/Marches (B4)	From the Baroccio circle, on the threshold of the Baroque.
Aretusi, Cesare	* Bologna 1549 † Bologna 1612	Bologna VI Emilia-Romagna (C4)	In the Mannerist sphere of influence of Tibaldi, Passerotti, and Sabatini. The formal severity of his religious paintings reflects the Counter-Reforma- tory spirit enforced by Cardinal Gabriele Paleotti Bologna.
Aretusi, Giovanni called Munari	active in Modena at the end of the 15th c.	Modena VI Emilia-Romagna (C2)	Father and tutor of Pellegrino A. A first-rate miniaturist.
Aretusi, Pellegrino Pellegrino Munari or Pellegrino da Modena	* active in Modena, turn of the 16th c. † 1523	Umbro-Roman VI Emilia-Romagna (B3)	Son and pupil of Giovanni Aretusi. Strongly influ- enced by Raphael, to whose workshop in Rome he was admitted.
Arrigo, Fiammingo Arrizzo Fiammingo, correctly Hendrick van den Broeck, or also Paludano	* Malines 1519 (?) † Rome 1597	I Tuscany (AB7)	Pupil of Fr. Floris. Initially active for Duke Cosimo in Florence. Here, he met Vasari and Salviati. Later adopted Venetian ideas. Worked in Umbria and in Rome.
Aspertini, Amico	* Bologna, around 1475 † Bologna 1552	Bologna VI Emilia-Romagna (B2)	Son of Giov. Antonio and brother of Guido A. Trained by Costa and E. Roberti (?); adopted ideas from all schools, however. An inventive eclecticist.
Aspertini, Giovanni and Guido see Aspertini, Amico			
Avanzi, Giacomo da Vanzo	active 1377 in Verona † around 1400	Verona VII Verona (B1)	Employee of Altichiero, also for the fresco painting of S. Giorgio in Padua.
Avanzi, Jacopo degli	* around 1370 † around 1450	Bologna VI Emilia-Romagna (C1)	Frescoes mostly destroyed. Paintings in the Pinacoteca Nazionale, Bologna.
Averara, Giambattista Avernaria	active around 1508 in Bergamo † 1548	Bergamo II Venice (A5)	Painted in the style of Titian. Worked in Veneto, and predominantly in Bergamo.
Bacciacca see Ubertini			
Baccio see Gotti			
Baccio della Porta see Bartolommeo, Fra			
Bachiacca see Ubertini, Francesco			
Badile, Antonio or Giovanni Antonio	* Verona, around 1516 † 1580	Verona VII Verona (B2)	Vasari describes him an assistant to Caroto; he was probably also in the Torbido workshop, however. Representative of the Classicist period of Veronese painting in the 16th c. Also influenced Veronese's development.
Badile, Giovanni	* Verona 1379 † Verona 1451	Verona VII Verona (B1)	Painted in the style of Michelino da Besozzo; also similarities with Stefano da Zevio.
Baglione, Cesare	* around 1550 † Parma 1613	Cremona V Lombardy (B6)	From Bologna or Cremona. Representative of Late Parmesan Mannerism. Bertoja circle.

Bagnacavallo, Bartolommeo
see Ramenghi

Bagnacavallo, Giov. Battista
see Ramenghi

Baietti, Antonio
see Domenico da Udine

Baldassare da Forlì	15th c.	Emilia VI Emilia-Romagna (B1)	From the workshop of Marco Palmezzano.

Baldassare di Biagio da Firenze
"Maestro di Benabbio"; see under Frediani, Vincenzo d' Antonio

Baldassare Estense Baldassare d' Este	* Ferrara, around 1432 † Ferrara 1504	Ferrara VI Emilia-Romagna (A1)	Illegitimate son of Niccolò III d' Este. Worked mainly for Francesco and Galeazzo Maria Sforza in Milan. From there, Borso d'Este summoned him back to Ferrara. There, he had a considerable influence on the development of local painting.
Baldini, Giovanni	* Florence, around 1500 † 1559	Florence I Tuscany (A6)	In 1499, he was in Rome, where lived with Garofalo. Vasari regarded him as a "very good master".
Baldovinetti, Alessandro	* Florence (?) 1425 † Florence 1499	Florence I Tuscany (B3)	Assistant to Castagno. Worked for the churches of Florence in particular. Stylistically allied to Filippo Lippi and Pesellino. His pupils included D. Ghirlandaio, Verrocchio, and Pollaiuolo.
Balducci, Giovanni Cosci	* Florence, around 1560 † Naples, after 1631	Florence I Tuscany (A7)	Naldini and F. Zuccaro determined his artistic course. Initially worked in Florence (Cardinal Alessandro de' Medici was one of his patrons) and Rome (1590). Moved to Naples around 1596, where he opened a workshop. Influence on Late Renaissance painting there.
Balducci, Matteo (di Giuliano di Lorenzo)	* Fontignano 1480/90 † (?)	Umbro-Tuscan I Tuscany (C6)	Pupil of Pinturicchio, later in the Sodoma studio in Siena.
Bandinelli, Baccio Bartolommeo di Michelangelo de' Brandini	* Florence 1493 † Florence 1560	Florence I Tuscany (B6)	Son of a Florentine goldsmith. Piloto encouraged him to take up sculpture. Trained in accordance with Donatello and Verrocchio. Favorite of the Medici after his return in 1512. Vasari regarded him as a great draughtsman. As such, he also influenced Salviati.
Barbagelata, Giovanni	* Genoa, around 1450 † Genoa 1508 (?)	Genoa V Lombardy (C2)	Active in Genoa btw. 1484 and 1508. Collaboration with Tommaso da Novara is documented, from 1484. Stylistically influenced by Foppa, Giov. Mazone, and Brea. Lorenzo Fasolo took over the workshop after his death.

Barbarelli, Giorgio
see Giorgione

Barbari, Jacopo de' Walch, Jakob	* Venice, around 1450 † around 1515, in the Netherlands	Venice II Venice (C2)	In 1505–08, resident in Germany (also in Nuremberg, where he worked for Emperor Maximilian). Emigrated to the Netherlands, at the Court of Philip I of Burgundy. Influenced Dürer, whom he knew from the latter's visit to Venice.

Barbeano see Gianfrancesco da Tolmezzo			
Bardi, Boniforte, Conte de'	1st half of the 15th c.	Liguria V Lombardy (C1)	Younger brother of Donato B.
Bardi, Donato, Conte de'	* Pavia, before 1426 † 1451	Liguria V Lombardy (C1)	Elder brother of Boniforte B. After the loss of their wealth, the two noblemen took up service in Liguria as painters.
Barisino da Modena see Tommaso da Modena			
Barna da Siena also Berna	* Siena † 1380	Siena I Tuscany (A2)	There is still uncertainty concerning the identity of this master. According to one hypothesis, Federico Memmi, brother of Lippo, may be behind this name. B. worked as a fresco executant in Siena, Florence, Cortona, and Arezzo. According to Vasari, he died as a result of an accident in the Cathedral of San Gimignano. He counts as one of Giotto's successors and had a profound influence on A. Vanni.
Barnaba da Modena	* Modena † around 1380	Tuscany / Liguria I Tuscany (B2)	In 1367, settled in Genoa, and was verifiably in Liguria and Piedmont until around 1380. Later, he probably completed the work of Andrea da Firenze at the Campo Santo in Pisa.
Baroccio, Federico (Barocci) also Barroccio, called Fiorida Urbino *pl. 54*	* Urbino, around 1535 † Urbino 1612	Urbino III Umbria / Marches (AB4)	Last important representative of Umbro-Roman Late Mannerism. Little is known about his early training. Trained in accordance with G. Genga, B. Franco, and Titian. Worked for die Della Rovere, and on the Cathedral of Urbino. Appropriated much from Correggio, but enhancing the latter's sentimentality, in which he approaches G. Reni.
Baronzio da Rimini, Giovanni	† before 1362	Rimini VI Emilia-Romagna (A1)	Successor to Giotto.
Bartolino de' Grossi see Jacopo Loschi			
Bartolo di Fredi Battilori	* Siena, around 1330 † Siena, around 1410	Siena I Tuscany (B2)	Active in Siena and in San Gimignano. Pupil of A. Vanni. Enormous talent as narrator and illustrator, but without the depth of feeling of, e.g., Luca di Tommé or Taddeo di Bartolo.
Bartolommeo da Miranda	active in Umbria btw. 1435 and 1475	Spoleto III Umbria / Marches (B3)	In the tradition of the local School of Spoleto. Collaboration (?) with Bartolommeo di Tommaso.
Bartolommeo della Gatta	* 1448 (?) † around 1502	Umbro-Tuscan I Tuscany (B5)	Painter and miniaturist. Assistant to Signorelli and Perugino. Strongly influenced by Piero della Francesca's frescoes in Arezzo.
Bartolommeo di Bindo see Lodovico di Angelo			
Bartolommeo di David	* Siena (?), around 1480 † 1544	Siena I Tuscany (C6)	This master was acknowledged only recently (Romeagnoli, before 1835, and Milanesi, 1854). Worked mainly in Siena and environs. Collaboration with Beccafumi, Giovanni di Lorenzo, and Baldassare Peruzzi is substantiated.

Bartolomeo di Giovanni Alunno di Domenico (Berenson)	doc. in Florence 1488	Florence I Tuscany (A5)	Identified only recently, on the basis of the *predelle* for a Ghirlandaio altar for the Ospedale degli Innocenti in Florence. Several works have been attributed to him in the meantime. Also worked under Botticelli's guidance.
Bartolommeo di San Marco, Fra called Baccio della Porta, also Bartolommeo del Fattorino	* Savignano 1472 † Florence 1517	Florence I Tuscany (BC5)	Apprenticeship together with Albertinelli (under Cosimo Roselli), with whom he later shared a workshop. Savonarola's addresses moved him so profoundly that he became a monk. Following a creative pause, he travelled to Rome and Venice. Here, the works of Giambellinis and Raphael had a detectable influence on him. Andrea del Sarto attributes to him the Venetian fusion of colour and shaded contours.
Bartolommeo di Tommaso da Foligno	2nd half of the 15th c.	Foligno III Umbria/Marches (B2)	Founder of the Foligno School. Worked in Ancona from 1425–33, and in Rome around 1450. Olivuccio di Ceccarello may have been his first tutor.
Bartolommeo Veneto Bartolommeo Veneziano	doc. in Venice 1502–55	Veneto-Lombard II Venice (A3)	A.Venturi attracted attention to this painter in 1899. According to him, he was a pupil of Gentile Bellini. He worked at the Court of the Grand Duke of Ferrara and elsewhere. There, he came under the influence of Lombard artists.
Basaiti, Marco Marcus Basitus or Baxaiti	* Venice (Friuli?) 1470/75 † Venice, after 1530	Venice II Venice (B4)	His name is indicative of Greek origin. Pupil of Alvise Vivarini; later, crucial formative influence from Giov. Bellini. A first-rate colourist.
Baschenis, Simone II	* Valle Averaria, around 1490 † Valle Averaria 1555	Bergamo (Trent) II Venice (5)	Son of Cristoforo di Simone. The most important artist from this Bergamasque painter dynasty of Trentese origin, which influenced the Trentese for nearly a century.
Bassano, Francesco (the Elder) Francesco da Ponte (the Elder)	* Bassano 1470/75 † Bassano, before 1541	Bassano II Venice (A4)	Founder of the famous painter dynasty in Bassano. According to Lanzi, Francesco received his training under Bellini, in Venice. Worked mainly in Bassano and environs.
Bassano, Francesco (the Youger) Francesco Giambattista da Ponte	* Bassano 1459 † Venice 1592	Bassano II Venice (A6)	Eldest son, pupil, and employee of Jacopo da Ponte. First independent work in 1574.
Bassano, Gerolamo da Ponte	* Bassano 1566 † Venice 1621	Bassano II Venice (A6)	Son of Jacopo and brother of the younger Francesco. Studied medicine in Padua, then turned to painting. Active in Venice and Bassano.
Bassano, Giambattista da Ponte	* Bassano 1553 † Bassano 1613	Bassano II Venice (A6)	Son of Jacopo B. Also collaborated with Luca Martinelli (1593) in Bassano and environs.
Bassano, Jacopo da Ponte Giacomo da Ponte *pl. 39*	* Bassano 1515/16 † Bassano 1592	Bassano II Venice (A5)	Son of Francesco (the Elder) and father of Francesco (the Younger), Gerolamo, Leandro, and Giambattista. The most important exponent of the Bassano School. After initial training under his father, he was admitted to Bonifazio Veronese's workshop in Venice. Under the influence of Vasari and Salviati, he approached Central Italian Mannerism, but always remained original, and occupies an exceptional position owing to the bucolic elements that are also found in his religious paintings.

Bassano, Leandro da Ponte	* Bassano 1557 † Venice 1622	Bassano II Venice (A6)	Youngest and most gifted son of Jacopo. Trained under his father. Initially worked in Bassano, only to settle permanently in Venice later on. Continued the work of his brother Francesco in the Doges' Palace after the latter's death. Distinct Late Mannerist influence in later works (F. Zuccari).
Bassetti, Marcantonio	* Verona 1588 † Verona 1630	Verona VII Verona (B3)	Pupil of Felice Brusasorci. Developed further in Venice, under Tintoretto's influence.
Bastiani, Lazzaro see Sebastiani			
Bastiano see Sebastiano Filippi			
Bastiano di Niccolò da M. Carlo see Sebastiano di Niccolò			
Battista da Como see Semino, Antonio			
Battista del Moro	1st half of the 16th c.	Verona VII Verona (B2)	Pupil of Torbido. His son, Marco, was chiefly a copperplate engraver.
Baudo, Luca da Novara	* Novara † Genoa 1509	Liguria V Lombardy (B3)	Presumably a pupil of Foppa. Verifiably in Liguria btw. 1491 and 1510. Mainly active in Genoa.
Bazzi see Sodoma			
Beccafumi, Domenico Domenico di Giacomo di Pace, called Mecarino	* Montaperti 1482/86 † Siena 1551	Siena I Tuscany (C5)	Vasari's information on B.'s early training is not very credible. He probably trained in the workshop of a certain Mecarino. Apart from journeys to Rome (1510), Genoa, and Pisa, he worked in Siena. Also had contact with Sodoma there. In Rome, Michelangelo and Raphael impressed him, as is evident in his portraits of women. He must have also taken account of Perugino's works in Rome.
Bedoli or Bedolli see Mazzola			
Bellini, Filippo	* Urbino around 1550 † Macerata 1603	Umbria III Umbria/Marches (B4)	Representative of Umbrian Late Mannerism. Mainly active in the Marches. On friendly terms with F. Zuccari, to whom he was in part indebted stylistically.
Bellini, Gentile	* Venice 1429 † Venice 1507	Venice II Venice (A1)	Son of Jacopo B. and elder brother of Giovanni. After initial collaboration with Giovanni, he later became independent. In his time he was nearly more famous than his brother, in part also owing to his large-format *vetutiste* of Venice. Period in Istanbul, at the Court of Sultan Mahomet II. Carpaccio came from his school. Titian, too, may have worked for a brief time (a few days?) in his workshop.
Bellini, Giovanni called Giambellino or Giambellini *plates 23, 24*	* Venice or Padua 1432 † Venice 1516	Venice II Venice (B2)	Son and pupil of Jacopo, and brother of Gentile B. Style crucially influenced by Mantegna and Antonello da Messina. Together with Titian, Giorgione, and Palma Vecchio, one of the grand masters of the Venetian School. His *Madonna* type had model character for later Venetians. His

86

			mature works, with their harmonious design, warm beauty, and technical perfection represent a point of departure for the art of Giorgione and Titian. A long creative period and a large studio carried Giambellino's influence far beyond Venice and the Veneto. Dürer was one of his admirers.
Bellini, Jacopo	* Venice, around 1400 † around 1470	Venice II Venice (A1)	Father and first tutor of Gentile and Giovanni B. Lived temporarily in Padua, where he came into contact with the Squarcione School. He took diverse inspiration from his numerous travels in Northern Italy (Pisanello, Gentile da Fabriano, Uccello) which he transmitted to his sons early on. Mantegna was his son-in-law.
Belliniano, Vittore see Vittore di Matteo			
Bello, Jacopo (Giacomo)	active in Venice, turn of the 16th c.	Venice II Venice (A2)	Came from the workshop of Lazzaro Sebastiani.
Bello, Marco Belli	* Girgenti or Venice, around 1500	Venice II Venice (C2)	Probably a pupil of Giambellino. In 1511, active in Udine.
Bellunello, Andrea actually Andrea di Bertolotto	* Belluno, around 1430 † San Vito al Tagliamento 1494	Friuli II Venice (C5)	Doc. in Fiumignano (1468) and Udine (1470). One of the grand masters of the Friuli in the 15th c. His style was directed towards the Vivarini, and also Crivelli and Giov. d'Alemagna. Other than Udine and San Vito, he also worked in Porderone, Spilimbergo, and Forni di Sopra.
Bembo, Andrea	doc. in Brescia btw. 1430 and 1459	Brescia VIII Brescia (B2)	Son of Giovanni B.
Bembo, Benedetto	* Brescia doc. 1462–89	Bergamo V Lombardy (C1) VIII Brescia (B1)	Moved from Brescia to Bergamo, and was active there from 1465. Younger brother of Bonifazio B.
Bembo, Bonifazio Fazio da Valdorno	* Brescia † Cremona, after 1477	Cremona V Lombardy (C2)	Son of Giovanni B. Active mainly in Cremona. Doc. between 1444 and 1477. There is a card game by him in the Brera that indicates contact with the art of Pisanello. Collaboration with Leonardo Ponzoni (1472).
Bembo, Gianfrancesco called il Vetraro (in Vasari: Giovanni Francesco Vetraio)	* btw. 1490 and 1500, in Cremona doc. until 1536 (1543?)	Cremona V Lombardy (C2)	Owing to frequent confusion over names, the biographies of the individual members of the large family of painters are difficult to reconstruct. According to Vasari, Gianfrancesco worked in Rome for Pope Leo X (1513–15). Thereafter active in Cremona.
Bembo, Lorenzo	active in Cremona, 15th c.	Cremona V Lombardy (C2)	Father of Gianfrancesco and brother of Bonifazio B.
Bembo, Pietro	active in Cremona, 16th c.	Cremona V Lombardy (C3)	Pupil of, and assistant to Boccaccio Boccaccino for the painting of frescoes for the Cathedral of Cremona (1505–18).
Benaglio, Francesco	* Verona 1432 † after 1482	Verona VII Verona (A2)	Mainly active in Verona. One of Francesco Bonsignori's tutors. Under the influence of Mantegna and Giambellini.
Benaglio, Girolamo	* Verona 1469	Verona VII Verona (A2)	Son of Francesco B.

Benedetto di Bindo Zoppo Benedetto da Siena	doc. in Siena 1411–17 † Siena 1417	Siena I Tuscany (B1)	Under the influence of Giotto and Simone Martini. Tutor of Sassetta.
Benvenuto di Giovanni di Meo del Guasta	* Siena (?) 1436 † 1518	Siena I Tuscany (A4)	Pupil and employee of Vecchietta. In 1453, worked in the Baptistry of Siena. Strongly influenced by the book illuminations of Liberale and Girolamo da Cremona. Some of his small panels (Washington) look like a naive anticipation of Mantegna. Last painting from 1509.
Bernadino de' Conti	* Pavia (?), around 1450 active btw. 1496 and 1522 in Milan	Milan V Lombardy (C2)	Pupil of Zenale. Mainly active in Milan. Influence from Leonardo. Numerous preserved portraits.
Bernardino d'Antonio del Signoraccio, called Detti	* Pistoia 1460 † Pistoia, after 1532	Tuscany I Tuscany (B5)	Tutor of Fra Paolino.
Bernardino da Asola	* Asola (?), around 1490 † Venice, around 1535/40	Venice II Venice (B5)	Son of Giovanni da Asola. His œuvre ist difficult to distinguish from that of his father. He fused elements of the Brescia School with influences from Titian and Dosso.
Bernardino di Castelletto Bern. di Castelletto di Massa	doc. 1481 and 1490	Lucca I Tuscany (B4)	In the tradition of the Lucca School. Borrowed from Filippo Lippi and D. Ghirlandaio.
Bernardino di Girolamo Roselli	* Florence, turn of the 16th c. active in Perugia from 1532–69	Florence III Umbria/Marches (A4)	From the Andrea del Sarto workshop in Florence.
Bernardino di Mariotto dello Stagno	* Perugia, around 1478 † 1566	Perugia III Umbria/Marches (A3)	Influence from Nicolò da Foligno, and especially from Crivelli. Mainly active in the Marches and in Sanseverino.
Bernazzano, Cesare(?) Christian name not verified. Possible confusion with Cesare da Sesto	active in Milan, turn of the 16th c.	Milan V Lombardy (A4)	According to Vasari, a first-rate painter of landscapes, animals, and plants. Collaboration with Cesare da Sesto. Francesco Melzi's paintings also feature flowers in B.'s style.
Berruguete, Alonso	* Paredes de Nava 1486 † Toledo 1561	Spain III Umbria/Marches (B3)	Arrived in Italy in 1507/08, where he came into Michelangelo and Raphael's sphere of influence. In 1512, in Florence, where was confronted with Andrea del Sarto's work and that of his pupils, Pontormo and Rosso. Later influences from Perin del Vaga and Polidoro. Returned to Spain around 1516.
Berruguete, Pedro	* Paredes, around 1450 † 1504	Spain III Umbria/Marches (A2)	Painter at the Court of Ferdinand the Catholic. Influences from Perugino are probably due to a period in Florence. Worked in the Ducal Palace of Urbino. Father of Alonso B.
Berto di Giovanni called Marco	active in Perugia from 1488 † before 1529	Perugia III Umbria/Marches (B3)	Pupil of, and assistant to Perugino. Collaborated with Sinibaldo Ibi on an altar for die Sant' Agostino brotherhood. Retained his tutor's style.
Bertoia, Jacopo Zanguidi	* Parma 1544 † Parma 1574	Parma V Lombardy (B6)	Pupil of Procaccini, later strongly influenced by Parmigianino.
Bertucci, Jacopo also Jacopone	* Faenza, around 1502 † 1579	Romagna / Rome VI Emilia-Romagna (A3)	Trained under his uncle, Girolamo. First doc. in Rome 1534, where he was in contact with Dosso and Battista Dossi. Later became an assistant to Taddeo Zuccari. His brother Michele B. was also a painter in Faenza, but died aged only 24.
Bertucci, Michele see Jacopo Bertucci			

Besozzo, Leonardo Molinari da also Bisuccio or Bissuccio	active 1st half of the 15th c., in Milan, † 1460 (?) in Naples	Milan V Lombardy (A1)	Son and pupil of Michelino da Besozzo.
Besozzo, Michelino da Michelino Molinari da B. (identical to Michele da Pavia?); also Bisuccio or Bissuccio	* Pavia (?) doc. 1388–1450	Milan V Lombardy (AB1)	Active in Milan 1420/25, Venice 1430/39, Milan 1439/42. Father of Leonardo da B. Numerous works in the Cathedral of Milan. Important Lombard master.
Bevilacqua, Filippo see Giovanni Ambrogio Bevilacqua			
Bevilaqua, Ambrogio also Giovanni Ambrogio, called il Liberale	* Milan (?), around 1450 doc. in Milan 1481–1512	Milan V Lombardy (AB2)	Lomazzo counts Giov. Ambrogio, together with his younger Brother Filippo, among the innovators of Lombard art. From 1481, active for the Court of Francesco Sforza. Counts as one of Foppa's successors. Some of his works were long attributed to Borgognone.
Bezzi, Giovanni Francesco called Nosadella	* Bologna, around 1530 † Bologna 1571	Bologna VI Emilia-Romagna (C4)	A member of the circle of Mannerists influenced by Raphael and Tibaldi, whose style is occasionally referred to as "Neoraphaelism".
Bezzi, Lorenzo also Beci, Becci, Berci, or Berti	* Cremona 16th c.	Cremona V Lombardy (BC3)	Pupil of Galeazzo Campi. Doc. in Cremona, 1517–21.
Bianchi, Giovanni called Bertone	doc. 1559–74	Emilia VI Emilia-Romagna (A4)	Active in Reggio Emilia, Zagarolo, and Rome. Circle of Lelio Orsi.
Bianchi-Ferrari, Francesco de' called il Frari	* 1457 † Modena 1510	Modena VI Emilia-Romagna (BC1)	Probably originated from the Tura School. Worked predominantly in Modena. Some of his paintings were attributed to Roberti and Mantegna. Considered one of Correggio's tutors.
Biazaci, Tommaso and Matteo	active btw. 1465 and 1490	Liguria / Piedmont V Lombardy (C2)	The brothers were active in Liguria and Piedmont. They probably received their training and artistic orientation from Pietro da Saluzzo.
Bicci di Lorenzo	* 1373 † Florence 1452	Florence I Tuscany (A2)	Son of, and assistant to Lorenzo di Bicci. Took over the running of the workshop (according to Frosini) around 1404. Collaboration with Domenico Veneziano is documented for frescoes for St Egidio (Florence, 1438–41).
Bicci, Lorenzo di	* Florence (?), around 1350 † 1427	Florence I Tuscany (A2)	The frescoes in Florence and Arezzo that some art historians (incl. Cavalcaselle) attribute to him are probably those of his son, Bicci di Lorenzo.
Bicci, Neri di	* Florence 1419 † Florence 1491	Florence I Tuscany (A3)	The best-known representative of this large painter dynasty. Maintained a large workshop, which also produced Cosimo Roselli and Fr. Botticini, amongst others.
Bigordi see Ghirlandaio			
Biliverti, Giovanni (Bilivert) also Bilivelti or Birivelti	* Maastricht 1576 † 1644 (?)	I Tuscany (C7)	The most important pupil of Cigoli in Florence, with whom he later went to Rome. Returned to Florence before Cigoli's death and worked at the Court of the Grand Duke. One of the outstanding Florentine painters on the threshold of the Baroque. A first-rate colourist.

Bisconti, Organtino
see Organtino di Mariano

Bissolo, Francesco (Bissuolo) also Pier-Francesco	* Treviso, around 1470 † Venice 1554	Venice II Venice (AB5)	Originated from the workshop of Giambellino, whose style of the last years of the 15th c. he retained.
Bisuccio, Leonardo da see Besozzo			
Bizzelli, Giovanni	* Florence 1556 † 1612	Florence I Tuscany (C7)	Pupil of A. Allori. Worked in Rome and Florence.
Blacci, Bernardino called il Blaceo	* Udine 1500/10 † Udine 1570	Friuli II Venice (C6)	Details of this artist (who was also a guilder) have only come to light in the last thirty years. In Pordenone's sphere of influence. Collaboration with Floreani is documented.
Boccaccino, Bartolommeo	active c. 1480–1520	Lombardy VI Emilia-Romagna (B2)	Pupil of Boccaccio B. The nature of the relationship is unclear.
Boccaccino, Camillo	* Cremona 1504/05 † Cremona 1546	Cremona V Lombardy (C3)	Son of Boccaccio B. Highly gifted, but died too young. Together with Giulio Campi he represents the apogee of the Cremonese School. Trained in Venice in accordance with the works of Titian, Sebastiano del Piombo, and Bordone (?). Shows many similarities to Correggio, despite never having been his pupil, however.
Boccaccio, Boccaccino (the Younger)	active mid-16th c.	Lombardy V Lombardy (C4)	Son of Camillo B. Studied under G. Campi.
Boccacino, Boccaccio pl. 73	* Ferrara (?), before 1466 † Cremona 1524/25	Cremona VI Emilia-Romagna (AB2)	His training under D. Panetti had little impact on his alliance to the School of Cremona, on which he had a crucial influence. Influences from Perugino are probably due to a period in Rome. Other than Camillo, his pupils included Garofalo and G. Campi.
Boccati, Giovanni also Boccatis or Boccato da Camerino pl. 45	* Camerino, around 1420 † 1487	Perugia III Umbria/Marches (A1)	In 1445, obtained citizenship in Perugia. Initially influenced by the Florentines Lippi, Fra Angelico, and Uccello, amongst others, later by the Sienese, in particular Domenico di Bartolo.
Boldrini, Leonardo	* Murano † 1497	Murano II Venice (C2)	Documented 1452–93. Clearly and formatively influenced by the Vivarini. Collaboration with Alvise Vivarini (?). Influence from Marco Zoppo.
Boltraffio, Giovanni Antonio also Beltraffio pl. 69	* Milan 1467 † Milan 1516	Milan V Lombardy (B3)	Came from a distinguished Milanese family. Leonardo had a lasting formative influence on him, as on his co-pupils Predis, Giampetrino, d'Oggione, and others. Became independent in 1498. Painted altarpieces and numerous portraits. An important master in succession to da Vinci.
Bonaccorsi see Perino del Vaga			
Bonacorso di Cino also Dicino	* Florence, active in Pistoia, 1347, and elsewhere	Florence I Tuscany (C1)	In Taddeo Gaddi's sphere of influence.
Bonamico di Cristofano see Buffalmacco			

Bonasia, Bartolommeo also Bonascia	* Modena, mid-15th c. † 1537	Lombardy / Emilia VI Emilia-Romagna (BC2)	Painter, wood-carver, and architect in Modena. Influenced by Mantegna and Piero della Francesca.
Bonasone, Giulio di **Antonio** also Buonasone	* Bologna, around 1498 † around 1580	Bologna VI Emilia-Romagna (B4)	His reputation is chiefly as a copperplate engraver. From the school of L. Sabatini.
Bonfigli, Benedetto (the **Elder)** also Buonfigli *pl. 44*	* Perugia, around 1420 † Perugia 1496	Umbria III Umbria / Marches (A1)	Training under Domenico Veneziano and influenced by Benozzo Gozzoli and Giovanni Boccati, amongst others. Painted beautiful faces; in total, however, somewhat cold and stiff in his composition. Amongst other things, he painted numerous standards for the guilds in Perugia.
Bonfigli, Benedetto (the **Younger)**	active around 1500, in Perugia	Umbria III Umbria / Marches (A1)	Son of Benedetto (the Elder)
Bonifazio Veronese see Pitati, Bonifazio			
Bono see Giambono, Michele			
Bono da Ferrara	active in Verona and Padua, 15th c.	VI Emilia-Romagna (B1)	Assistant to Pisanello, and later to Squarcione and Mantegna. Identity with an artist of the same name, who was active between 1442 and 1461 in the Cathedral of Siena, is unlikely.
Bonomo, Jacobello di	active in Venice, 2nd half of the 14th c.	Venice II Venice (A1)	Together with Francesco Jacobello, one of the very early masters of the Venetian School.
Bonone, Carlo also Bononi	* Ferrara 1569 † Ferrara 1632	Ferrara VI Emilia-Romagna (B4)	Painter and book illuminator. Pupil of Carracci. Later, further training in Rome, Parma, and Venice (Tintoretto); remained true to the Carracci style, however.
Bonsignori, Fra Girolamo	* Verona, around 1440 † Mantua, around 1519	Verona VII Verona (A2)	Brother of Francesco Bonsignori. Initially orien- tated towards Mantegna and Leonardo; later, he reflected Fra Angelico. Some of his paintings have occasionally been attributed to Caroto.
Bonsignori, Francesco in Vasari, erroneously Monsignori	* Verona 1455 † Caldiero 1519	Verona VII Verona (A2)	Training under Liberale, whose painting style he retained, until he moved to Mantua in 1490, and also received ideas from Mantegna. Worked for Francesco II Gonzaga.
Bonvicino (Buonvicino) see Moretto			
Bordone, Paris also Bordon *pl. 40*	* Treviso 1500 † Venice 1571	Venice II Venice (C5)	Training under Titian from around 1515; later under Giorgione, whose style he approached. Worked mainly in Venice, Belluno, and Vicenza; much travelled. Periods in France and possibly in Augsburg (1540). A great painter, but not an in- novator. One of Tintoretto's tutors.
Borgognone, Ambr. di **Giorgione**	* Pavia, mid-15th c.	Pavia V Lombardy (B2)	Painted in Ambrogio di Stefano's style, with whom he is occasionally confused. Pupils?
Borgognone, Ambrogio Ambrogio di Stefano da Fossano; in Italy, also Bergognone *pl. 62*	* Fossano around 1453 † 1523	Milan VI Lombardy (B2)	Pupil of Foppa. Leonardo had hardly any influence on him. His youthful *Madonnas* are deeply per- ceived and are evidence of the naive piousness of their creator. Reserved in his use of colour, with

			fine silver tone, typical of Lombard painting. Together with Foppa, the greatest painter of the Milanese School.
Borgognone, Bernadino Bernardino di Stefano da Fossano	* Fossano, around 1465 † after 1524	Piedmont V Lombardy (B2)	Probably the brother of Ambrogio B.
Boscoli, Andrea	* Florence † 1606	Marches I Tuscany (AB7)	Pupil of Santi di Tito. Worked mainly in the southern Marches; Journeys to the Veneto, the Liguria, and the Emilia are verified, however. His Early Baroque style had a considerable influence on painting in the Marches.
Boselli, Antonio	* San Giovanni Bianco 1470/75 † Bergamo, btw. 1527 and 1532	Bergamo II Venice (A5)	Painter and wood-carver. From a large artistic family, he is considered one of the main representatives of Bergamasque painting at the turn of the Cinquecento. Influences from Palma and L. Lotto.
Bosilio, Antonio and Manfredino	active 2nd half of the 15th c.	Piedmont V Lombardy (C2)	Brothers from the Tortona region. Engaged by Lodovico Sforza for the decoration of the Sala della Balla in the Castel of Milan. Influenced by Foppa, Braccesco, Brea, and Corso.
Bosis, Daniele de'	active in Milan, 2nd half of the 15th c. † 1505	Lombardy V Lombardy (C2)	A partnership with Giacomo Dal Pozzo is documented (1496), for the execution of an altarpiece. In 1490, together with other painters, entrusted by Lodovico Sforza with the decoration of the Sala della Balla. Otherwise active in Biella and Novara.
Botticelli, Sandro Alessandro di Mariano Filipepi *pl. 7, 8*	* Florence 1445 † Florence 1510	Florence I Tuscany (AB5)	His tutor was, in fact, Filippo Lippi. Participation (as apprentice or assistant) in the Verrocchio workshop is considered verified. Independent from around 1470. Collaboration with the Pollaiuolo brothers in Florence, and on frescoes in the Sistine Chapel (1481). Came under Savonarola's influence, with distinct consequences for his later work. To a great degree, his art embodies the Florentine tradition, and yet he attained an exceptional position with his brilliant sense of outline, his refined interpretation, and his ponderous sentimentality. Despite many pupils, including his tutor's son, Filippino Lippi, he remained the first and last of his painterly world.
Botticini, Francesco	* Florence 1447 † Florence 1497	Florence I Tuscany (C5)	Pupil of his father, Giovanni di Domenico; later in the workshop of Neri di Bicci and Verrocchio, together with Botticelli and Leonardo (?). His style is strongly influenced by Botticelli, to whom various paintings by Botticini have also been attributed.
Botticini, Raffaelo	* Florence 1477 † after 1520	Florence I Tuscany (C5)	Son and pupil of Francesco B. Other than his father, influenced by Perugino and D. Ghirlandaio. His style is occasionally reminiscent of L. Credi.
Braccesco, Carlo di Giovanni Carlo da Milano, Carlo di Mantegna	* Pavia active in Liguria btw. 1478 and 1501	Liguria V Lombardy (B2)	Adopted diverse ideas during numerous journeys, which makes it difficult to ascribe his works correctly. Only in 1942 did R. Longhi draw attention to B. and recognize him as the creator of some hitherto "anonymous" paintings (still disputed nevertheless).

Bragadin, Donato di Giovanni Donato Veneziano	doc. 1438–73	Venice II Venice (B1)	According to Longhi, aside from Jacopo Bellini (with whom he collaborated for a time) and Antonio Vivarini, "the only name worthy of mention btw. 1440 and 1460". The family produced a series of 15th-c. Venetian painters, incl. Antonio di Bernardo, Domenico, Giacomo di Donato, and Tommaso di Donato.
Bramante, Donato Donato d'Angelo Lazzari, Bramante da Urbino	* Fermignano 1444 † Rome 1514	III Umbria / Marches (B2)	Better known as a master-builder (incl. St Peter's in Rome) than as a painter. In his youth – probably influenced by Alunno and the Florentines – he brought the Tusco-Umbrian heritage to Milan. Here, his influence can be seen most clearly in Borgognone and Bramantino.
Bramantino see Suardi, Bartolommeo			
Brea, Ludovico	* Nice, around 1443 † 1520	Nice / Liguria V Lombardy (C2)	Provencal influences came to Liguria through him. Jean Miralhet and Jacopo Duranti are believed to have been his tutors. The works of his later career, not always uniform in quality, are indicative of a large workshop.
Brescianino see Andrea del Brescianino			
Brini, Francesco and Giovanni	* Florence 1540 (?) † Florence 1586	Florence I Tuscany (A6)	With his brother, Giovanni, pupil under Michele Tosini.
Bronzino, Angelo Agnolo di Cosimo Allori pl. 19	† Monticelli 1503 † Florence 1572	Florence I Tuscany (A6)	Pupil of, and assistant to Pontormo, after an early apprenticeship under Raffaelino del Garbo. Court Painter to Grand Duke Cosimo I. Undeniably the greatest Florentine portraitist of the 16th c. Impressive treatment of expensive materials. Tutor of Alessandro Allori.
Brusasorci, Agostino see Felice Brusasorci			
Brusasorci, Domenico Domenico del Riccio pl. 100	* Verona 1516 † Verona 1567	Verona VII Verona (A2)	Representative of Veronese Proto-Mannerism, based on Raphael, Parmigianino, and Giulio Romano. Berenson refers to Domenico's "purely painterly" interpretation, which he still developed before the Venetians. Had a great influence on the Veronese School through his pupils Zelotti, India, and Paolo Farinati.
Brusasorci, Felice Felice del Riccio	* Verona 1542 † Verona 1605	Verona VII Verona (A3)	Son of Domenico B. and nephew of Agostino B., from whom he received his initial training. Later subject to the direct influence of the Florentine Mannerists Rosso, Vasari, and Naldini.
Buffalmacco actually Bonamico di Cristofano	* Florence † after 1351	Florence I Tuscany (B1)	Pupil of Tafo and a contemporary of Giotto. Worked on the Campo Santo in Pisa, amongst other things.
Bugatti, Zanetto	doc. in Milan, from 1458 † Milan 1476	Milan V Lombardy (A1)	Fresco painter and portraitist, who also worked for the Sforza Court. Distinguished portraitist and medallist. Closer contacts with Bonifazio Bembo and V. Foppa, as well as contact with Flemish art (v.d. Weyden).

Bugiardini, Giuliano di Piero also Buggiardini	* near Florence 1475 † Florence 1554	Florence I Tuscany (A5)	From D. Ghirlandaio's workshop. Later, collaboration with Albertinelli (with whom he shared a studio). Strongly influenced by Raphael, but also by Fra Bartolommeo.
Buonaccorsi, Pietro see Perino del Vaga			
Buonaiuti see Andrea da Firenze			
Buonarotti see Michelangelo			
Buonaventura see Segna di Buonaventura			
Buonconsiglio, Giovanni called il Marescalco	* Montecchio Maggiore c. 1465 † Venice 1536/37	Venice II Venice (B2)	In 1495, moved from Vicenza to Venice. Kept his own workshop there. In the tradition of Giambellini and Antonello. Contacts with Montagna. Sometimes reminiscent of the Veronese School.
Buoninsegna see Duccio			
Buontalenti, Bernardo called delle Girandole	* Florence 1536 † 1608	Florence I Tuscany (A7)	Painter, sculptor, architect, and miniaturist. Training under Salviati, Vasari, and Bronzino. Highly regarded at the Court of the Grand Duke of Tuscany, Cosimo I.
Buti, Domenico	* Florence † 1590	Florence I Tuscany (A6)	In Bronzino's sphere of influence. Also worked in the Pal. Vecchio (Studiolo of Francesco I).
Butinone, Bernardino Jacopi called Bernardo da Treviglio (also as Buttinone) *pl. 66*	* Treviglio, before 1436 † after 1507	Milan V Lombardy (B2)	Son of Jacopo da Treviglio. Worked together with the other pupil of Foppa, Bernardo Zenale. Influences from Mantegna. Tutor of Bramantino.
Butteri, Giovan-Maria	* btw. 1535 and 1540 † Florence 1606	Florence I Tuscany (BC7)	Active in Florence from 1567. Assistant to Bronzino, together with Alessandro Allori, with whom he later collaborated.
Cagnoli, Francesco also de Cagnolis or Cagnola	* Novara active in Piedmont and the Tyrol around 1500	Piedmont V Lombardy (C4)	In the circle of Gaudenzio Ferrari.
Cagnoli, Sperindio also de Cagnolis or Cagnola	doc. 1505–21	Piedmont V Lombardy (C4)	Active in Novara und environs. Training in the workshop of his father, Tommaso, together with his brother, Francesco. Influenced by Gaudenzio Ferrari, with whom collaboration is verifed.
Calcar, Giovanni da Jan-Stephan von Calcar	* Cleves 1499 † Naples 1556/50	Holland / Venice II Venice (C5)	Pupil of Titian and friend of Vasari. Training in the Netherlands; nevertheless, completely dependent on Titian. Renowned for his anatomical panels, which he painted for Karl V's physician, Vesalius.
Caldara, Polidoro called Polidoro da Caravaggio	* Caravaggio 1499/1500 † Messina 1543 (?)	Umbro-Roman III Umbria / Marches (A3)	Entered Raphael's workshop in Rome around 1515. Worked in the circle of Perino del Vaga, Giulio Romano, Maturino, and Pedro Machuca in the Vatican loggias. Later influenced by Michelangelo, Parmigianino, and Rosso Fiorentino. In connection with the Sacco di Romea, he moved to Naples in 1527 to join Andrea da Salerno. Last worked in Sicily, where he was murdered shortly before his planned return to Rome.

Caliari, Benedetto	* Verona 1538 † 1598	Verona VII Verona (B3)	Youngest brother of Paolo C., and his assistant. Specialized in architectures and ornaments.
Caliari, Carletto	* Venice 1570 † Venice 1596	Verona VII Verona (B3)	Son of Paolo C., who arranged an apprenticeship for him under Bassano.
Caliari, Gabriele	* Venice 1568 † Venice 1631	Verona VII Verona (B3)	Adopted the style of his father, Paolo C. Collaborated with his brother, Carletto, and his uncle, Benedetto.
Caliari, Paolo see Veronese			
Calisto Piazza see Piazza			
Calvaert, Denys (Dionisio) also Calavart or Calwaer	* Antwerp 1540 (?) † Bologna 1619	Bologna VI Emilia-Romagna (C4)	In 1556, listed in the register of the Lukas Guild of Antwerp. Pupil of Christiaen van den Queckborne. In Bologna, he was a pupil of Prospero Fontana and Sabatini, with whom he went to Rome. Returned to Bologna after two years. His pupils included Domenichino, Reni, Fr. Albani, and others. He is in contrast to the Carracci School. "Graceful in his composition, correct in his draughtsmanship, flawless in his perspective" (Wurzbach). One of the grand masters of the Bolognese School.
Calvi, Lazzaro	* Genoa, around 1510 † Genoa 1602	Genoa V Lombardy (A5)	Training together with his brother Pantaleo under Perino del Vaga. They were also del Vaga's assistants for the painting of frescoes for the Pal. Doria in Genoa. Both retained the Tusco-Roman style of the first half of the 16th c.
Calvi, Pantaleo	* Genoa, around 1510 † Genoa 1595	Genoa V Lombardy (A5)	Brother of Lazzaro and father of a generation of Genoese painters in the second half of the 16th c. (Aurelio, Benedetto, Felice, Marcantonio C.)
Cambiaso, Giovanni Giovanni di Bartolommeo	* Cambiaso 1495 † Genoa 1579	Genoa V Lombardy (B4)	In 1527, he worked in Moneglia, where his son Luca was born. He painted in the style of the Tusco-Roman Mannerists Perin del Vaga, Beccafumi, and Porderone.
Cambiaso, Luca Luchetto da Genova, also le Cangiage pl. 76	* Moneglia 1527 † El Escorial 1585	Genoa V Lombardy (B6)	Son and pupil of Giovanni C. Trained in Florence and Rome under Raphael and Michelangelo. Long active in Genoa, where he produced his best works. Emigrated to Spain and was active for Philipp II (ceiling frescoes in the Escorial). Brilliant technique and a highly gifted draughtsman. Collaboration with G.B. Castello over many years.
Cambiaso, Orazio	* active in Spain, 2nd half of the 16th c. 1585 back in Genoa	V Lombardy (C6)	Son and pupil of Luca C., after whose death he remained for a time at the Court of Philip.
Campagnola, Domenico	* Venice 1500 (?) † Padua 1564	Venice II Venice (B5)	Son of a German shoemaker. Apprenticeship under Giulio Campagnola. Like Campagnola, he became a famous and extremely productive engraver. In his painting, he retained the style of his mentor, Titian.
Campagnola, Giulio	* Padua 1481 † 1516	Venice II Venice (B5)	A period in Titian's workshop is likely. Chiefly active as miniaturist and engraver. Tutor of Domenico Campagnola.

Campi, Antonio Cavaliere Antonio	* Cremona 1523 † Cremona 1587	Cremona V Lombardy (C4)	Second son of Galeazzo C. His initial works remain close to the style of his brother, Giulio, and that of Camillo Boccaccino. His graphic works exhibit influences from Parmigianino and Emilian sculpture. In 1560, he abandoned collaboration with his brother Giulio and began to develop more independently. Probable contacts with Peterzano in the last decade, whose Reformist style he approached.
Campi, Bernardino	* Cremona 1522 † Reggio Emilia 1591	Cremona V Lombardy (C5)	Not directly related to Galeazzo Campi or his sons Giulio, Antonio, and Vincenzo. Nevertheless, assistant to Giulio. Influenced by Giulio Romano.
Campi, Galeazzo	* Cremona 1477 † Cremona 1536	Cremona V Lombardy (C3)	Pupil of Boccaccio Boccaccini. Father of Giulio, Antonio, and Vicenzo C. Close contacts with Tommaso Aleni are assumed, owing to the stylistic alliance. Influences from Giambellini and Perugino in his landscapes.
Campi, Giulio	* Cremona, after 1507 † 1572	Cremona V Lombardy (C4)	Eldest son of Galeazzo Campi. His first altarpieces reveal ideas from Brescia and the Emilia. Collaboration with Camillo Boccaccino. Later influenced by Giulio Romano and Porderone. Worked chiefly in Cremona.
Campi, Vincenzo	* 1536 † 1591	Cremona V Lombardy (C5)	Youngest son of Galeazzo C.; trained under his brother Giulio. He is also believed to have painted numerous still-lifes and genre scenes.
Canavesio, Giovanni	* Pinerolo (?), around 1425/30 † after 1500	Liguria / Piedmont V Lombardy (C1)	Active in Liguria and Piedmont. Distinctly influenced by Provencal and Flemish models (incl. the Master of Flémalle).
Candido, Pietro Peter Candid de Witte (Wit)	* Bruges (?) around 1548 (1540 ?) † Munich 1628	Florence I Tuscany (A7)	In 1559, already in Florence. In 1564, he went with Vasari to Rome and worked with him in the Vatican (staircase). In 1577, collaboration with Vasari on the cupola painting of the Cathedral of Florence (completed by F. Zuccari in 1579). In 1579, he went to Bavaria, where he entered into the service of Albert V. Collaboration with Sustris and Hans van Aachen. Maximilian I appointed him as a lifelong Court Painter.
Canera, Anselmo	* Verona, around 1530 † after 1584	Verona VII Verona (A3)	Assistant to Caroto, whose style he adopted. Collaboration with Bern. India in Vicenza (Pal. Thiene). Together with Palladio, he assisted in the decoration of the Villa Rotonda.
Canozi, Cristoforo and Lorenzo see Lendinara			
Caporale, Bartolommeo also Caporali *pl. 46*	* Perugia, around 1420 † Perugia 1505	Perugia III Umbria / Marches (B1)	Ancestor of a large painter dynasty. Mainly active in Perugia. Fra Angelico and Benozzo Gozzoli profoundly influenced his work. Father of Giovanni Battista C.
Caporale, Giovanni Battista also Caporali, called Bitti or Bitte	* Perugia, around 1476 † 1554	Perugia III Umbria / Marches (B1)	Son of Bartolommeo C. After initial training under his father and uncle, Giapeco (miniaturist), he soon came into contact with the art of Perugino and Pinturicchio. The latter summoned him to Rome, where he also adopted influences from Signorelli and Peruzzi.

Caporali, Giacomo called Giapeco	active in the 15th c., in Perugia	Perugia III Umbria/Marches (B1)	Brother of Bartolommeo C. Miniaturist.
Capriolo, Domenico Domenico di Bernardino, also Caprioli	* Venice (?) 1494 † Treviso 1528	Venice II Venice (B4)	Most probably a pupil of his father-in-law, P. M. Pennacchi. Workshop periods with Giorgione and Titian are probable. Despite his early (violent) death, he left behind an extensive body of work.
Caravaggio Actually Michelangelo da Merisi *pl. 77*	* Caravaggio 1560/65 † 1609	V Lombardy (B6)	Nothing is known about his artistic training, and, moreover, it cannot be interpreted from his work. His œuvre stands in isolation and has nothing in common with Mannerism. His naturalism and his light-dark manner, combined with a brilliant technique, made him a most attractive painter with a considerable influence on European painting. He does not really belong in a handbook on the Renaissance; since, however, his œuvre still falls within the Late Renaissance, a comparison of his work with that of his contemporaries is most revealing.
Caravaggio, Francesco **Prato da** see Prato, Francesco			
Cardi, Ludovico see Cigoli			
Cariani, Giovanni Giovanni de' Busi	* Fulpiano 1485/90 † Fulpiano 1547	Bergamo II Venice (B5)	Of Bergamasque origin; he mainly worked in Venice, however. Contacts with Giambellini, Giorgione, and the youthful Titian. Stylistically, he owed the most to his tutor, Palma.
Carli, Raffaelino de' see Raffelino del Garbo			
Carlo da Camerino	active around 1400	Marches III Umbria/Marches (A1)	A "crucifixion" in San Michele (Macerata) bears his signature. An important master in the transition from the Trecento to the Quattrocento. Know- ledge of Giottesque models can be assumed.
Carnevali, Fra **Bartolommeo** Bartolommeo di Givanni Corradini	† Cavallino 1484	Urbino III Umbria/Marches (B3)	Dominican monk. Painted altarpieces in Urbino.
Caroto, Giovanni also Carotis *pl. 99*	* Verona 1488 (?) † after 1562	Verona VII Verona (A2)	Pupil of Liberale, to whom he remained true in his early work. In Mantua, he came into personal contact with Mantegna, which led to a modifi- cation of his style. Also adopted ideas from Titian and Raphael. Berenson describes him as an eclec- ticist. His great pupil, Veronese, seems to have benefited from this.
Carpaccio, Vittore also Carpatio or Carpazio, Scarpaza, Scarpatio	* Venice (?) 1450/65 † before 1526	Venice II Venice (A3)	Pupil of, and possibly assistant to Gentile Bellini, whom he soon surpassed in his *vedute* of Venice. He was a great narrator, with meticulous repro- ductions of Venetian architecture and typical street and canal scenes. Much of what we know of the Venice of the 15th and 16th centuries is due to his paintings. His religious paintings are of lesser importance. C. is one of the most important of Venetian painters.

Carpi, Girolamo da Girolamo Sellari	* Ferrara 1501 † Ferrara 1556 (?)	Ferrara VI Emilia-Romagna (AB3)	Apprenticeship under Garofalo (according to Vasari), whose style he did not adopt, however. Orientated towards Correggio, Parmigianino, Raphael, and in particular Dosso, to whom he was probably also an assistant.
Carpi, Tommaso da	* Carpi active in Ferrara, 1st half of the 16th c.	Ferrara VI Emilia-Romagna (A3)	Father and first tutor of Girolamo.
Carracci, Agostino	* Bologna 1557 † Parma 1602	Bologna VI Emilia-Romagna (AB4)	Elder brother of Annibale, cousin of Ludovico, and father of Antonio C. Temporarily collaborated with Annibale in the Pal. Farnese in Rome (1597–1600). Training under the engraver Domenico Tibaldi, and under Prospero Fontana. His achievements are somewhat overshadowed by those of Annibale and Ludovico. His pronounced naturalistic tendencies, which he combines with expressive gestures and a sense of plasticity, are remarkable.
Carracci, Annibale	* Bologna 1560 † Rome 1609	Bologna VI Emilia-Romagna (B4)	Younger brother of Agostino. Trained in Parma and Venice (Veronese), before going to Rome in 1595. The most important representative of the Carracci family. Developed in parallel with the Mannerists and, eschewing their pathos, developed a style of Classical Realism. Influence on Poussin.
Carracci, Antonio-Marziale	* Venice 1583 † Rome 1618	Bologna VI Emilia-Romagna (C4)	Illegitimate son of Agostino C. After the death of the latter, he was in the Annibale workshop.
Carracci, Francesco called Franceschino	* Bologna 1559 † Rome 1622	Bologna VI Emilia-Romagna (AB4)	Brother of Agostino and Annibale. Training under Ludovico C.
Carracci, Ludovico *pl. 92*	* Bologna 1555 † Bologna 1619	Bologna VI Emilia-Romagna (AB4)	Cousin of Agostino and Annibale. Training under Prospero Fontana, whose style he initially retained. Later under Passignano in Florence. Visited Parma, Venice, and Rome; mainly worked in Bologna, however. Together with his cousins, he founded the Carracci Academy, which had a great influence on the development of Reni, Albani, Zampieri, and others.
Carrari, Baldassare	doc. 1489–1516	Forlì VI Emilia-Romagna (B2)	Active in Forlì and Ravenna. Trained in accordance with Melozzo da Forlì and Palmezzano. He came into contact with Venetian painting as a result of Rondinelli's intercession.
Carrucci, Jacopo see Pontormo			
Casanova see Agostino da C.			
Casella, Francesco called Casellano	* Cremona (?) active in the 16th c.	Cremona V Lombardy (B3)	Pupil of Galeazzo Campi.
Caselli, Cristoforo called de' Temperelli	* Parma around 1460 † Parma 1521	Venice II Venice (C3)	Until 1488, he was in Venice, in the Giambellini workshop, amongst others. Together with Giambellini, Alvise Vivarini, Fr. Bissolo, Lattanzio da Rimini, and Vincenzo da Treviso, he was involved

in the decoration of the Sala del Maggior Consiglio in the Doges' Palace. In total, Venice than influenced him more than did the native art.

Casentino, Jacopo del see Landini			
Casolani, Alessandro called Alessandro della Torre	* Mensano 1552/53 † Siena 1607	I Tuscany (A7)	Trained in the Ippolito Agostini studio, where he became acquainted with the works of Sodoma and Beccafumi. Further training under A. Salimbeni and Roncalli.
Castagno, Andrea del Andrea di Bartolommeo di Simone	* Castagno, around 1421 † Florence 1457	Florence I Tuscany (A3)	Strongly and formatively influenced by Masaccio and his friend, Domenico Veneziano. The works of Donatello inspired him towards a hitherto unknown plastic, realistic manner of representation. Initiated the "dramatic phase of Florentine painting" (Venturi). Transferred the monumental style of his frescoes to his panel paintings. Influence on Mantegna, especially however on the Pollaiuoli.
Castello, Giovanni Battista called il Bergamasco	* Gandino 1509 † Madrid 1579	V Lombardy (C5)	Employee of Luca Cambiaso.
Catena, Vincenzo Vincenzo di Biagio	* Venice or Treviso, around 1480 † Venice 1531	Venice II Venice (C4)	Probably from a distinguished Venetian family. Training in the Bellini workshop and under Giorgione, whose style in particular he appropriated. Elements from Antonello's art are also evident in his work, possibly due to the intercession of Giambellini or Alvise Vivarini.
Caterino, Veneziano	active in Venice in the 14th c.	Venice II Venice (BC1)	From Paolo Veneziano's sphere of influence.
Cavallini, Pietro	active btw. 1250 and 1330	I Tuscany (C1)	Pupil of Cimabue. Active mainly in Rome and Naples. Freed himself from Byzantine ties, without breaking completely with the tradition. Of significance for the further development of Gothic art in Rome. Frescoes in Assisi?
Cavalori, Mirabello see G. Macchietti			
Cavazzola, Paolo il Actually Paolo Moranda	* Verona 1486/88 † Verona 1522	Verona VII Verona (A2)	Assistant to Francesco Morone. Moved stylistically between Bellini (imparted by his tutor) and the Lombards (Foppa, Solario). Orientation towards Mantegnesque models in his composition, and also towards Raphael in later years.
Cavedone, Giacomo also Cavedoni	* Sassuolo 1577 † Bologna 1660	Bologna VI Emilia-Romagna (AB4)	Together with Reni, Zampieri, and Guercino, one of the end points of the great Bolognese School, which carried elements of the Renaissance into the Baroque. With respect to his use of colour, he trained in accordance with Titian's paintings. His fresco technique especially impressed Guido Reni, who, according to Vasari, wanted to collaborate with him in Rome.
Caversegno, Agostino da	* Caversegno active 1st half of the 16th c.	II Venice (C5)	Pupil of L. Lotto.

Caylina, Paolo Probably identical to Paolo da Bressa	* Brescia 1480/85 † after 1545	Brescia VIII Brescia (A1)	A relation of Foppa and documented as his proxy (*procuratore*) in Milan and Pavia. Training in the circle of V. Civerchio (possibly Giovan Pietro da Cemmo).
Ceccarelli, Naddo or Ceccherelli	active in Siena in the 14th c.	Siena I Tuscany (A1)	Circle of Simone Martini.
Cecchino da Verona Probably identical to the "Master of the Paris Judgement"	active mid-15th c.	Verona VII Verona (B1)	Doc. in Siena (1432) and Verona (1447 and 1464). Tuscan and Veronese influences can be substantiated. No definitive attribution of this master's work has been made to date.
Cenni di Francesco di Ser Cenni	doc. in Florence 1410–15	Florence I Tuscany (C2)	Pupil of Spinello Aretino.
Cennini, Cennino di Drea	* Colle di Valdensa, around 1370	I Tuscany (B2)	Assistant to Agnolo Gaddi over many years.
Ceraiolo, Antonio del Cerajolo or Ceraiuolo	active in Florence, 1s half of the 16th c.	Florence I Tuscany (B6)	Pupil to, and assistant of L. Credi and Ridolfo Ghirlandaio.
Cerano see G.B. Crespi			
Ceri, Andrea de'	active in Florence btw. 1368 and 1398	III Umbria/Marches (B3)	Tutor of Perino del Vaga.
Cerva, Giovanni Battista della	active in Milan † after 1548	Piedmont V Lombardy (C3)	Employee of Gaudenzio Ferrari.
Cesa, Antonio see Matteo Cesa			
Cesa, Donato see Cesa, Matteo			
Cesa, Matteo also Cessa	* Belluno, around 1430 (?) † after 1491	Belluno II Venice (B2)	Son of Donato and father of Antonio Cesa. Influenced by the Murano School. Active mainly in Belluno and environs.
Cesare da Conegliano	* Conegliano † after 1583	Venice II Venice (A5)	Dependent on Bonifazio Veronese.
Cesi, Bartolommeo	* Bologna 1556 † Bologna 1629	Bologna VI Emilia-Romagna (BC4)	In earlier years, a pupil of Nosadella. Earliest known work from 1574. In the circle of the Bolognese Late Mannerists. Influenced by C. Tibaldi and Proccaccini, with whom he had collaborated.
Chigi, Agostino	† 1524	Venice II Venice (C5	Circle of Paris Bordone. Collaboration with Tocco Marconi.
Chimenti, Jacopo Jacopo da Empoli	* Empoli 1554 † 1640	Florence I Tuscany (B7)	Pupil of Tommaso Manzuoli da San Friano, whose style he adopted. Later under Alessandro Allori. In time, his style became softer and more relaxed. Combined good draughtsmanship with carefully planned design. One of the outstanding Florentines on the threshold of the Baroque.
Chiodarolo, Giovanni-Maria also Chiodaruolo	active at the end of the 15th/turn of the 16th c.	Bologna VI Emilia-Romagna (B2)	Pupil of Fr. Francia. In the sphere of influence of Costa and Aspertini in Bologna.
Cianfanini, Giovanni see Tommaso			

Cigoli, Lodovico Cardi da	* Cigoli 1559 † Rome 1613	Florence I Tuscany (BC7)	Apprenticeship under A. Allori (c. 1574–78), later under Santi di Tito. On friendly terms with Gregorio Pagani. Trained in accordance with the works of Michelangelo and Pontormo, also taking ideas from F. Barocci. Correggio and Venetian painting fascinated him, however, as his work shows. One of the great Tusco-Roman Late Mannerists.
Cima, Carlo da Conegliano	* end of the 15th c.	Venice II Venice (A3)	Son of Giovanni Battista, whose style of painting he made completely his own.
Cima, Giovanni Battista da Conegliano *pl. 36*	* Conegliano, around 1459 † after 1517	Venice II Venice (A3)	Lived in Venice for more than twenty years, where he trained under Giambellini in particular. His paintings, with their serious-looking *Madonnas*, are not always easy to distinguish from those of Bellini and Montagna.
Cimabue Giovanni Gualtieri called Cenni di Pepo	* Florence mid-13. c. † after 1302	Florence I Tuscany (B1)	His painting in a fresco in Santa Maria Novella in Florence is probably as legendary as his life's description in Vasari. Although still partly in the Byzantine tradition, he must be regarded as one of the first Florentine painters to break away from traditional schemata and pave the way for Giotto. He can be considered the forefather of Tusco-Umbrian painting. Giotto is traditionally regarded as his pupil.
Cione, Andrea di see Orcagna			
Cione, Jacopo di Jacopo Orcagna di Cione	active btw. 1365 and 1398	Florence I Tuscany (C2)	Brother of Andrea (Orcagna) and Nardo di Cione.
Cione, Nardo di Bernardo di Cione	active 1346/48 until 1365 † Florence 1366 (?)	Florence I Tuscany (C2)	Younger brother and close employee of Andrea. There is no documentary evidence of his œuvre. The works that are attributed to him likewise identify him as an important master.
Circignani, Nicolì called il Pomarancio	* Pomarance 1517/24 † after 1597	Umbria III Umbria / Marches (A4)	Assistant to Santo di Tito and employee of G. de' Vecchi in Rome. Later worked almost exclusively in Umbria.
Civerchio, Vincenzo **(the Elder)** called il Fornaro	* Crema, around 1470 † around 1544	Crema V Lombardy (C2) VIII Brescia (A1)	The most outstanding representative of the Cremanese School. After early training in Milan, he was in Brescia from 1491. Vincenzo's eclectic style was developed in accordance with Foppa, Butinone, and copperplate engravings from the north. Later influences from Lotto and Bordone. Collaboration with Zenale.
Civitali, Matteo see Frediani, Vincenzo di Antonio			
Clovio, Giulio Juraj Julije Klovic	* Grizane 1498 † Rome 1578	Umbro-Roman III Umbria / Marches (A4)	Came as a young man from Croatia to Venice, where Cardinal Dom. Grimani sponsored him. In 1516, he was in Rome, where he probably came into contact with the painters in Giulio Romano's circle, who also influenced his style. Periods in Hungary, Mantua, Candiana, and Perugia. Raphael and Michelangelo were formatively influences in

his mature phase. Until his death, he was on friendly terms with El Greco, who also gained his admission to the Grimani circle.

Cocchi, Pompeo di Piergentile	* Corciano (?), before 1490 † Perugia 1552	Perugia III Umbria/Marches (A3)	Mainly painted altarpieces, in Perugia and environs. Contemporary of D. Alfani and G.B. Caporali. Influences from Perugino and Raphael.
Cola dell Amatrice Nicola di Filotesio	* Amatrice 1489 † Ascoli 1559	Marches III Umbria/Marches (A3)	Pupil of C. Crivelli, to whose style he fundamentally remained true. Also influenced by Signorelli. Mainly active in the Marches.
Coltellini, Michele also Cortellini	* Ferrara, around 1480 † around 1559	Ferrara VI Emilia-Romagna (C3)	Probably trained in the circle of Ercole Roberti (Dom. Panetti). Strong influences from Costa and Francia.
Conegliano, Sebastiano da see Sebastiano Florigerio			
Contarini, Giovanni or Contarino	* Venice 1549 † around 1604	Venice II Venice (A6)	Under the influence of Titian and Tintoretto. A favoured painter of Emperor Rudolph II.
Conte, Jacopino del (Jacopo)	* Florence 1510 † Rome 1598	Florence I Tuscany (B6)	Pupil of Andrea del Sarto. Went early to Rome and stayed there for the rest of his life. Known for his numerous papal portraits.
Conti, Bernardino de'	* Pavia (?), around 1450 † around 1525	Milan V Lombardy (C2)	Pupil of Zenale, later under the influence of Leonardo.
Coppi, Giacomo del Meglio	* Peretola 1523 † Florence 1591	Florence I Tuscany (A7)	One of Vasari's assistants in Florence.
Coppo di Marcovaldo	* Florence (?) 1225/30 † around 1300	Florence I Tuscany (BC1)	Contemporary of Cimabue. Within the scope of Byzantine criteria, efforts towards a more realistic representation are already recognizable. Outlined architectures replace the Byzantine weave of lines. From this art, too, the Florentine painting of the Trecento took its point of departure.
Corona, Leonardo Leonardo da Murano	* Venice 1561 † Venice 1605	Venice II Venice (B6)	Assistant to his father, Michele (book illuminator). Typical Venetian Mannerist, orientated towards Titian and Tintoretto in particular.
Correggio, Antonio actually Antonio Allegri *plates 78, 88, 89*	* Correggio, around 1489 † Correggio 1534	Emilia VI Emilia-Romagna (B3)	His very early paintings reveal the influence of Costa and Mantegna, which would be in accordance with a presumed apprenticeship under Fr. Bianchi. Around 1518, the encounter with the work of Leonardo and Raphael led to a decisive change in style. However, he fused what he adopted to a style all his own, influenced by elaborate use of light, refined colour composition, and Leonardesque *sfumato*. Although C. did not found a school in a real sense, he had a considerable influence on subsequent generations of painters in Italy, especially the Mannerists and the Bolognese, and Roman representatives of the Early Baroque.
Corso, Nicolò Nicolò di Lombarduccio	* Pieve di Vico, Corsica, 1446 † 1513	Liguria V Lombardy (C2)	From 1469, he was in Genoa. Active in Pietrasanta, Alessandria, and Savona. Partnership with Francesco da Pavia. He was in the Mazone workshop in Alessandria. Also stylistically allied to Carlo Braccesco.
Corte, Cesare	* Genoa 1550 † Genoa 1613	Genoa V Lombardy (C6)	Came from a distinguished family that was originally from Pavia. Dependent on Luca Cambiaso.

Cosci
see Balducci, Giovanni

Cosimo, Piero di
see Piero

Cossa, Francesco del pl. 81	* Ferrara 1435 † Bologna 1477	Ferrara VI Emilia-Romagna (A1)	One of the ancestors of the Emilian School. Considered to be a pupil of Piero della Francesca and took much from Squarcione and Mantegna. Stylistically allied to Tura, but less bizarre. In 1470, he moved from Ferrara to Bologna and determined the development of painting there. His frescoes in the Pal. Schifanoia in Ferrara are his best-known work. Lorenzo Costa was one of his pupils.
Costa, Ippolito	* Mantua 1506 † Mantua 1561	Ferrara VI Emilia-Romagna (BC3)	Son and sole heir of Lorenzo C. Pupil of his father and assistant to Girolamo da Carpi. Active in Mantua for the Court of the Gonzaga.
Costa, Lorenzo (the Elder) pl. 83	* Ferrara 1460 † Mantua 1535	Ferrara VI Emilia-Romagna (A2)	Probably a pupil of Ercole Roberti. Settled in Bologna around 1483, where he was active for the Bentivoglio. Closely collaborated with Francia. In 1507, he went to the Gonzaga Court at Mantua. He was a tutor of Dosso Dossi and Aspertini, among others.

Costantino da Vaprio
see Zanino

Cozzarelli, Guidoccio **(Guido)**	* Siena 1450 † Siena 1517	Siena I Tuscany (A4)	Miniaturist and panel painter. Employee of, and successor to Matteo di Giovanni. Later, he approached Pietro Orioli stylistically.
Credi, Lorenzo di Lorenzo d'Origo, also Barduccio or Sciarpelloni (Vasari)	* Florence 1459 (?) † Florence 1537	Florence I Tuscany (C5)	Pupil, and for many years employee of Verrocchio, to whose legacy he remained true. Leonardo's influence is restricted to details and compositional elements. His groups of people are mostly individual figures assembled in a schematic pose, although with beautiful faces. A not unimportant representative of the Florentine School, but without inventive power.
Crespi, Giovanni-Battista called il Cerano	* Cerano 1557 † Milan 1633	Milan V Lombardy (B6)	A Late Mannerist, who trained in Venice and Rome. Native influences are due to Gaudenzio Ferrari. Later in contact with C. Proccaccini, who cannot have been his tutor, however.
Crespi, Giovanni-Pietro	active in the 16th c., in Busto Arsizio	Milan V Lombardy (AB5)	Grandfather of Giovanni Battista C.

Cresti, Domenico
see Passignano

Cristiani, Giovanni di Bartolommeo	active in Pistoia c. 1340–98	Pistoia I Tuscany (C2)	Stylistically allied to Nicolò di Tommaso.
Crivelli, Carlo pl. 37	* Venice 1430/35 † Venice 1493/95	II Venice (A2) IV Padua (AB2)	From the school of Bart. Vivarini and Squarcione in Padua. Long active in the Marches. Collaboration with G. Schiavone. Developed his own style, in which Bellinesque-Mantegnesque traits were combined with a garland fruit decor and sculptured pilaster. Owing to their very fine technique – which is reminiscent of enamel work – the panels

Crivelli, Jacopo	active in Venice around 1450	Venice IV Padua (A2)	Father of Carlo C.
Crivelli, Protasio Protasio Chirillo Milanese (in De Dominici, 1742)	* Milan doc. in Naples btw. 1497 and 1506	Naples V Lombardy (A2)	Lombard Artist in Naples. Influenced by Melozzo da Forlì and Palmezzano.
Crivelli, Vittorio	* Venice, around 1440 † Fermo 1501/02	Venice II Venice (A2)	Brother, pupil (?), and imitator of Carlo C. A long period in Zara, from 1469 to 1476. Documented in 1481, in Montelparo (Marches). Thereafter, settled in Fermo.
Crocefissaio Simone dei Crocefissi, Simone di Filippo di Benvenuto, Simone da Bologna	* Bologna, around 1330 † Bologna, around 1399	Bologna VI Emilia-Romagna (B1)	Pupil and imitator of Vitale da Bologna.
Crocefissaio, il see Macchietti, Girolamo			
Da Mel see Giovanni da Mel			
Daddi, Bernardo	* Florence, end of the 13th c. † around 1350	Florence I Tuscany (B2)	Training under Giotto has not been documented. He probably served an apprenticeship under one of Giotto's pupils. Other than the latter, also influenced by Pietro Lorenzetti. One of the better painters in the generation after Duccio and Giotto.
Daddi, Daddo	active in Florence, mid-14th c.	Florence I Tuscany (B2)	Son of Bernardo D.
Dalmasio, Lippo di Dalmasio Scannabecchi, called Lippo della Madona	* Bologna 1352 active 1376–1410 in Bologna	Bologna VI Emilia-Romagna (AB1)	One of the early Bolognese masters. Probably from the Vitale workshop.
Daniele da Volterra see Ricciarelli, Daniele			
Danti, Gerolamo	* Perugia 1547 † Perugia 1580	Perugia III Umbria/Marches (A4)	Gifted, but prematurely deceased offspring of an artists' dynasty in Perugia. His Mannerist style is primarily orientated towards Michelangelo. Son of Giulio, and brother of Vincenzo and Egnazio D.
Dario da Treviso Dario di Giovanni, Dario da Udine, Dario da Porderone, Dario da Asolo	* Porderone 1420 † 1498	Padua IV Padua (A1)	Pupil of Squarcione, thereafter in the Paduan workshop of Pietro Maggi. Employee of Mantegna. Active in Treviso, Asolo, Bassano, Serravalle, Conegliano, and elsewhere.
Delitio, Andrea	active btw. 1430 and 1480	Marches III Umbria/Marches (B1)	Probably from the Abruzzi. Active in Norcia, Sulmona, and elsewhere. Tuscan-trained under Uccello and Domenico Veneziano.
Della Corna, Antonio	doc. in Cremona 1469–94	Cremona V Lombardy (BC1)	Pupil of Mantegna. Active in Cremona, Asola, Milan (Sala della Balla), and elsewhere.
Demio, Giovanni De Mio	* Schio 1510/20 † around 1570	Venice II Venice (C6)	Circle of G.B. Franco. Also worked as mosaicist in Venice and Pisa.
Detti see Bernadino d'Antonio			

Diamante, Fra (di Feo)	* Terranova, around 1430 † Florence, after 1498	Florence I Tuscany (B3)	Employee of Fra Filippo for many years, after whose death he completed the frescoes in the Cathedral of Spoleto. Later, also involved in the painting of the Sistine Chapel under Pope Sixtus IV. Probably also Filippino Lippi's first tutor.
Diana, Benedetto Benedetto Rusconi	* Venice, around 1460 † Venice 1525	Venice II Venice (B3)	Companion of Carpaccio and Mansueti. Open to diverse influences (Dürer, Lotto, Moretto, etc.). Later experimented in Giorgione's style.
Doceno, il see Gherardi, Cristofano			
Domenichino see Zampieri			
Domenico da Tolmezzo	active at the turn of the 16th c., in Friuli	Friuli II Venice (C5)	In the sphere of influence of Giambellini and Pellegrino da San Daniele.
Domenico da Udine called lu Domine	* Udine, active in Trieste around 1425 † around 1447	Friuli II Venice (C5)	Active in Trieste, and elsewhere. Collaboration with Antonio Baietti.
Domenico di Bartolo Domenico Ghezzi	* Asciano, around 1400 † Siena, before 1447	Siena I Tuscany (A2)	Some of his paintings were long attributed to his tutor, Taddeo di Bartolo. He painted one of the most beautiful panels of the Early Renaissance, the *Madonna dell' Umiltà* (Siena). His frescoes in the Spedale della Scala (Siena) sometimes exhibit an expressive realism that is reminiscent of O. Dix. Tutor of Piero della Francesca.
Domenico di Michelino Actually Domenico di Francesco	* Florence 1417 † Florence 1491	Florence I Tuscany (B3)	Named himself after his master, a certain Michelino. Painterly training under Fra Angelico, whose assistant he also became. His style is similar to that of Filippo Lippi and Pesellino.
Domenico di Zanobi see Poggini			
Domenico Veneziano see Veneziano, Dom.			
Donati, Alvise de'	* Montorfano (?), active btw. 1491 and 1512	Lombardy V Lombardy (AB3)	Documented in Lombardy and Piedmont as a sculptor and painter. Came from an artistic family. In 1494, mentioned as an assistant in the workshop of Eliazaro Oldoni. Influences from Bramantino, Foppa, and Borgognone.
Donato da Pavia	active at the end of the 15th c.	Pavia V Lombardy (AB1)	Nordic influences recognizable.
Doneto	active in Venice in 14th c.	Venice II Venice (BC1)	In the sphere of influence of Paolo Veneziano.
Doni, Adone Dono de' Doni	* Assisi, around 1510 † Assisi 1575	Umbria III Umbria/Marches (B4)	Pupil of Perugino, to whose colourism he remained true. Later came under the influence of Michelangelo.
Donzello, Ippolito (Polito) also Donzelli	* Florence 1456 † Naples (?), around 1494	Florence I Tuscany (A3)	Came from the workshop of Neri di Bicci. Until 1480, active together with his brother Piero in Florence. Went with Piero to Naples, where they produced their most important works. Both were of significance in connection with the development of Neapolitan painting.

Donzello, Piero see Donzello, Ippolito			
Dossi, Battista Battista de' Luteri	* 1497 † Ferrara 1548	Ferrara VI Emilia-Romagna (A3)	Brother and close employee of Dosso Dossi. Occasionally, it is difficult to distinguish between their respective individual achievements.
Dossi, Dosso Giovanni di Nicolì de' Luteri *pl. 86*	* Dosso 1480/90 † Mantua 1542	Ferrara VI Emilia-Romagna (A3)	Pupil of Costa (according to Vasari). Worked predominantly in Ferrara. After his encounter with Giorgione's and Titian's work, the Ferrarese heritage receded into the background, and D. developed a romanticism all his own. His influence on the development of Ferrarese painting in the 16th c. is important. His younger brother, Battista, mostly worked at his side.
Duccio di Buoninsegna	* Siena, around 1255 † 1319	Siena I Tuscany (A1)	One of the great masters who tried to break with the iconographic tradition. His *Madonnas* exhibit humanity and melancholic tenderness without losing their Byzantine majesty. He was a tutor of Simone Martini and also the first tutor of Segna di Bonaventura.
Empoli see Chimenti, Jacopo da			
Erri, Agnolo	doc. 1447–82	Modena V Lombardy (A2)	Son of Benedetto and brother of Bartolommeo Erri. Both are regarded as outstanding representatives of a large family of painters. Influenced by Cossa and Piero della Francesc.
Erri, Bartolommeo	active in Modena, 2nd half of the 15th c.	Modena V Lombardy (A2)	Brother of Agnolo (cf. above).
Estense, Baldassare see Baldassare			
Eusebio da San Giorgio Eusepius Jacobi Cristofori	* Perugia, around 1478 † Perugia, after 1535	Perugia III Umbria/Marches (B3)	Considered a pupil of Fiorenzo di Lorenzo. In 1496, he was in a workshop together with Berto di Giovanni, Sinibaldo Ibi, Lodovico d'Angelo, and other artists.
Eusebio Guidetto di Romagnano	active at the turn of the 16th c.	V Lombardy (BC4)	Identity with Pseudo-Giovane is questionable.
Evangelista da Milano	active in Genoa around 1544	Genoa V Lombardy (A5)	Influences from Correggio.
Evangelista da Pian di Meleto	* Pian di Meleto, around 1458 † Urbino 1549	Umbria III Umbria/Marches (B3)	Pupil of Giovanni Santi and assistant to Timoteo Viti.
Fabriano see Gentile da Fabriano			
Falconetto, Angelo	* Rovereto 1504 † Verona 1567	Verona VII Verona (AB2)	Painter and engraver. Worked predominantly in the Trent region. Nephew of Gian-Maria F.
Falconetto, Gian Antonio	* Verona, around 1470 † Rovereto	Verona VII Verona (A2)	Son and pupil of Jacopo Falconetto.
Falconetto, Giovanni Maria	* Verona 1468 † Padua 1534	Verona VII Verona (A2)	The most famous offspring of the Falconetti artists' dynasty. Brother of Gian-Antonio and son of Jacopo, with whom he also trained. Adopted Liberale's style and that of Melozzo da Forlì. Perfect perspective in his painted architectures.

			Later devoted exclusively to architecture (incl. villas in Veneto).
Falconetto, Jacopo	active in the 2nd half of the 16th c.	Verona VII Verona (A2)	Son of Giambattista and father of Gian-Antonio and Gian-Maria F.
Falconi, Bernardo	active in the 2nd half of the 14th c.	Pisa I Tuscany (AB1)	Influences from both Simone Martini and Giotto verifiable.
Falzagalloni, Stefano see Stefano da Ferrara			
Farinati, Paolo also Farinato	* Verona 1524 † Verona 1606	Verona VII Verona (AB2)	Uncle of Giambattista Zelotti.
Fasolo, Bernardino also Fazoli or Fazola da Pavia	* Pavia, around 1489 † Genoa, after 1526	Genoa V Lombardy (A4)	Son and pupil of Lorenzo Fasolo, who moved to Genoa in 1495/96. According to Bernardino, he trained for three years under L. Baudo. Stylistically allied to Borgognone.
Fasolo, Giovanni Antonio	* Vicenza, around 1530 † 1572	Verona VII Verona (B3)	Training under Batt. Zelotti and Paolo Veronese. Worked mainly in Vicenza and environs. Influenced by the Veronese Mannerists, especially Brusasorci.
Fasolo, Lorenzo also Fazoli, called Lorenzo da Pavia	* Pavia † before 1520	Genoa V Lombardy (A2)	Foppa School. Active in Liguria and Lombardy between 1463 and 1516/18. Father of Bernardino F. Active for Lodovico Sforza and others in Milan (incl. Sala da Ballo). From 1502–03, partnership with Lodovico Brea and Giovanni Barbagelata.
Fedeli see Matteo dei Fideli			
Fei, Alessandro di Vincenzio Alessandro del Barbiere	* Florence 1538/43 † Florence 1592	Florence I Tuscany (B7)	Trained under Ridolfo del Ghirlandaio and P.F. Foschi. Collaboration with Maso da San Friano. Distinctly reminiscent of the naturalistic tendencies of A. del Sarto and T. Zuccari.
Fei, Paolo di Giovanni see Paolo di Giovanni Fei			
Feltre see Morto da Feltre			
Feltrini, Andrea Andrea di Cosimo or del Fornaio	* Feltre (?), around 1490 † around 1554	Florence II Venice (A4)	Training under Morto da Feltre and Piero di Cosimo, whose influence overlaid the Venetian heritage. Collaboration with Ridolfo Ghirlandaio, in the Pal. Vecchio in Florence.
Fernandez, Pedro see Pseudo-Bramantino			
Ferramola, Benedetto	* Brescia 1541 † after 1588	Brescia VIII Brescia (A2)	Son and pupil of Giov. Giacomo F.
Ferramola, Floriano (Fioravante)	* Brescia, before 1480 † Brescia 1528	Brescia VIII Brescia (B1)	Son of Lorenzo Ferramola and the most important of this family of painters. Tutor of Moretto. Mainly worked in Brescia.
Ferramola, Giovanni Giacomo I	active in Brescia around 1513	Brescia VIII Brescia (A1)	Probably the brother of Floriano.
Ferramola, Giovanni Giacomo II	* Brescia 1508 † Brescia 1568	Brescia VIII Brescia (B2)	Son of Floriano F.

Ferramola, Lorenzo	active in Brescia 15th/16thC.	Brescia VIII Brescia (AB1)	Father of Floriano and Giovanni Giacomo F.
Ferrara, Stefano da Stefano Falzagalloni	* Ferrara before 1430 † Padua 1500	Padua VI Emilia-Romagna (AB1)	According to Vasari, a close friend of Mantegna. Stylistic characteristics of Giambellini. Little of his work is preserved; he must have been highly regarded in his time, however. Important fresco, *Madonna with Child*, in S. Antonio in Padua.
Ferrari de' Giuchis, Cristoforo	active in Caravaggio, 1504–06	V Lombardy (BC2)	In the sphere of influence of Zenale and Borgognone.
Ferrari, Defendente *pl. 71*	* Chivasso, around 1490 † after 1531	Piedmont V Lombardy (B4)	Initial training under Martino Spanzotti, whose style he initially retained. Later Flemish and German influences, which can be traced back to graphic models. Probably influenced by the works of Gaudenzio, in the twenties he was more open to influences from the Veneto.
Ferrari, Eusebio	* Vercelli, before 1470 † after 1533	Piedmont V Lombardy (B2)	Doc. in Vercelli, 1508–33. Collaborated with Gaudenzio Ferrari, among others. Initially allied to Bramantino and Cesare da Sesto. Later, Central Italian influences verifiable, attributable to a journey to Rome (with Gaudenzio?).
Ferrari, Francesco de'	active in Liguria btw. 1476 and 1494	Genoa V Lombardy (C2)	First documented in 1476, in Genoa. Collaboration with Francesco Grasso, for works in the Pal. San Giorgio in Genoa. Later collaboration with Nicolò Corso in the Capella Sta. Maria in Passione (1493).
Ferrari, Gaudenzio Gaudenzio Milanese (Vasari)	* Valduggia 1475/80 † Milan 1546	Piedmont V Lombardy (B3)	There is no documentary evidence of his training. He probably visited the workshop of somewhat mysterious Lombard painter Stefano Scotti, which also produced Luini. Borrowings from Bramante and Zenale are recognizable. In Milan, he received ideas through Bramantino. The digestion of elements of the "maniera morna" indicates a period in Rome. Gaudenzio is the most important exponent of the Piedmont School.
Filippino Lippi see Lippi, Filippino			
Filippo Lippi see Lippi, Filippo			
Finiguerra see Pollaiuolo, Antonio			
Fiore see Jacobello del Fiore			
Fiorentino see Rosso Fiorentino			
Fiorentino, Stefano Stefano da Ponte Vecchio	* Florence 1301 * 1350	Florence I Tuscany (AB1)	Pupil of Giotto, with influence on the young Pietro Lorenzetti.
Fiorenzo di Lorenzo *pl. 47*	* Perugia, around 1445 † Perugia, around 1525	Umbria III Umbria/Marches (A2)	Important master of the Umbrian School, whose workshop produced Perugino (?) and Pinturicchio. Mainly painted religious themes. He developed his style in accordance with Benozzo Gozzoli; in

			Florence, with Antonio Pollaiuolo and L. Signorelli. Provincial traits again become dominant towards the end of his œuvre.
Fiorini, Giovanni Battista	* Bologna, around 1535 † Bologna, around 1599	Bologna VI Emilia-Romagna (C3)	Assistant (employee?) of Cesare Aretusi in Bologna. Collaboration with C. Procaccini is also verified. Worked mainly in Bologna, also in Parma and Rome (Vatican), however, at the beginning of the sixties.
Flacco, Orlando	* Verona, around 1527 † Verona 1591/93	Verona VII Verona (A3)	A highly regarded portraitist in his time. Few preserved works. Stylistically allied to B. India.
Floreani, Francesco	* Udine 1510/15 † Udine 1595	Friuli II Venice (C6)	Came from a family of painters and wood-carvers. Pupil of Pellegrino da San Daniele. Highly regarded portraitist. Classified among the Raphael-orientated Mannerists. Temporary collaboration with G.B. Grassi.
Floreano, Giovanni called delle Cantinelle	* Udine † Udine 1511	Friuli II Venice (C3)	Father of Francesco F. and tutor of Gaspare Negro.
Florigerio, Sebastiano also Florigorio (Bastianello)	* Conegliano, around 1500 † Udine, around 1545	Friuli II Venice (C4)	Pupil and son-in-law (?) of Pellegrino da San Daniele. Active in Udine (from 1524), Padua, and Cividale, and elsewhere. One of the gifted Friulian masters, yet some of his figures look as though they have been cut out of other paintings and inserted into a new scene. Some of his work is reminiscent of Dossi.
Fogolino, Marcello	* Vincenza (?) 1483/88 † Trent (?) around 1558	Trent II Venice (C4)	His training was possibly under Carpaccio in Venice. A period in Rome (1515) is likely. Emigrated in 1527 with his brother Matteo to Trent. After Romanino and Dossi left Trent, F. remained the most sought-after painter in the Trentino. Mannerist approaches are recognizable in his frescoes from the forties on.
Fogolino, Matteo	* Vicenza doc. 1525–55, in Trent and elsewhere	II Venice (C4)	Younger brother of Marcello F., with whom he closely collaborated.
Fontana, Lavinia Lavinia Zappi (after her marriage in 1577)	* Bologna 1552 † Rome 1614	Bologna VI Emilia-Romagna (A4)	Daughter of Prospero F. Initially pursued the eclectic style of her father in the Tusco-Roman tradition. Influenced by the Counter-Reformation. Later orientation towards the Campi and Carracci. Receptive to Venetian use of colour. A great portraitist.
Fontana, Orazio	* Urbino † after 1571	III Umbria/Marches (A4)	Miniaturist and painter of porcelain.
Fontana, Prospero	* Bologna 1512 † Bologna 1597	Bologna VI Emilia-Romagna (A4)	Pupil of Innocenzo da Imola. Went with Girolamo da Treviso to Genoa, where he worked until 1539. Later in Rome, where he came into contact with Perino del Vaga. Giulio Romano and Porderone also influenced his style. Worked in Rome, Florence, and Bologna, and elsewhere. In the last period of his œuvre, he followed the artistic guidelines of the Council of Trent.
Foppa, Vincenzo de *plates 63, 64*	* Brescia btw. 1425 and 1430 † Brescia 1515/16	Lombardy V Lombardy (B1)	The most important representative of the Lombard School in the second half of the Quattrocento. The roots of his style: Verona (Pisanello), Venice (J. Bellini), and Padua (Mantegna). He came from

Brescia to Milan, where he worked for the Sforza (also in Genoa). He returned to Brescia in his sixties. His influence extends to both Schools, e.g. to Zenale, Macrino d'Alba, Borgognone, and de' Conti in Milan, as well as to V. Civerchio and F. Ferramola in Brescia.

Forlì, Ansuino da see Ansuino			
Forlì, Melozzo da see Melozzo			
Foschi, Pierfrancesco Pierfrancesco di Jacopo	* Florence 1502 † Florence 1567	Florence I Tuscany (B6)	From the workshop of Andrea del Sarto. Later orientation towards Sogliani (composition), and especially Pontormo.
Foschi, Sigismondo	doc. in Faenza, 1520 † 1532/36	Faenza V Lombardy (A5)	Few preserved works, which are indicative of Florentine influences (Fra Bartolommeo, Andrea del Sarto).
Fossano see Borgognone			
Fra Paolino see Paolino			
Francesca see Piero della Francesca			
Franceschi, Francesco de'	doc. in Venice 1443–68	Venice II Venice (AB1)	His principal work, *Polyptych of St Peter*, is today in the Museo Civico in Padua. Otherwise, little is preserved. Stylistically in the circle of the Vivarini.
Francesco d' Antonio	* Florence † Florence, after 1433	Florence I Tuscany (B3)	Doc. in Florence btw. 1393 and 1433. Pupil of Lorenzo Monaco (according to Vasari), whose style he initially retained. Later softer in outline, and stylistic approach to Masolino and Masaccio.
Francesco da Milano Francesco Pagani	doc. in Veneto 1502–48	Lombardy/Venice V Lombardy (A5)	Trained under the influence of Zenale and Civerchio; active in Veneto and Friuli, however. Here, he adopted ideas from Porderone.
Francesco da Volterra identical to Francesco Neri da Volterra	* Volterra, active in Pisa in the 14th c.	Tuscany I Tuscany (A1)	From the Giotto circle.
Francesco di Bartolomeo Alfei see Maestro della Osservanza			
Francesco di Gentile	* Fabriano, active in the 2nd half of the 15th c.	Fabriano III Umbria/Marches (B1)	Son of Gentile da Fabriano (?)
Francesco di Giorgio Martini Francesco Maurizio di Giorgio Martino Pollaiuolo	* Siena 1439 † 1502	Siena I Tuscany (C4)	One of the more important (true) Sienese in the second half of the Quattrocento. Active as painter, miniaturist, sculptor, architect, and engineer. From the Vecchietta workshop (initial training probably under Sano di Pietro). Collaboration with Liberale da Verona and Girolamo da Cremona. Through numerous commissions for fortresses (Urbino, Milan, Naples), he came into contact with many artists, from whom he received ideas. Mantegna and Donatello greatly impressed him. In spite of

his efforts towards greater plasticity and meticulous reproductions of landscapes and architecture, he remains bound to the Late Gothic Sienese tradition; he lost only its warmth. An influential tutor (incl. B. Peruzzi, Neroccio di Landi).

Francesco di Simone	15th c.	Florence I Tuscany (C4)	Pupil of Verrocchio.
Francesco di Simone da S. see Santacroce			
Francesco di Stefano see Pesellino			
Francesco Jacobello	active in the 14th c.	Venice II Venice (A1)	Tutor of Jacobello di Bonomo.
Francesco Napoletano	* Naples, active in Milan around 1500	Milan V Lombardy (A3)	In the circle of Leonardo da Vinci. Influence from Cesare da Sesto.
Francesco Neri da Volterra see Francesco da Volterra			
Francesco Prato (Prata) da Caravaggio	* Caravaggio, active in Brescia † after 1527	VIII Brescia (AB2)	Pupil of Romanino.
Franchi, Rosello di Jacopo identical to "il Compagno di Bicci"	* Florence, around 1377 † 1456	Florence I Tuscany (B2)	Influenced by Lorenzo Monaco and Starnina. Active in Florence, Empoli, and Prato, and elsewhere.
Francia, Francesco Francesco di Marco di Giacomo Raibolini *pl. 84*	* Bologna 1450 † Bologna 1517	Bologna VI Emilia-Romagna (B1)	Began as a goldsmith and probably first came to painting through the encounter with L. Costa. Regular training under M. Zoppo has not been substantiated. He collaborated for a time with Fr. Bianchi. Francia quickly became famous, because he painted in a very pleasing manner. Much of his work is reminiscent of Perugino, which is due more to allied interpretations than to imitation, however. He worked mostly for churches in Bologna, for the Bentivogli, but occasionally further afield as well (e.g., in Lucca). His pupils included Aspertini. F. also had an influence on the early work of Correggio.
Francia, Giacomo	* Bologna, before 1486 † Bologna 1557	Bologna VI Emilia-Romagna (C2)	Son and pupil of Fr. Francia. Maintained a workshop together with his brother, Giulio. Barely broke away from his father's style, even though approaches towards an increased dramatic sense are occasionally recognizable.
Francia, Giulio	* Bologna 1487 † Bologna 1545	Bologna VI Emilia-Romagna (BC2)	Collaboration with his brother, Giacomo. (cf. above)
Franciabigio Francesco di Cristofano or Francesco Bigio	* Florence 1482 † Florence 1525	Florence I Tuscany (B5)	Trained under Albertinelli, which is also expressed in his early work. He later felt attracted to Raphael, from whose portraiture he learnt. His approach towards Michelangelo, especially detectable in his frescoes, supports the hypothesis of a period in Rome around 1519. Collaboration with Andrea del Sarto and Pontormo is documented, in Poggio a Caiano (1521).

Franco, Giov. Battista il Semolei	* Venice 1510 (?) † Venice 1561	Venice II Venice (C6)	Painter, engraver, and a first-rate draughtsman; went to Rome aged twenty, where he came under the influence of Michelangelo (Vasari). In Florence, he was engaged by Cosimo de' Medici. 1541/42 back in Rome, 1545 in Urbino, at the Court of Guidobaldo, where he completed designs for Majolika tiles. Active in Osimo and elsewhere in the Marches. Commissions in Venice (1559/60) for the Signoria.
Francucci, Innocenzo di Pietro Innocenzo da Imola	* Imola, around 1490 † Bologna, around 1549	Bologna VI Emilia-Romagna (A3)	Participation in the Francia workshop is documented (1508). Vasari also mentions a period in Florence (with Albertinelli). Stylistic borrowings from the Florentine School seem to support this. An important master of the Bolognese School. Prospero Fontana was his pupil.
Frediani, Vincenzo di Antonio	doc. in Lucca, 1481–1505	Lucca I Tuscany (A5)	Circle of Baldassare di Biagio da Firenze (Maestro di Benabbio) and Matteo Civitali. Influenced by Ghirlandaio, Filippino Lippi, and Botticelli.
Fuluto, Pietro	* Tolmezzo † around 1520	Friuli V Venice (C5)	Training under Gianfrancesco da Tolmezzo. Active in Friuli.
Fungai, Bernadino	* Siena 1460 † Siena 1516	Siena I Tuscany (A5)	Initial apprenticeship under Giovanni di Paolo has not been substantiated, in contrast to his time as an assistant to Benvenuto di Giovanni. Later he showed influences from Orioli and Signorelli. Mainly active in Siena, where he counts as one of the more important masters.
Gaddi, Angelo di Taddeo also Agnolo	* Florence, after 1333 † Florence 1396	Florence I Tuscany (B2)	Son of Taddeo G.
Gaddi, Gaddo di Zanobi	* Florence, around 1260 † Florence 1333 (?)	Florence I Tuscany (C1)	On friendly terms with Cimabue, and father of Taddeo G. Painter and mosaicist. Is believed to have worked on the mosaics of St Peter's in Rome.
Gaddi, Taddeo di Gaddo	* Florence, around 1300 † Florence 1366	Florence I Tuscany (C1)	Pupil of his father, Gaddo, then employee for many years of his godfather, Giotto. Few of his many works are preserved. Developed a decorative style with adventurous architectures and efforts towards a portrayal of depth. Stronger spiritualization of interpretation towards the end of his creative period. Taddeo represents a step towards the Renaissance.
Galassi, Galasso (the Younger) also Galasso di Matteo Riva	* Ferrara, around 1423 † around 1473	Ferrara VI Emilia-Romagna (AB1)	Perhaps the son of G.G. (the Elder). In Cossa's sphere of influence.
Galasso, Galassi (the Elder)	* Ferrara, around 1438 active until c. 1480	Ferrara VI Emilia-Romagna (AB1)	According to Vasari, already active in 1404. His existence is doubtful, however.
Galdino da Varese	active c. 1480 - c.1520	Varese V Lombardy (A2)	Remarkable painter of the local School of Varesotto. Contacts with the glass painters of the Milan Cathedral. Stylistically allied to Cristoforo de Mottis and Nicolì da Varallo.
Galeazzi, Agostino	* Brescia 1523 active in Brescia and Vicenza	Brescia VIII Brescia (A 2)	Pupil of Moretto. Mainly active in Brescia and Vicenza. Tutor of Fr. Ricchino.

Galizzi
see Santacroce (Rizzo)

Gambara, Lattanzio also Gambaro	* Brescia, around 1530 † around 1574	Brescia VIII Brescia (A2)	Pupil of Romanino and Giulio Campi. One of the most important representatives of Brescian Mannerism.
Gambetello, Girolamo Girolamo da Fano	* Fano 16th c. † Rome (?)	III Umbria/Marches (A4)	Active in the Vatican.
Gandini, Giorgio Gandini del Grano	* Parma, around 1489 * Parma 1538	Parma V Lombardy (A4)	Assistant to Correggio. Orientation towards Parmigianino in his design.
Gandolfino da Roreto identical (?) to Gandolfino d' Asti	active at the end of the 15th/turn of the 16th c.	Piedmont V Lombardy (AB4)	Training in Liguria, possibly in the Brea circle. Later under the influence of Martino Spanzotti and Deffendente Ferrari. In 1523, collaboration with Pascale Oddone in Savigliano.

Garbo, Raffaelino del
see Raffaelino

Garelli, Tommaso d' Alberto called Masacodo	active in Bologna, 2nd half of the 15th c.	Bologna VI Emilia-Romagna (A2)	Still Gothic in style, but his saints are full of personality. (Triptych from 1477 in S. Petronio, Bologna.) On friendly terms with Marco Zoppo.
Garofalo Benvenuto Tisi *pl. 87*	* Ferrara, around 1476 † Ferrara 1559	Ferrara VI Emilia-Romagna (BC3)	Training under D. Panetti and, from 1497, under Boccaccino. Approached the Proto-Classicist style of Costa and Francia. Venetian influences (Giorgione) are evident in his landscapes. Between 1520 and 1530, his use of colour reveals influences from Dosso and Titian. In Rome, he took ideas from Raphael's frescoes. Many pupils, including Niccolò Abbate and Girolamo da Carpi. Influence on the Fontainebleau School. Important representative of the Ferrarese School.
Gatta, Bartolommeo della Don Pietro Dei	* Florence (?), 1448 † around 1502	Florence I Tuscany (B5)	Calmadolensian monk in Florence, later Arezzo. Between 1479 and 1486, he collaborated with Signorelli and Perugina on the decoration of the Sistine Chapel in Rome. Also achieved fame as a miniaturist, showing influences from Piero della Francesca (Antiphonal, Urbino).
Gatti, Bernardino il Soiaro	* Pavia or Cremona, around 1496 † Cremona 1575	V Lombardy (A4)	Pupil of Correggio and Porderone. Initially a pure imitator of Correggio, he increasingly developed his own personality. Later, he also drew on the early Lombard tradition, while at the same time a familiarity with Giulio Romano's frescoes in Mantua is recognizable.

Gaudenzio
see Ferrari, Gaudenzio

Genga, Girolamo	* Urbino, around 1476 † Urbino 1551	Umbria III Umbria/Marches (A3)	Pupil of Signorelli and Perugino. Journeys to Siena, Florence, and Rome, where he was confronted with the works of the Tusco-Roman Renaissance. Around 1510, he broke away more and more from Signorelli's example and acknowledged Perugino's influence. Collaboration with Timoteo Viti was also productive. Important representative of the Umbrian School.
Gentile da Fabriano Gentile di Nicolò Massi *pl. 42*	* Fabriano, around 1370 † Rome 1427	Fabriano III Umbria/Marches (A1)	Coming from the Marches, Gentile developed his style in accordance with models of Umbro-Sienese art. He was first documented in Venice, later in

Brescia and Florence, where he belonged to the local artistic cliques. From elements of the "ars nova" (Nordic influences?), he developed a precious, courtly style, greatly distancing him from the memorial paintings of his contemporaries. Exemplary is the *Adoration of the Magi* (Uffizi), which identifies him as one of the pioneers of the Renaissance. Of great influence on all Northern Italian Schools, especially on Pisanello.

Gerini, Lorenzo di Niccolò Lorenzo di Niccolò	active in Florence btw. 1350 and 1400	Florence I Tuscany (B2)	Son of Niccolò di Pietro G. Like his father, from the Orcagna circle.
Gerini, Niccolò di Pietro	active in Florence † 1415	Florence I Tuscany (BC2)	Initial training probably under T. Gaddi, then in the workshop of Spinello and Jacopo Orcagna. Father of Lorenzo G.
Gerino da Pistoia	* Pistoia 1480 † after 1529	Umbria III Umbria/Marches (A3)	Vasari describes him as a close friend of Pinturicchio and as an assistant to Perugino. Worked in Sansepolcro, Pistoia, Poggibonsi, and Porciano di Lamporecchio.
Gherardi, Cristofano il Doceno	* Borgo San Sepolcro 1508 † Borgo San Sepolcro 1556	Florence I Tuscany III Umbria/Marches (B4)	Training under Raffaelino del Colle, from the Giulio-Romano circle. Later, in Florence, he became an assistant to Vasari. In 1537, he was banned from Florence and went to San Sepolcro. In Bologna, too, and later in Rome, he worked together with Vasari. His Mannerist style was orientated towards Raphael, Perugino, and Parmigianino.
Gherardo di Giovanni del Fora identical to the "Maestro del Trionfo della Castità"	* Florence 1444/45 † Florence 1497	Florence I Tuscany (A5)	A painter first rediscovered by Fahi (1967/1976) from the artists' circle of Lorenzo il Magnifico. Vasari describes him as extremely versatile. Gherardo maintained a large workshop and painted both large-format panels and miniatures. Influences from D. Ghirlandaio and Botticelli (?).
Ghezzi, Domenico see Domenico di Bartolo			
Ghiberti, Lorenzo di Cione called Bartoluccio	* Florence 1370 (Sculptor) † Florence 1455	Florence I Tuscany	As a sculptor, also had a crucial influence on the development of young Florentine painters, as did Donatello. According to Vasari, as a trained goldsmith, he served for a time as painter and stuccoist, until he won a competition for the construction of the bronze doors of the Baptistry after returning to his native town. He had a crucial influence on Masolino and Uccello. One of the outstanding artists of the Florentine Renaissance.
Ghirlandaio, Benedetto actually Bigordi	* Florence 1458 † Florence 1497	Florence I Tuscany (AB5)	Youngest brother and pupil of, and assistant to Domenico G., in whose style he painted.
Ghirlandaio, Davide actually Bigordi	* Florence 1452 † Florence 1525	Florence I Tuscany (AB5)	Brother and close employee of Domenico G. Also worked as a mosaicist in Siena, Florence, and Orvieto.
Ghirlandaio, Domenico Domenico Currado Bigordi	* Florence 1449 † Florence 1494	Florence I Tuscany (B5)	The most important member of this artistic family and one of the most important painters of the Florentine School. Training as a goldsmith under his father, as a painter under Baldovinetti. Strongly influenced by Verrocchio. Close collaboration with Bastiano Mainardi, his brother-in-law. Other than

			Florence, Domenico worked (also as mosaicist) in Rome (Sistine Chapel), San Gimignano, and Pisa. His workshop produced notable artists, including his son Ridolfo, Michelangelo, Francesco Granacci, and Jacopo del Sellaio.
Ghirlandaio, Ridolfo Ridolfo di Domenico	* Florence 1483 † Florence 1561	Florence I Tuscany (AB5)	Son of Domenico G. Pupil of his uncle David and Cosimo Roselli. Also came under the direct influence of Raphael. Lasting influence on the Tusco-Roman Mannerists (Tosini, Salviati, Alessandro Fei, and others).
Ghisoni, Fermo also called Fermo da Caravaggio	* Mantua (?) † Mantua 1575	III Umbria/Marches (AB4)	Came from a Caravaggio family of painters. Pupil of Lorenzo Costa; from 1527, assistant to Giulio Romano for works in the Pal. Te and in the Ducal Palace. Combined influences of his master with those of Parma (Correggio, Bedoli).
Giacomo da Milano Giacomo di Domenico	active in Perugia btw. 1525 and 1539	Lombardy / Umbria V Lombardy (A5)	Influences from Raphael and Signorelli.
Giacomo della Pieve	active in Umbria around 1500	Umbria III Umbria/Marches (B2)	Pupil of, and assistant to Perugino.
Giacomo di Nicola da Recanati	active 1414/15 to 1466	Marches III Umbria/Marches (B1)	Active in Fermo's and Recanati's sphere of influence. Still strongly bound to the Gothic style.
Giambattista di Jacopo Rossi see Rosso Fiorentino			
Giambono, Michele Giovanni Michele di Taddeo Bono, also Zambono	* turn of the 15th c. active in Venice, 1420–62	Venice II Venice (B1)	Representative of the International Gothic, with Venetian influences (Jacobello del Fiore). Contacts with Gentile da Fabriano also possible.
Giampietrino (Giampedrini) Gian Pietro Ricci, also Giampetrino	active in Milan, first half of the 16th c.	Milan V Lombardy (AB4)	Considered a pupil of, and assistant to Leonardo, whose style he imitated. Probably also worked from the master's cartoons. One of the noteworthy painters in the Milanese Leonardo circle.
Gianfrancesco da Tolmezzo Giovanni Francesco del Zotto, called il Barbeano	* Tolmezzo, around 1450 doc. 1482–1510	Friuli II Venice (C5)	Painter and "intagliatore". Pupil of, and assistant to Domenico da Tolmezzo. Surpassed the master and many of his Friuli contemporaries in the assurance of his draughtsmanship and in the correctness of the painterly execution. Worked exclusively in Friuli (in Udine, Mione, Forni, Osais, Provesan, and elsewhere). Porderone is believed to have been one of his pupils.
Giangiacomo da Lodi	* Lodi 1420/30 † around 1500	Lodi V Lombardy (AB1)	Late Gothic painter, who only came into contact with Foppa'a art at a late stage (around 1487).
Giannicola di Paolo identical (?) to Gian Niccolò da Perugia	* Perugia, around 1460 † Perugia 1544	Perugia III Umbria/Marches (B3)	Stylistically dependent on Perugino and Pinturicchio. Later approached the style of Fra Bartolommeo and Albertinelli.
Giolfino, Niccolò (Nicola)	* Verona 1476 † Verona 1555	Verona VII Verona (B2)	Co-pupil of Caroto and Torbido in the Liberale workshop. His early work is not preserved. He combines Raphaelesque influences with an increased plasticity, possibly in connection with the wood-carving tradition of his family.
Giorgio d'Andrea Bartoli see Andrea di Bartolo			

Giorgione da Castelfranco Giorgio Barbarelli, also called Zorzo *plates 27, 28*	* Castelfranco 1477 † Venice 1510	Venice II Venice (B4)	More has been written about G. than is known about him. An outstanding artist of the Venetian Renaissance, a splendid portraitist, and a "prime landscapist" of Italy. Few works can be attributed to him with any certainty. This may be due to his alliance to Titian (collaboration), but also to the zeal of his pupils and contemporary colleagues in attempting to copy or surpass him. His greatest contribution is considered to be his treatment of landscape as an independent object of painterly representation. His influence on Titian and subsequent generations of painters in Venice and other Ital. Schools cannot be overestimated. Even in the case of Giambellini, an influence from the much younger G. can be verified. Palma the Elder, Lorenzo Lotto, Sebastiano del Piombo, and Porderone are greatly indebted to him stylistically.
Giottino, Tommaso Giotto di Maestro Stefano	active in Tuscany 1324–64	Florence I Tuscany (C2)	Pupil and conscientious imitator of Giotto.
Giotto da Bondone Ambrogio da Bondone *pl. 2*	* Colle di Vespignano 1266 † 1337	Florence I Tuscany (B1)	Pupil of Cimabue. Considered a pioneer of Renaissance painting in Italy, with a considerable influence on subsequent generations of painters. Even during his lifetime, he was admired and highly regarded for his naturalism and his expressive representative art. His frescoes can still be found in Padua (Arena Chapel), Florence (S. Croce), Rimini, Rome, and Naples. There is doubt concerning the extent of his participation in the frescoes in S. Francesco in Assisi. Both Lorenzetti and also Gaddo Gaddi and Taddeo Gaddi are believed to have been among his pupils.
Giov. Batt. di Bartolommeo Alberti, see Landi, Neroccio			
Giovan Pietro da Cemmo see Caylina, Paolo			
Giovanni Agostino da Lodi identical to Pseudo-Boccaccino	active in Milan from c. 1490 † after 1520	Lodi V Lombardy (AB2)	Identity with the so-called Pseudo-Boccaccino (a designation chosen by Wilhelm von Bode for Giov. Agostino, stylistically similar to B. Boccaccino, but still not identified at that time) is meanwhile no longer contested. He was a pupil of Marco d' Oggione.
Giovanni Angelo da Camerino Giovanni Angelo di Antonio da Camerino	* Camerino doc. in Siena, 1451	III Umbria / Marches (B1)	Perhaps identical to the master of the Barberini panels. Contacts with Giovanni Boccati.
Giovanni Antonio da Pesaro	doc. 1462–1511	Marches III Umbria / Marches (A2)	Influenced by Late Gothic painting in Emilia, to which he also remained true after his return to the Marches.
Giovanni Battista della Cerva	active in Milan † after 1548	V Lombardy (C3)	Tutor of G.P. Lomazzo.
Giovanni d'Alemagna Zuane da Murano	* Germany † Padua 1450	Murano II Venice (C1)	Brother-in-law and partner of Antonio Vivarini. Moved to Padua in 1437. Still bound to the linear,

			Late Gothic style (Cologne School?), while the style of his partner Antonio reveals Renaissance traits.
Giovanni da Asola	* Asola, around 1465 (?) † Venice 1531	Venice II Venice (B5)	Father of Bernardino da Asola. From 1512, he was in Venice. Influenced by the young Titian and Dosso.
Giovanni da Lodi identical to Bongiovanni Lupi	active in Milan and Lodi † 1525	V Lombardy (AB2)	In Leonardo's sphere of influence. Pupil of Marco d' Oggioni.
Giovanni da Mel	* Cadore, around 1480 † Belluno 1549	Friuli II Venice (B4)	Son of Antonio Rosso and elder brother of Marco da Mel. Predominantly active in Belluno; influences from Jacopo da Valenza. Also reminiscent of Francesco Vecellio and Porderone, however.
Giovanni da Milano Giovanni di Jacopo di Guido da Raverzaio, or da Como	* around 1370	Florence I Tuscany (B2)	Pupil of Taddeo Gaddi and stylistically allied to Giottino.
Giovanni da Murano see Alemagna			
Giovanni da Padova	active in Padua in the 14th c.	Padua IV Padua (B1)	Worked on the Campo Santo of Padua with his brother, Antonio. Both were probably from the workshop of Giusto de' Menabuoi.
Giovanni da Udine Giovanni di Ricamatore	* Udine 1487 † Rome 1561	Venice II Venice (A5) III Umbria / Marches (A3)	Pupil of, and assistant to Giov. Martini (c. 1502–06). Then influenced by Cima and Carpaccio and, according to Vasari, engaged in Giorgione's workshop. He was in the Raphael circle in Rome. His style is characterized by an uninhibited naturalism.
Giovanni dal Ponte Giovanni di Marco, Giovanni da Santo Stefano	* Florence 1385 † after 1437	Florence I Tuscany (B1)	Smeraldo di Giovanni was his assistant. Both probably trained under Bufalmacco. Towards the end of his creative period, he was typical of the fusion of the Late Gothic style with elements of the Early Renaissance.
Giovanni de Cramariis	doc. in Friuli from 1470 † 1533	Friuli II Venice (C4)	Active in Friuli and Siena. Brother-in-law of Pellegrino da San Daniele. Influence from Girolamo da Cremona and Liberale da Verona.
Giovanni de' Grassi Giovannino de' Grassi	active in Milan in the 14th c. † Milan 1398	Milan V Lombardy (A1)	In Giotto's sphere of influence. First doc. as book illuminator in 1389.
Giovanni de' Sacchi see Porderone			
Giovanni del Biondo dal Casentino	active in Florence 1356–92	Florence I Tuscany (C2)	Pupil of Andrea Orcagna.
Giovanni dell' Abbate see Niccolò dell' Abbate			
Giovanni di Francesco Giovanni di Francesco di Giovanni del Cervelliera	doc. in Florence btw. 1439 and 1459	Florence I Tuscany (C5)	Identical to Giovanni da Rovezzano (mentioned by Vasari). Assistant to Castagno and temporarily partner of Filippo Lippi. Stylistically allied to Pesellino and Fra Diamante.
Giovanni di Giorgio	* Germany (?) 1472 (?) † Perugia (?) 1527	Umbria III Umbria / Marches (A3)	Mainly active in Perugia. Care in detail is indicative of Nordic influences. Of provincial significance only.

Giovanni di Paolo di Grazia called Giovanni del Poggio	* Siena, around 1399 † Siena 1482	Siena I Tuscany (A2)	Doc. from 1417 as a book illuminator. Franco-Flemish and Lombard influences (Michelino da Besozzo). Recourse to the compositions of Gentile da Fabriano. Imaginative narrator (illustrations for Dante's *Divine Comedy*). Mainly worked for churches and monasteries in Siena.
Giovanni di Piamonte (Pimonte)	doc. in Città di Castello, 1456	Florence I Tuscany (B4)	Training in the circle of Piero della Francesca, and one of his assistants. Later went to Arezzo and Umbria. Influences from Masaccio and Castagno.
Giovanni di Pietro also Nanni di Pietro	active btw. 1439 and 1468 † before 1479	Siena I Tuscany (B3)	Brother of Vechietta. Collaboration with Matteo di Giovanni. Orientation towards Simone Martini (also copies).
Giovanni di Pietro da Napoli	* Naples active in Pisa in the 14th/15th c.	Pisa I Tuscany (A2)	Collaboration with Martino di Bartolommeo.
Giovanni di Pietro Falloppi Giovanni da Modena	doc. in Bologna, 1409–56	Bologna VI Emilia-Romagna (A1)	Remarkable representative of Late Gothic painting in Emilia. Strongly influenced by Lombard examples of the International Gothic.
Giovanni di Ser Giovanni called lo Scheggia	* Florence 1406 † Florence 1486	Florence I Tuscany (A3)	Pupil of Masaccio. Stylistically, more graceful and playful than his tutor. Also worked as a painter of *cassoni*.
Giovanni di Taldo see Landi, Neroccio			
Giovanni Donato da Montorfano see Montorfano			
Giovanni Francesco di Simone da Rimini	doc. 1441–70	Rimini III Umbria/Marches (B2)	Probably assistant to Matteo da Gualdo (B. Berenson) and influenced by Boccati and Bonfigli.
Giovanni Martini see Martini, Giovanni			
Giovenone, Amadeo see Giuseppe il Giovane			
Giovenone, Giovanni Battista	active in Vercelli in the 16th c.	Piedmont V Lombardy (AB5)	Altarpiece in Trivero near Biella.
Giovenone, Girolamo	* Barengo, around 1490 † Vercelli 1555	Piedmont V Lombardy (BC4)	Training under Martino Spanzotti and influenced by Defendente Ferrari. Later, distinct orientation towards Gaudenzio Ferrari. From *c.* 1534, collaboration with Bernadino Lanino (whose daughter he married) is documented. Father of Giuseppe, Amadeo, and Giov. Paolo.
Giovenone, Giuseppe (the Younger) Giuseppe il Giovane	* Vercelli, around 1524 † Vercelli, after 1589	Piedmont V Lombardy (AB5)	Son of Girolamo G. Active almost exclusively in Vercelli and environs. In Gaudenzio Ferrari's sphere of influence. Works of very variable quality. His brother Amadeo was probably his assistant (and imitator).
Giovenone, Paolo Paolo Battista Giuseppe	* Vercelli, around 1525 † before 1609	Piedmont V Lombardy (B5)	Son of Girolamo and brother-in-law of B. Lanino.
Giovenone, Raffaelo	active in Novara, Biella, and Quaregna † 1604	Piedmont V Lombardy (A6)	Son of Giovanni Battista G. Principal work in Biella.

Girolamo da Brescia Fra Girolamo di Antonio	* Brescia doc. in Florence 1490 † 1529	Brescia/Florence I Tuscany (A3)	In 1490, he entered the Carmelite Order and there enjoyed certain privileges, which made it easier for him to work as an artist. His only signed work is today in the Pinacoteca Civica in Savona. There are influences from Civerchio and Foppa evident in this triptych (adoration of the child with saints and donators).
Girolamo da Carpi Girolamo Sellari	* Ferrara 1501 † Ferrara 1556 or 1569	Ferrara VI Emilia-Romagna (AB3)	Named after his father's birthplace. According to Vasari, he trained under Garofalo. Documented in Bologna from 1525. Assistant to Biagio Pupini and Girolamo Borghese. Active in Rome, from where he returned to Bologna in 1527. Later back in Rome (active for Julius II). Combined Ferrarese and Venetian influences with Raphaelesque ideas.
Girolamo da Cremona	* Cremona active btw. 1451 and 1483	Venice II Venice (A1)	Active in Padua, Mantua, Siena, and Venice. Artistic training in Veneto around 1450 with contacts with the workshops of Mantegna and the Vivarini.
Girolamo da Fano see Gambetello			
Girolamo da Treviso (the Elder) see also Pennacchi	active in the 2nd half of the 15th c.	Treviso II Venice (BC3)	There is doubt concerning the identity of this painter, since two are documented: Girolamo di Bartolomeo Strazarolo da Aviano (doc. 1476–97), and Girolamo di Giovanni Pennacchi, elder brother of Pier Maria P. (doc. 1488–97 in Treviso).
Girolamo da Udine Girolamo di Bernardino	active in Friuli, turn of the 16th c. † 1512	Friuli II Venice (C3)	Assistant to Cima and Pellegrino da San Daniele. Close collaboration with both makes it difficult to ascribe his works with certainty.
Girolamo da Vicenza	active around 1500	Venice II Venice (B3)	In Giovanni Bellini's sphere of influence.
Girolamo dai Libri	* Verona 1474 † Verona 1556	Verona VII Verona (B2)	Son of the book illuminator Francesco dai Libri. Training in the workshop of D. Morone, and closely associated with the latter's son, Francesco. Also an outstanding miniaturist (Vasari). Somewhat stiff in his composition, but lovingly and most carefully crafted reproductions of the animal and plant world.
Girolamo del Pacchia see Pacchia			
Girolamo di Benvenuto see Guasta, Girolamo			
Girolamo di Bernardino see Girolamo da Udine			
Girolamo di Giovanni Camerino Girolamo Camerino di Giovanni	active btw. 1449 and 1469	Camerino III Umbria/Marches (A1)	Pupil of Giovanni Boccati. Important representative of the art of the Marches in the Quattrocento. Strongly influenced by Piero della Francesca.
Girolamo Miruoli see Miruoli			
Girolamo Pennacchi see Pennacchi			

Girolamo and Giovanni da Murano
see Andrea da Murano

Giulio Romano Giulio di Pietro di Gianuzzi Pippi *pl. 53*	* Rome 1499 (?) † Mantua 1546	Umbro-Roman III Umbria/Marches (A4)	Came early into Raphael's workshop, where became his favorite pupil. As his assistant, he collaborated on the Vatican Stanze and loggias. Collaboration with Gianfrancesco Penni and other artists on diverse altarpieces. Completed works begun by Raphael after Raphael's death (1520). In 1524, he went to the Court of the Gonzaga at Mantua, where he produced his principal works as architect and painter (Palazzo Te, etc.). Extensive draughting work. His panel paintings are rare. Had a considerable influence on Roman and Northern Italian Mannerism and the Early Baroque.
Giuochi, Giuliano also Giuliano d'Arrigo, called Pesello	* Florence 1367 † Florence 1446	Florence I Tuscany (C3)	Mainly active as sculptor and architect. A gifted painter of animals. Tutor of Pesellino.
Giusto d'Allamagna Justus von Ravensburg	active 1451 in Genoa	Genoa V Lombardy (B2)	A fresco by him exists as a signed work in S. Maria di Castello in Genoa (annunciation), which shows a relationship to the Rhenish School. Giusto's influence on other painters of the Genoese School is unmistakable.
Giusto de' Menabuoi Giusto di Giovanni de' M., called Giusto Padovano or Giusto Fiorentino	* Florence, first half of the 14th c. † Padua 1393	Florence IV Padua (B1)	Imitator of Giotto. Possibly trained under B. Daddi or Maso di Banco. Numerous frescoes in Padua, which probably must be attributed in part to his pupils Giovanni and Antonio da Padua, however. Signed house altar in London (N.G.).

Gobbo, il
see Solario

Gotti, Bartolommeo also Goti	active in the 16th c. (in France and elsewhere)	Florence I Tuscany (AB6)	Pupil of Ridolfo Ghirlandaio.
Gozzoli, Benozzo Benozzo di Lese di Sandro *pl. 43*	* Florence 1420 † Pistoia 1497	Florence III Umbria/Marches (B1)	Assistant to Ghiberti for the work on the Baptistry doors. Painting style influenced by Fra Angelico, whom he accompanied to Rome as an assistant. Owing to his constant activity in Orvieto, Montefalco, Perugia, and San Gimignano, he had a profound influence on the development of the Umbrian School. His principal work in the Pal. Riccardi-Medici in Florence (*Medici family as the Magi*) confirms a great narrative talent, assured draughtsmanship, and a masterful use of colour.
Grammorseo, Pietro	* Mons (?) † Casale, before 1531	Piedmont V Lombardy (B4)	Born in Flanders. Trained in the School of the Spanzotti, son-in-law of Francesco S. Documented in Casale Monferrato btw. 1521 and 1527. Dependent on Leonardo, but also open to Nordic influences (Dürer). Influence on both Volpi.
Granacci, Francesco	* Villamagna 1469 † Florence 1543	Florence I Tuscany (A5)	According to Vasari, a friend and admirer of Michelangelo, with whom he was a member of the Ghirlandaio workshop. Retained the style of his master. In spite of their friendship of many years, Michelangelo apparently declined an offer of collaboration on the frescoes of the Sistine Chapel.

			G. later adopted some of the vastness and monumentality of Fra Bartolommeo. Influence on Ridolfo Ghirlandaio.
Grandi, Ercole Ercole da Ferrara, occasionally confused with Ercole Roberti (Grandi)	* Ferrara, around 1463 † Ferrara 1531	Ferrara VI Emilia-Romagna (A2)	Many works were long attributed to other painters (e.g., Garofalo, Costa).
Grandi, Girolamo	* Ferrara, end of the 15th c. † 1562	Ferrara VI Emilia-Romagna (A2)	Painter and graphic artist (wood-carvings). Son of Ercole Grandi.
Grassi, Giambattista di Raffaelo	* Udine 1525 † 1578	Friuli II Venice (C5)	Initially retained the painting style of Pellegrino and Porderone. Later influenced by Michelangelo and Vasari. (The latter gave biographical notes on Porderone and other Friuli artists.) Also active as an architect.
Grasso, Francesco	doc. btw. 1465 and 1500	Liguria V Lombardy (C3)	Active in Liguria and Lombardy, also in collaboration with his brothers Giovanni and Francesco de Ferrari. Paduan influences are evident towards the end of his creative period.
Gregorio di Cecco di Luca	* Lucca, before 1389 † Siena, after 1424	Siena I Tuscany (A3)	Adoptive son of Taddeo di Bartolo and possibly tutor of the "Master of the Osservanza" (Graziani, 1948).
Grifo di Tancredi see Master of San Gaggio			
Grimaldi, Lazzaro	* Reggio Emilia 1472 † before 1516	Emilia VI Emilia-Romagna (A2)	In 1493/94, documented in Reggio Emilia; from 1499, employee of B. Boccaccino in Ferrara for the execution of the frescoes of the Cathedral there. Influences from L. Costa and Francia.
Gualdo see Matteo da Gualdo			
Gualtieri di Giovanni da Pisa called Dellunigiana. Identical to the "Maestro della Vita di Maria"	* Pisa active in Siena, 1409–11	Siena I Tuscany (A3)	Collaboration with Niccolò Naldo in the Cathedral of Siena. Somewhat stiff and awkward in his anatomical depiction. Digested ideas from Taddeo di Bartolo and Paolo di Giov. Fei.
Guariento, Ridolfo	* Padua † before 1378	Padua IV Padua (B1) II Venice (C1)	Participation in the initial decoration of the great councillors' hall in the Doges' Palace (1365). Frescoes in Padua (Eremitani).
Guarinoni, Giovanni Battista	* Averara, around 1548 † Bergamo 1579	Bergamo II Venice (A6)	Mainly active as a Bergamasque fresco executant. Provincial Mannerist, reminiscent of Bassani's naturalism.
Guasta, Girolamo Girolamo di Benvenuto di Giovanni del Guasta	* Siena 1470 † 1524	Siena I Tuscany (BC5)	Son and close employee of Benvenuto di Giovanni. Possibly identical to the Maestro della Pala Bagatti-Valsecchi.
Guasta, Benvenuto di Giovanni Benvenuto di Giovanni di Meo del Guasta	* Siena (?) 1436 † around 1518	Siena I Tuscany (A4)	First documented in 1453, on the occasion of the collaboration with Vecchietta in the Baptistry of Siena, and regarded as his pupil. As a miniaturist, strongly influenced by Liberale da Verona and Girolamo da Cremona, of whom his landscapes in particular are reminiscent. Principal work, *The Resurrection*, in the Pinacoteca Nazionale in Siena.

Guercino, il Giovanni Francesco Barbieri	* Cento 1591 † Bologna 1666	Bologna VI Emilia-Romagna (A4)	After G. Reni's death, the greatest Bolognese painter of the 17th c. His œuvre is of uneven quality. The last of the Bolognese School, his Renaissance roots are still recognizable.
Guidaccio da Imola	doc. 1463–1508 † before 1510	Romagna VI Emilia-Romagna (A1)	Son of Giovanni Checchi da Imola. Influenced by Mantegna and Cossa.
Guido da Siena Guido da Senis	active in Siena, 2nd half of the 13th c.	Siena I Tuscany (A1)	His *Madonnas* reveal a distinct "Byzantine tradition." His Stations of the Cross (Pinacoteca Nazionale, Siena) is already imbued with a new dramatic spirit. G. had a great influence on the subsequent generation of the Sienese School.
Ibi, Sinibaldo	* Perugia, around 1475 † after 1548	Gubbio III Umbria/Marches (B3)	In 1496, he opened a workshop together with Berto di Giovanni, Lattanzio di Giovanni, and Eusebio di San Giorgio. Worked mainly in Gubbio. In his time, much sought after as an artist; however, his work did not go far beyond an imitation of Perugino and Raphael.
Imola, Innocenzo Francuccida see Francucci			
India, Bernardino also Bernardo	* Verona 1528 † Verona 1590	Verona VII Verona (A3)	Training under Brusasorci, in Caroto's sphere of influence. Developed a Mannerist style with leanings toward Giulio Romano and Parmigianino. His style is very decorative, but reveals little power of innovation.
India, Tullio	active in Verona around 1530	Verona VII Verona (B3)	Nephew of Bernardino I. Imitator of Paolo Veronese.
Inganatio, Pietro also Pietro degli Ingannati	active in Venice in the 16th c.	Venice II Venice (A5)	In the sphere of influence of Seb. del Piombo.
Jacobello del Fiore	* Venice, around 1370 † Venice 1439	Venice II Venice (A1)	One of the important Venetians between Gothic and Renaissance. Under the influence of Gentile da Fabriano, elegance and individualization increasingly superseded Byzantine rigidity. Possibly the tutor of Michele Giambono.
Jacobello di Antonello see Antonello da Messina			
Jacobello di Bonomo	active in Venice in the 14th c.	Venice II Venice (A1)	Pupil of Francesco Jacobello. (Works in Cesena and Torre di Palme.) Influence on Jacobello del Fiore.
Jacometto Veneziano	active in Venice from 1472 † Venice, before 1498	Venice II Venice (C2)	In the circle of Antonello da Messina. Mainly active as a miniaturist and painter of smaller panels. Flemish influences, probably due to Antonello's intercession.
Jacone Jacopo di Giovanni	* Florence 1495 † Florence 1554	Florence I Tuscany (A6)	Vasari mentions him in connection with Aristotele da Sangallo. Pupil of Andrea del Sarto, and later influenced by Polidoro da Caravaggio and Pontormo. Merchants may have exported some of his works to Germany.
Jacopino de' Mottis see Bernardino Lanzani			
Jacopo da Empoli see Jacopo Chimenti			

Jacopo da Valenza Jacomo Davalenso, or also Giacomo da Valencia	active btw. 1485 and 1509 † after 1509	Venice II Venice (C2)	Originated from the Belluno region. Pupil of Bartolommeo and Alvise Vivarini. Later worked mainly in Umbria. Always remained true to the style he adopted in his youth.
Jacopo del Casentino Jacopo Landini, also called Jacopo da Prato Vecchio	* Prato Vecchio (?) 1297 † Prato Vecchio 1358	Florence I Tuscany (B2)	Pupil of Taddeo Gaddi, with whom he went to Florence. Went in 1354 to Arezzo, where he worked as a painter and architect. Tutor of Agnolo Gaddi.
Jacopo del Sellaio see Sellaio			
Jacopo di Cione see Orcagna			
Lamberti see Lambertini			
Lambertini, Michele di Matteo Michele di Matteo da Bologna	doc. in Bologna, 1410–69	Bologna VI Emilia-Romagna (C1)	Mainly active in Bologna (S. Petronio); also documented in Venice however, in 1447. Influenced by Gentile da Fabriano and Nordic masters (?).
Landi, Neroccio de' Neroccio di Bartolommeo di Benedetto de' Landi	* Siena 1447 † Siena 1500	Siena I Tuscany (C5)	Painter and sculptor, probably from the Vecchietta workshop. From 1468 until 1475, partner of Francesco di Giorgio. Mainly painted devotional paintings, including *Madonnas* of a delicate and poetic interpretation. Maintained a very productive workshop. Known employees include: Marioto da Volterra, Giovanni di Taldo, Giov. Batt. di Bartolommeo Alberti, and Girolamo del Pacchia.
Lanino, Bernadino	* Vercelli, around 1512 † Milan 1583	Piedmont V Lombardy (A3)	Father-in-law of Gerolamo Giovenone. After an initial apprenticeship under Baldassare de Cadighis di Abbiategrasso, assistant to Gaudenzio Ferrari, who had a profound influence on his style. Numerous frescoes in Vercelli. Close collaboration with G. Giovenone.
Lanzani, Bernardino	* St. Colombano al Lambro † after 1526	Milan V Lombardy (B2)	Pupil of Jacopino de' Mottis in Borgognone's sphere of influence. Doc. between 1490 and 1526. Mainly active as a fresco executant, in Milan, Lodi, Pavia, Pieve di Porto Morone, Bobbio, and elsewhere.
Lanzani, Polidoro di Paoli called Polidoro Veneziano	* Venice 1515 † 1565	Venice II Venice (B6)	Pupil and imitator of Titian. A good landscapist.
Lattanzio da Rimini	active in Venice, end of the 15th c.	Venice II Venice (B2)	Assistant to Giovanni Bellini. There is a beautiful polyptych by him (St Martin) in the Piazza Brembana (Bergamo).
Lattanzio di Giovanni	active in Perugia, turn of the 16th c. † Perugia 1534	Umbria III Umbria/Marches (AB2)	Pupil and employee of Bartolommeo Caporali.
Lattanzio di Niccolò di Liberatore	active in Foligno, 15th/16th c.	Umbria III Umbria/Marches (B2)	Son of Niccolò da Foligno, called Alunno. Close collaboration with his father, e.g., in Todi and Foligno. Also influenced by Pinturicchio.
Lazzari see Bramante			

Lendinara, Cristoforo Canozi da	doc. from 1448 † 1491	Modena VI Emilia-Romagna (B1)	Together with his brother Lorenzo mainly documented as an intarsia cutter (e.g., in Modena Ferrara and Parma). Formative influence from Piero della Francesca.
Leonardo da Pistoia Leonardo Grazia (Grassi)	* Pistoia 1505 † Naples?	III Umbria/Marches (A4)	Vasari describes him as an assistant to Giov. Francesco Penni. Active in Lucca, Rome, and especially in Naples.
Leonardo da Vinci *plates 1, 12, 13*	* Vinci 1452 † Amboise 1519	Florence I Tuscany (B5)	Pupil of Verrocchio, in whose workshop he participated until 1480. The latter probably had a profound influence not only on Leonardo's artistic development, but also on the shaping of his personality. Leonardo's work as painter, sculptor, architect, engineer, and inventor developed in the field of tension between breathtaking versatility and an overwhelming perfectionism. There was much that he did not complete; however, in what has come down to us, he proved himself to be one of the most brilliant artistic personalities of the occident. In the quest for the perfect reproduction of beauty, he penetrated deeper than all other painters before and after him. His *sfumato*, his *Madonna* type, his interpretation of landscape, and his treatment of light were a formative influence on two generations of painters. The actual Leonardo School developed in Milan, where its influence rapidly overlaid the Lombardy-Foppan tradition. The following stand out from his large circle of pupils and imitators: B. Luini, Sodoma (pupil?), Boltraffio, Ambrogio de' Predis, Cesare da Sesto, and Andrea Solario.
Leonello da Crevalcore Antonio da Crevalcore	* Bologna active end of the 15th c.	Bologna VI Emilia-Romagna (C2)	Painter of flowers and still-lifes in Bologna.
Leonoro dell' Aquila l'Aquilano	* Aquila doc. from 1497–1512 in Genoa	Liguria V Lombardy (BC3)	In 1497, active in Genoa, together with Battista da Verona. Also active as engraver. Stylistically difficult to classify, but allied to the style of Borgognone. Contacts with Pietro de Saliba da Messina, whom he engaged as a subcontractor for a commission in Genoa.
Liberale da Verona Liberale di Jacopo dalla Biava *pl. 96*	* Verona, around 1445 † Verona 1526/29	Verona VII Verona (AB2)	One of the main representatives of the Veronese School. Formatively influenced by Pisanello and Mantegna. His painting is of variable quality. His miniatures for Monteoliveto and Siena (1467–76) are renowned. From 1492 in Verona, where his studio produced outstanding masters of the Veronese School: Giolfino, Torbido, Caroto, and others.
Liberatore see Niccolò da Foligno			
Libri see Girolamo dai Libri			
Licinio, Bernardino	* Venice, around 1485 † Venice, after 1549	Venice II Venice (BC5)	Distant relative of Porderone and perhaps his pupil. Developed under the influence of the later Giambellino and Giorgione. Like Palma, he favoured compositions with half-length panels of figures.

Licinio, Giovanni Antonio see Porderone			
Licinio, Giovanni Antonio (the Younger) il Sachiense	* Porderone (?), around 1515 † Como, around 1576	Venice II Venice (B5)	Brother of Giulio L., nephew and pupil of Porderone.
Licinio, Giulio il Romano	* Porderone (?) 1527 † after 1593	Venice VII Venice (C5)	Brother of Giov. Antonio and, like him, probably a pupil of his uncle, Porderone.
Lippi, Filippino pl. 9	* Prato 1457 † Florence 1504	Florence I Tuscany (A5)	Son of Fra Filippo Lippi. Pupil of Fra Diamante, and later assistant to Botticelli. Remained in the tradition of his father and never suprassed his tutor, Sandro. Nevertheless, a great master who inherited his sense of outline and compositional balance from his father, while in total seeming more serious. Perugino is far behind him in the sincerity of his perception, as conspicuously evi- dent in the *The Deposition* in Florence (Accademia), which Filippino began and which Perugino com- pleted. Raffaelino del Garbo was one of his Pupils.
Lippi, Fra Filippo di Tomaso plates 5, 6	* Florence, around 1406 † Spoleto 1469	Florence I Tuscany (B3)	Carmelite monk, whose tutor is considered to be Lorenzo Monaco. Fra Angelico, and later Masaccio, also had a crucial influence on his development. Although the monastery could not contain him, and he initiated a minor scandal through an affair with a nun, with major reper- cussions, he remained a monk for his entire life. With respect to Vasari's description of Lippi's life not everything should be taken at face value. As an artist, he enjoyed the highest regard, and the Florentine Renaissance would have been poorer without him. The innocent charm of his *Madonnas* and his chubby-faced infant Christ figures became the outward distinguishing characteristics of his art. His significance also lies, however, in his formal assurance, in his luminous use of colour, and especially in the harmonious integration of the landscape. The frescoes in the Cathedral of Prato are considered his principal work. His son, Filippino, was not yet 13 at the time of his death and apart from craftsman's skills can only have learnt little from him. Together with Botticelli, however, Filippo left his mark as a tutor.
Lippo di Benivieni	active in Florence in the 14th c.	Florence I Tuscany (C1)	In the Giotto circle.
Lippo di Dalmasio Dalmasio Scannabecchi or Lippo della Madona	* Bologna 1352 † Bologna, after 1410	Bologna VI Emilia-Romagna (AB1)	Earliest time of the Bolognese School. Probably a pupil of Vitale da Bologna. Temporarily active in Pistoia. Works in London (N.G.) and Bologna.
Livio da Forlì see Modigliani, Livio			
Lodi, Giov. Agostino see Giovanni Agostino da Lodi			
Lodovico di Angelo di Baldass.	active in Città di Castello in the 14th c.	Umbria III Umbria/Marches (AB2)	Workshop of Fiorenzo di Lorenzo. Collaboration with Bartolommeo di Bindo is documented, from 1382.

Lomazzo, Giovanni Paolo	* Milan 1538 † Milan 1600	Milan V Lombardy (C4)	Painter and art historian. Painterly training under Giov. Batt. della Cerva, thereafter assistant to Gaudenzio Ferrari, his uncle. Further trained in the style of Michelangelo and the Roman Mannerists. His most important literary works include *Trattato dell' Arte della Pittura* and *Idea del Tempio della Pittura*.
Lombardelli, Giovanni Battista	* Montenovo (Ostra Vetere) † Perugia 1592	Umbria VI Emilia-Romagna (B4)	Probably a pupil of Marco da Faenza, under whose influence his early works originated. In Rome, he came into in the wake of the local Mannerists (including Marco Marchietti).
Longhi, Barbara	* Ravenna 1552 † Ravenna 1638	Ravenna VI Emilia-Romagna (A4)	Daughter and pupil of Luca Longhi. She left behind a series of small-format works, particularly with the depiction of saints and the Madonna with Child.
Longhi, Francesco	* Ravenna 1544 † Ravenna 1618	Ravenna VI Emilia-Romagna (A4)	Son of Luca Longhi. Owing to his stylistic similarity to his father, it is difficult to reconstruct his artistic development. Influences from the Vasari circle (Naldini, Poppi) are recognizable, however.
Longhi, Luca called Raffaelo da Ravenna	* Ravenna 1507 † Ravenna 1580	Ravenna VI Emilia-Romagna (A3)	Stylistically strongly rooted in the 15th c. and not very open to Mannerist tendencies. Worked almost exclusively in Ravenna, where he produced numerous altarpieces. Possibly a somewhat underrated master, overshadowed by the splendid Venetians and the witty Mannerists. In the tradition of Roberti, Francia, and Giambellino, he was also responsible for the artistic training of his eight children, of whom Francesco and Barbara were the most successful.
Longobardi, Marco also Marco dei Lombardi	doc. in Bologna 1388–1430	Milan V Lombardy (A2)	Documented are at least contacts with Matteo de' Fedeli (1482). A triptych in the Brambilla Collection (Milan) ist signed "Marci Longobardi et Joannis Auroni Canturiensis opus", and, stylistically, can probably be classified to the beginning of the Cinquecento.
Lorentino d' Andrea	doc. in Arezzo, from 1463 † 1506	Arezzo I Tuscany (C4)	Pupil of Piero della Francesca, to whose style he remained true. Mainly active in Arezzo and environs.
Lorenzetti, Ambrogio	* Siena 1280/90 † Siena 1348	Siena I Tuscany (AB1)	Possibly the younger of the two brothers, who both came from the workshop of Simone Martini. Giotto's example is unmistakable in both his frescoes and panel paintings. The frescoes in the Palazzo Pubblico in Siena are considered his principal work.
Lorenzetti, Pietro also Laurati	* Siena 1280/90 † Siena 1348	Siena I Tuscany (B1)	More than his brother, Ambrogio, dependent on Duccio and Giotto, and, in total, drier and more serious. Worked in Siena, Arezzo, and Assisi (Lower Church). Collaboration with his brother on various altarpieces. Both probably fell victim to the Black Death of 1348. The Lorenzetti are counted among the greatest painters of Italy, and, with their art, paved the way for the great representatives of the Early Renaissance.

Lorenzetti, Ugolino
see Ugolino da Siena

Lorenzo da Viterbo Lorenzo di Jacopo di Pietro Paolo da Viterbo	* Viterbo, around 1444 † Viterbo 1472 (?)	Viterbo III Umbria/Marches (B1)	Dependent on B. Gozzoli and Melozzo da Forlì. Important provincial painter. Frescoes in Viterbo (S. Maria della Verità).

Lorenzo di Bicci
see Bicci

Lorenzo di Niccolò
see Gerini

Lorenzo di Pietro
see Vecchietta

Lorenzo Monaco Piero di Giovanni	* Siena around 1370 † Florence 1425	Florence I Tuscany (C2)	Camaldolensian monk. Painted several altarpieces for the order in Florence, e.g., the high altar of S. Maria degli Angeli (1414). Important forerunner of Fra Angelico in the tradition of T. Gaddi and the Lorenzetti. Collaboration with Angnolo Gaddi ist documented. His style as a book illuminator is reminiscent of Orcagna. Lorenzo is the last great representative of the Florentine Late Gothic. Fra Angelico and Filippo Lippi owed much to him stylistically.

Lorenzo Veneziano
see Veneziano

Loschi, Bernardino also Losco	* Parma 1489 † Carpi 1540	Carpi V Lombardy (C3)	Son and pupil of Jacopo d' Ilario.
Loschi, Jacopo d' Ilario also Losco	* Parma 1425 † Carpi 1503	Carpi V Lombardy (C1)	In the Lombard tradition, with Paduan elements. Father of Bernardino L. and brother-in-law and tutor of Bartolino de' Grossi (doc. in Parma btw. 1425 and 1462).
Lotto, Lorenzo *pl. 32*	* Venice 1480 † Loreto 1556	Venice II Venice (C4)	Initially influenced by Antonello da Messina, Giov. Bellini, and Alvise Vivarini. Already documented as a master in Treviso at age 18. During periods in Bergamo, Rome, Venice, and the Marches, he adopted many different ideas; these never diluted his Venetian origins, however. B. Berenson recognizes a distinct Nordic influence in his early portraits. In his landscapes and female figures, he has much in common with Palma Vecchio, with whom he had personal contact. After the latter's death, he came increasingly under Titian's influence (use of colour and painting technique). Among his very psychoanalytically interpreted portraits are some of the most beautiful ever painted. His landscapes have a realistic warmth. Weaker in scenes with many figures, which, although dramatically imbued, are anatomically uncertain, while the association of figure and background is not always harmonious.
Luca di Tommé	* Siena 1330 † Siena, after 1389	Siena I Tuscany (A1)	In total, a successor to Simone Martini and Pietro Lorenzetti, but also influenced by the Florentine Realists (Orcagna, Spinello). His works can be found in Tuscany and in the Marches. A partnership with Niccolò di Ser Sozzo is documented.

Luciano, Sebastiano
see Piombo, Sebastiano del

Luini, Ambrogio	active in Milan, turn of the 16th c.	Milan V Lombardy (B4)	Brother and pupil of Bernardino L.
Luini, Aurelio	* Luino, around 1530 † Milan 1593	Milan V Lombardy (C4)	Son of Bernardino L.
Luini, Bernardino also Lovino *pl. 68*	* Luino (?), around 1475 † 1532	Milan V Lombardy (B3)	The most important Lombard artist at the turn of the 16th c. Training under Borgognone, whose influence gradually receded in the face of the influential power of Leonardo, since 1482 in Milan. L. adopted Leonardos "*sfumato*", his *Madonna* type, and borrowed from his composition, without achieving much depth, however. L.'s complaisance and tendency towards sweetness is balanced by his careful technique. His frescoes look more powerful and independent (some of which are today in the Brera, Milan). Was also active in Saronno, Lugano, and Chiaravalle. Father of Aurelio L., the most gifted of his sons.
Luini, Giovan Pietro	active in Milan, 16th c.	Milan V Lombardy (C4)	Son of Bernardino L.
Lunetti, Tommaso di Stefano	* Florence, around 1490 † Florence 1564	Florence I Tuscany (C6)	Painter and architect. In Vasari, described as an assistant to Lorenzo di Credi, which can also be recognized in his style. Additionaly influenced by Fra Bartolommeo, Bacchiacca, and Pier Francesco Foschi.

Lupi, Bongiovanni
see Giovanni da Lodi

Lutero
see Dossi

Maccagnino, Angelo Actually Angelo di Pietro da Siena	doc. 1439–56	Ferrara VI Emilia-Romagna (A2)	Active in Siena and Umbria, until his appointment to the Court d'Este in Ferrara. His frescoes in the Studiolo of Pal. Belfiore are lost. No verified works. Identity with the "Master of the Wedding Banquet of Boston" (with a representation of the encounter between Salomon and the King of Saba) has not yet been substantiated. Stylistically allied to Cossa.
Macchiavelli, Zenobio di Jacopo called Zanobi	* Florence 1418 † 1479	Florence I Tuscany (C4)	Pupil of, and assistant to B. Gozzoli. Highly regarded by Vasari.
Macchietti, Girolamo called del Crocefissaio	* Florence 1535 † Florence 1592	Florence I Tuscany (AB7)	Training under Michele Tosini. Collaboration with Mirabello Cavalori. Many of the works mentioned in Vasari are lost. Preserved drawings reveal his occupation with the graphic work of Pontormo.
Macrino d'Alba Giangiacomo Fava de Alladio	* Alba, around 1470 † before 1528	Piedmont V Lombardy (B2)	After initial training in Vercelli, an employee in Foppa's workshop. Umbro-Tuscan influences are attributed to a period in Rome (not substantiated). Active in Alba, Pavia (Certosa), Asti, and elsewhere. Considered one of Gaudenzio Ferrari's tutors.

Maestro d. Natività di Castello	active in Florence, 3rd quarter of the 15th c.	Florence I Tuscany (BC4)	A designation used by B. Berenson for the anonymous painter of the *Castello Adoration*, today in the Accademia in Florence. It has similarities to a painting by Filippo Lippi on the same theme. Also stylistic affinity to Fra Angelico and Baldovinetti.
Maestro degli Arcangeli see Maestro di Pratovecchio			
Maestro del desco di Boston see Maccagnino			
Maestro del Tondo Lathrop Presumably identical to Michelangelo di Pietro 'Mencherini' (or Mencarini)	active in Lucca btw. 1490 and 1520	Lucca I Tuscany (B4)	The Tondo (*Madonna with Child and Saints*) is today in the Getty Museum in Malibu. It shows orientations toward D. Ghirlandaio. Influences from Fra Filippo and Botticelli in other works.
Maestro dell' Osservanza Francesco di Bartolomeo Alfei(?)	active in the 2nd quarter of the 15th c.	Siena I Tuscany (A3)	Name refers to a triptych in the Basilica S. Osservanza near Siena. Until 1940, the works of this master were attributed to Sassetta. He counts as one of the most important artists of Siena in the first half of the 15th c. Strongly influenced by Sassetta. Training perhaps under Gregorio di Cecco. Very Sienese in his interpretation and more committed to the Gothic tradition of Masolino than to the innovations of Masaccio.
Maestro della Pala Bagatti see Girolamo di Benvenuto			
Maestro di Macchirolo	active in Milan, 2nd half of the 14th c.	Milan V Lombardy (B1)	Gothic painter under Giotto's influence.
Maestro di Pala Sforzesca	active around 1500, in Milan	Milan V Lombardy (A2)	Named after the altarpiece from the Sant' Ambrogio ad Nemus in the Brera. The most diverse hypotheses have been put over the years concerning the painter's identity. Among those considered were Ambrogio de' Predis, Francesco Napoletano (Jacobsen), and Bernardino de' Conti (Berenson and Morelli). It is fairly certain that he was a painter from the Leonardo circle, whose Lombard tradition is clearly evident, however. Possibly, "he" may have been a group of collaborators. Since the family of Lodovico il Moro is represented as donator, the Duke is presumed to have been a commissioner.
Maestro di Pratovecchio Identical to the "Maestro degli Arcangeli"(?)	active in Florence, mid-15th c.	Florence I Tuscany (A4)	According to Longhi, identical to the "Master of the Archangel" (Berlin). Contacts with Giovanni Francesco del Cervelliera. Stylistically influenced by Castagno, Verrocchio, and Piero della Francesca.
Maestro Esiguo ident. to Amadeo da Pistoia(?)	active end of the 15th / turn of the 16th c.	III Umbria/Marches (AB2)	Stylistically allied to Matteo da Gualdo (Jacobsen) and Benozzo Gozzoli (Berenson). Active in Umbria and Tuscany.
Magistris, Giovanni Andrea de	* Caldarola, 16th c.	Marches III Umbria/Marches (A4)	Father of Simone.

Magistris, Simone de called Toscani	* Caldoroli 1534 † after 1600	Marches III Umbria/Marches (A4)	Active in the Marches (Ascoli, Orsino, Caldaroli). Workshop together with his brothers Giovanni Francesco and Polomino.
Magni, Cesare	doc. in Milan before 1530–33	Milan V Lombardy (BC4)	His first tutor may have been Cesare da Sesto; this has led to subsequent confusion. Like da Sesto, he belonged to the more intimate Leonardo circle, where he also received ideas from Marco d' Oggione.
Mainardi, Sebastiano Bastiano di Bartolo	* San Gimignano, around 1460 † Florence 1513	Florence I Tuscany (A5)	Brother-in-law, pupil, and employee of Domenico Ghirlandaio, to whom he is stylistically indebted the most.
Maineri, Gian Francesco de'	doc. in Mantua and Parma from 1489 † after 1506	Ferrara VI Emilia-Romagna (B2)	Book illuminator and painter, in the sphere of influence of Ercole Roberti and Francia. Longhi and Zamboni (1975) presume him to be a pupil of Ercole.
Mancini, Domenico called Smicca	* Treviso active in Venice turn of the 16th c.	Venice II Venice (BC4)	Influenced by Giovanni Bellini and Giorgione.
Mansueti, Givanni di Niccolò	active in Venice from 1485 † Venice 1527 (?)	Venice II Venice (B3)	Pupil of Gentile Bellini and strongly influenced by Carpaccio. Nevertheless, developed a personal style in his most religious paintings, in particular expressed by his treatment of light, which may have been derivative of Giorgione. More sparing than Carpaccio in his use of colour.
Mantegna, Andrea Andrea di Biagio *plates 55, 57, 58, 59*	* Padua 1431 † Mantua 1506	Padua VI Padua (B1)	One of the greatest Italian Renaissance masters, to whom the Squarcione School in Padua essentially owes its reputation. Already took on his first commissions at seventeen. After works in Padua, Verona, and Venice, in 1459 he was appointed to the Gonzaga Court at Mantua, where worked for the rest of his life. Classiscal models and the sculptural work of Donatello had a profound influence on him. His draughtsmanship is firm and assured, his use of colour restrained; under the later influence of the Venetians, it becomes livelier and warmer, however. The stylistic exchange with his brother-in-law, Giovanni Bellini, was productive for both and created the basis for some of the most important works of the Early Renaissance.
Manzuoli, Tommaso d'Antonio called Maso da San Friano	* San Friano 1536 † Florence 1571	Florence I Tuscany (B7)	According to Borghini (1584), a pupil of C. Portelli; according to Vasari, of P.F. Foschi. Stylistically allied to Pontormo, his style was also formed by the contact with other Tusco-Roman Mannerists (Santo di Tito, Vasari, Bronzino). Alessandro Fei and J. Chimenti trained under him.
Marchesi, Girolamo Marchesi da Cotingnola	* Cotignola, around 1490 (?) † Bologna, after 1531 (1559 ?)	Romagna VI Emilia-Romagna (C2)	His work is so clearly divided into two phases that, for a time, two painters were presumed. Initial training most probably in the Zaganelli workshop (which, under Francesco, was later relocated to Ravenna). Raphaelesque influences become apparent with the stay of Raphael's pupil G. Genga in Romagna (1513–10). Contacts between the two artists are documented, but not a formal collaboration. The second phase of his artistic career

			began with intensive travel between Bologna, Rome, and Naples, and an approach to the young Parmigianino.
Marchietti, Marco Marco da Faenza	active in Rome and elsewhere, mid-16th c. † Faenza 1588	VI Emilia-Romagna (A4)	Trained in the spirit of Roman Mannerism. In Rome together with his countryman Jacopo Bertucci, in Florence assistant to G. Vasari for work in the Palazzo Vecchio. He painted his famous grotesques in the town hall of Faenza.
Marco da Mel see Giovanni da Mel			
Marco da Montepulciano	* Montepulciano; active in Tuscany in the 15th c.	Tuscany I Tuscany (B2)	Stylistically reminiscent of Fra Angelico.
Marco dei Lombardi see Longobardo, Marco			
Marco del Buono Giamberti see Appolonio di Giovanni			
Marco del Moro see Battista del Moro			
Marconi, Rocco	* Treviso 1470/75 † Venice 1529	Venice II Venice (A4)	Training in the workshop of Giovanni Bellini, where he was one of the more gifted assistants. After Giambellino's death (1516), in the studio of Palma Vecchio, which also had stylistic repercussions for his work.
Marcovaldo see Coppo di Marcovaldo			
Marescalco see Buonconsiglio, Giovanni			
Marescalco, Pietro called lo Spada	* Feltre, around 1520 † Feltre 1589	Venice II Venice (B5)	Venetian Mannerist, influenced by J. Bassano, Tintoretto, and Schiavone. Little credible dramatic sense, in a playful and decorative context.
Mariano d'Antonio di Francesco Nutoli	* Perugia active in Perugia 1433–68	Perugia III Umbria/Marches (A2)	Still very Gothic, with Florentine influences (Cimabue). Later dependent on Alunno.
Mariano di Ser Austerio called Mariano da Perugia	* Perugia, around 1470	Perugia III Umbria/Marches (B3)	Documented in Perugia from 1493 until 1527. Assistant to Perugino. Stylistic affinity to Spagna and Bernardino di Mariotto.
Marinoni	active mid-15th until mid-16th c.	Bergamo V Lombardy (B2)	A large Bergamasque artistic family with a workshop in Desenzano sul Serio. Its most important representative was Giovanni M. († around 1512). His son Antonio (independent from 1496) took over the workshop, which after his death (around 1545) came into the hands of his brothers, Bernardo and Pietro. Ambrogio and Francesco, Antonio's sons, took up their father's heritage after the sons of Pietro and Bernardo (Francesco and Giuliano) gave up their careers as painters.
Mariotto da Volterra see Landi, Neroccio			

Mariotto di Cristofano	active in Florence 1393–1457	Florence I Tuscany (B2)	From the school of Bicci di Lorenzo. Detectable influence from Fra Angelico in composition and use of colour. Brother-in-law of Masaccio.
Mariotto di Nardo	active in Florence btw. 1394 and 1424	Florence I Tuscany (C2)	Pupil of Lorenzo di Niccolò Gerini, and probably the son of Nardo Cione.
Marmitta, Francesco	* Parma, around 1460 † around 1506	Bologna VI Emilia-Romagna (C2)	Collaboration with Francesco Bianchi Ferrari, to whom some of his paintings were attributed. Reminiscent of Francia.
Marti, Agostino see Zacchia il Vecchio			
Martinelli, Luca see Bassano, Giambattista			
Martini see Francesco di Giorgio			
Martini, Giovanni not identical to Giovanni da Udine	* Udine 1470/75 † Udine 1535	Friuli II Venice (C5)	Son of Martino and nephew of Domenico da Tolmezzo. Training in the workshop of Alvise Vivarini. Important Friulian painter and woodcarver, with distinct influence from Venice (Cima).
Martini, Simone called Simone di Memmi	* Siena 1283 † Avignon 1344	Siena I Tuscany (A1)	Probably a pupil of Duccio, in whose spirit he painted. In early years, at the Court in Naples; from 1320 at the latest, back in Siena, where he worked for the town hall and the cathedral. His frescoes in Assisi are also important. After completing a diplomatic commission in Avignon, he remained at the Papal Court (friendship with Petrarca) until his death. Simone cannot necessarily be regarded as a forerunner of the Renaissance, yet the Florentine School is greatly indebted to him: the outline as a design tool. Simone can be regarded as the founder of the School of Avignon. Lippo Memmi, with whom he also collaborated, was his brother-in-law.
Martino da Udine see Pellegrino da San Daniele			
Martino di Bartolommeo	active in Pisa 1389–1435	Siena I Tuscany (A2)	The last Sienese master of the Trecento, to which his style can still be classified. Strongly influenced by Taddeo di Bartolo. Collaboration with Francesco da Valdambrino, amongst others, is documented.
Martorelli, Giovanni di Jacopo	doc. in Bologna 1439–80	Bologna VI Emilia-Romagna (A1)	Possibly from the Lombardy. Still bound to the Late Gothic style. Stylistic alliance to Michele di Matteo. His art is typical of the impoverishment of Bolognese painting that can be observed from 1450 on.
Marziale, Marco	* Venice, around 1440 † Venice, after 1507	Venice II Venice (B2)	Pupil of Gentile Bellini, but also strongly influenced by the Bellini's brother, for whom he carried out commissions in Venice (e.g., for the decoration of the Sala Grande in the Doges' Palace). Moved to Cremona around 1500, where he painted various altarpieces.

Masaccio Tommaso di Ser Giovanni di Simone Guidi *pl. 3*	* 1401 S. Giovanni Valdarno † Rome 1428	Florence I Tuscany (A3)	Pupil and employee of Masolino da Panicale, from whom he has less, however, than from Giotto, active three generations earlier. In the Brancacci frescoes (S. M. del Carmine, Florence), begun by Masolino, we encounter an uncompromising protagonist of the new spirit. He gained expression and depth from a clearer, more definite form, and from a monumental interpretation that does not lose itself in inessential details. He is the first great master of the Early Renaissance whose work influenced the development of the subsequent generation. It is hard to imagine Piero della Francesca without his example. He seems to be about two generations ahead of Fra Filippo, who carried on the work in the Carmelite Church.
Maso da San Friano see Manzuoli			
Maso di Banco	active btw. 1320 and 1350	Florence I Tuscany (BC2)	Pupil of Giotto, whose style he continued and varied. Typical of this are the frescoes in the Bardi Chapel (S. Croce, Florence). He influenced Giottino profoundly. Vasari still held Maso and Giottino to be one and the same painter.
Masolino da Panicale Tommaso di Cristofano Fini	* Panicale 1383 † Florence 1447 (?)	Florence I Tuscany (B2)	A painter still dependent on Gentile da Fabriano, rooted in the Late Gothic, who also worked under Ghiberti as an assistant. Around 1425, he left the remaining decoration of the Brancacci Chapel to his pupil, Masaccio, and went to Hungary two years later. He also worked in Castiglione d' Olona, Empoli, and Todi. (One of his early *Madonnas* is in the Kunsthalle Bremen.)
Matteo da Gualdo Matteo di Pietro di Giovanni di Ser Bernardo	* Gualdo Tadini, around 1435 † 1507	Marches III Umbria / Marches (B2)	Training as a painter in the circle of Gerolamo di Giovanni da Camerino and Bartolommeo di Tommaso da Foligno. Distinct Paduan influences. Active in Assisi, Gualdo Tadini, and Nocera Umbra, and elsewhere. Probably the tutor of Giov. Francesco da Rimini.
Matteo dei Fideli	active in Lombardy 1450–1502	Lombardy V Lombardy (A2)	Ferrarese and Umbrian influences are verifiable. Collaboration with Marco dei Lombardi, amongst others.
Matteo di Giovanni **di Bartolo** Matteo da Siena	* Borgo San Sepolcro, around 1430 † Siena 1495	Siena I Tuscany (AB4)	Training under Domenico di Bartolo or Vecchietta, whom he resembles stylistically. Later, however, clearly open to Florentine innovations. Collaboration with Giovanni di Pietro over many years. One of the outstanding masters of Siena in the 15th c. Compared with his Florentine contemporaries (A. Pollaiuolo, Baldovinetti, Castagno), however, his œuvre came to fruition very late.
Matteo di Pacino	active in Florence 1359–94	Florence I Tuscany (BC1)	As the son and pupil of Pacino di Bonaguida, a successor of Giotto.
Maturino da Firenze "the mysterious"	* Florence 1490 † 1527 / 28	Florence / Rome III Umbria / Marches (A3)	Pupil of Raphael and tutor of Polidoro da Caravaggio, with whom he long collaborated in Rome. Left behind an extensive body of graphic work.

Mazone, Giovanni also Massone	* Alessandria, around 1433 † Savona (?) 1512	Liguria V Lombardy (C2)	From a large Piedmont family of painters. Active in Savona and Genoa (1453). His style developed on the basis of Lombard (Foppa) and Paduan (Mantegna) models. His later work also exhibits Nordic influences.
Mazzaforte, Pietro see Niccolò da Foligno			
Mazzieri, Antonio	* Florence, active around 1520	Florence I Tuscany (BC6)	From the Franciabigio workshop. Mainly painted landscapes and battle scenes.
Mazzieri, Donnino and Angelo di Domenico, ident. to Maestro di Santo Spirito	active in Florence, 15th c.	Florence I Tuscany (A5)	From the workshop of Cosimo Roselli.
Mazzo, Bartolommeo	* Parma, 15th c.	Parma V Lombardy (C2)	Father of Filippo M. and grandfather of Parmigianino.
Mazzola Bedoli, Girolamo	* Viadana 1500 (?) † Parma around 1569	Parma V Lombardy (B5)	Initial training probably in the Mazzola studio, with Parmigianino, whose employee he later became and whose surname he adopted in 1538. Formative influence from Parmigianino and the contact with Correggio's œuvre. In Mantua, he adopted Mannerist ideas through Giulio Romano.
Mazzola, Filippo called Filippo del Erbette	* Parma, around 1460 † Parma 1505	Parma V Lombardy (C3)	Son of Bartolommeo Mazzo and father of Parmigianino. Considered an imitator of Giovanni Bellini, to whom he was probably introduced by his tutor Tacconi (Bellini pupil). His brothers Michele and Pierilario were also painters.
Mazzola, Girolamo Francesco see Parmigianino			
Mazzola, Michele	* Parma, around 1469 active tog. with Pierilario M. in Parma	Parma V Lombardy (C3)	Son of Filippo M.
Mazzola, Pier Ilario	* Parma, around 1476 † 1545	Parma V Lombardy (B3)	Son of Filippo and brother of Michele and Parmigianino.
Mazzolino, Ludovico also Mazzuoli or Manzulin da Ferrara	* Ferrara around 1480 † after 1528	Ferrara VI Emilia-Romagna (B2)	Close contacts with Ercole Roberti's workshop are documented, as are those with B. Boccaccino. His work also reflects the direct influence of Costa and the contact with transalpine art. Later Raphaelesque tendencies, especially in his pictorial design, can be attributed to a period in Rome.
Mazzuoli, Giuseppe called il Bastarollo	* Ferrara, around 1536 † 1589	Ferrara VI Emilia-Romagna (A4)	Pupil of Dosso Dossi. Mainly worked for churches and public buildings in Ferrara, where numerous works by him are preserved.
Master of St. Caecilia	active in the 14th c.	Tuscany I Tuscany (C1)	Successor of Giotto.
Master of St. Magdalena	active in the 13th c.	Tuscany I Tuscany (C1)	Successor of Cimabue.
Master of the Madonna Strauss	2nd half 14th c. / turn of the 15th c.	Tuscany I Tuscany (B2)	From the school of Agnolo Gaddi, whose refined Neogiottesque style is reflected in the work of this anonymous master.

Master of the Paris Judgement see Cecchino da Verona			
Master of San Gaggio ident. to Grifo di Tancredi	active in the 13th c.	Tuscany I Tuscany (C1)	In Cimabue's and Giotto's sphere of influence.
Meloni da Carpi, Marco	* Carpi, around 1470	Carpi / Ferrara VI Emilia-Romagna (C2)	Pupil of Bianchi-Ferrari and influenced through Francia.
Meloni, Altobello dei see Altobello			
Melozzo da Forlì Melozzo di Giuliano degli Ambrosi *pl. 85*	* Forlì 1438 † Forlì 1494	Forlì VI Emilia-Romagna (B1)	Direct contact with Piero della Francesca is almost beyond controversy, and can be recognized in his work. One of the outstanding artists of Central Italy in the second half of the 15th c. From Piero, he learned in particular the definite outline, which he further developed for the representation of gestures and movement. Illusionary spatial composition by means of his tremendous command of perspective. His career and artistic course are still very obscure; in his time, however, he must have been a highly regarded master.
Melzi, Francesco	* Milan, around 1493 † Milan 1570	Milan V Lombardy (A4)	Pupil, assistant, and confidant of Leonardo da Vinci, whom he also followed to France. Clearly dependent on his master.
Memmi, Federico see Barna			
Memmi, Lippo Filippo di Memmo di Filippuccio	* Siena (?), around 1285 † Siena after 1361	Siena I Tuscany (A2)	Son and pupil of Memmo di Filippuccio. Close employee of Simone Martini, who was also his brother-in-law. Influence of the latter, in particular his culture of outline, is unmistakable in Lippo's œuvre. Whether or not he followed Simone to Avignon is uncertain.
Memmo di Filippuccio see Memmi, Lippo			
Mencherini (or Mencarini) see Maestro del Tondo Lathrop			
Menzocchi, Francesco also Manzocchi	* Forlì 1502 † Forlì 1574	Umbria III Umbria / Marches (A4)	Already at sixteen, an employee of Girolamo Genga, who determined his artistic development. Later adoption of Venetian influences, incl. those of Porderone, with whom he collaborated in 1539. From *c.* 1560, participation of his sons, Sebastiano and Pier Paolo, in the workshop.
Menzocchi, Pier Paolo	* Forlì 1535 doc. until 1589 (Florence)	Umbro-Tuscan I Tuscany (A6)	The more important son of Francesco M. Early training probably in Florence, in the Vasari circle.
Meo di Guido da Siena	* Siena active in Perugia in the 14th c.	Siena I Tuscany (A1) III Umbria / Marches (A1)	In the Trecento, he made a major contribution to the dissemination of the Sienese style in Umbria.
Messina, Antonello da see Antonello da Messina			
Messina, Piero (Pino) da	15th / 16th c., Venice and Sicily	Venice / Sicily II Venice (C2)	Pupil of Antonello da Messina.

Messina, Raffaelo da
see Alibrando

Miani, Pietro	active in Cividale in the 16th c.	Friuli II Venice (C5)	Friulian painter of only local significance.
Michelangelo Buonarroti Michelangelo di Lodovico *pl. 14*	* Caprese 1475 † Rome 1564	Tuscany / Rome I Tuscany (A5)	Sculptor, painter, and architect, who, in all disciplines, showed the way for the development of art in Italy and Europe in the 16th and 17th c. Initial training in the workshop of D. Ghirlandaio, where he studied Giotto and Masaccio, amongst others. Hence, he was a member of the circle of artists who studied classical sculpture in the Medici gardens under the guidance of Bertoldo di Giovanni. First sculptural commissions in Florence and Rome. Fresco commissions in the Sala del Gran Consiglio of the Pal. Vecchio (*Battle of Cascina*) as a counterpart to Leonardo's *Battle of Anghiari*. Here, Michelangelo's monumental interpretation and dynamic style is already evident. Culmination of his painterly œuvre: the ceiling and altar wall of the Sistine Chapel in the Vatican. His greatest works as sculptor include *David* (Florence), Medici tombs (Florence), *Pietà* (Rome), and the planned figures for the Tomb of Julius II (Rome). The culmination of his architectural œuvre is the cupola of St Peter's. Other than Florence, M. also worked in Siena and Bologna, primarily however in Rome, where he served seven popes. An uncompromising will and a gigantic level of achievement characterized his life. His letters are of literary quality, and his sonnets of high poetic rank. M. is one of the outstanding artistic figures of the occident. He influenced the greater part of the subsequent generation of painters, in particular the Florentines Pontormo and Bronzino, the Bolognese Mannerists, and also the Tusco-Roman Mannerists (incl. Vasari and his circle).
Michele da Verona	* Sommacampagna, around 1470 † Verona, around 1536	Verona VII Verona (AB2)	Pupil of Domenico Morone, concurrently with the latter's son, Francesco. Training in the spirit of the Paduan School, whose style he essentially retains, with the addition of some eclectic elements.
Michele di Matteo da Panzano also da Bergamo	active in Bologna in the 15th c.	Bologna VI Emilia-Romagna (A1)	Influences from Melozzo da Forlì.
Michele di Matteo Lambertini see Lambertini			
Michele di Ridolfo see Tosini			
Michelino da Besozzo see Besozzo			
Michieli, Andrea dei called il Vicentino	* Vicenza, around 1544 † Venice, around 1619	Venice II Venice (C6)	Stylistic characteristics indicate training under Giov. Antonio Fasolo in Vicenza. In Venice, he remained true to Titian and Tintoretto. Left behind an extensive body of work in the churches of Venices and the Veneto.

Mino da Siena Mino di Graziano	active in Siena 1289–1321	Siena I Tuscany (AB1)	Brother and probably pupil of Guido da Siena.
Mirola see Miruoli, Girolamo			
Miruoli, Girolamo also Mirola or Miruola	active btw. 1535 and 1570 in Bologna, Parma, and Modena	Bologna VI Emilia-Romagna (C4)	Circle of the Bolognese Mannerists. Pupil of Pellegrino Tibaldi. Active in Bologna, Parma, and Modena.
Modena see Erri, Agnolo			
Modigliani, Gianfrancesco Francesco da Forlì	doc. in Forlì from 1598 † Rimini (?) 1609	Tusco-Roman III Umbria/Marches (AB4)	Son of Livio M., in whose workshop he was active. Their respective paintings are difficult to distinguish from one another.
Modigliani, Livio Livio da Forlì	* Forlì doc. 1561–1606	Tusco-Roman III Umbria/Marches (B3)	Father of Gianfrancesco M. Training probably in Florence, in the Vasari workshop together with Poppi and Naldini. Roman influences (T. Zuccari) are also detectable in his paintings, however.
Mombello, Luca also Mombelli	* Orzivecchi 1520 active in Brescia	Brescia VIII Brescia (AB2)	Pupil of, and assistant to Moretto and F. Ricchini. Mainly worked in Brescia.
Monaco, Lorenzo see Lorenzo			
Moneta, Giovanni Battista	* Bergamo 1530	Bergamo VIII Brescia (B2)	Pupil of Giov. Batt. Moroni. Like his tutor he was particularly successful as a portraitist, even when his works are rare today.
Montagna, Bartolommeo Actually Bartolommeo Cincani *pl. 35*	* Vicenza (?), around 1449 † Vicenza 1523	Vicenza II Venice (AB3)	The family came from the Brescia region. Initial training presumably under D. Morone in Verona. Distinct Venetian influence, probably in Giambellino's studio. He may also have adopted the Mantegnesque severity. His occasional obsession with detail is reminiscent of Carpaccio. He was active in Venice (Scuola di San Marco) and in Verona, mainly however in Vicenza. Powerful use of colour (zinc plating), symmetrical picture composition, and marked light-dark contrasts are his distinguishing characteristics. The Friulian School (Pellegrino and Porderone) is indebted to him.
Montagna, Benedetto	* Vicenza, around 1480 † 1555/58	Vicenza II Venice (A4)	Son and pupil of, and assistant to Bartolommeo M. Remained stylistically allied to his father, supplemented by Nordic characteristics, which may be explained by his study of graphic works. Was a productive engraver even in early years.
Montagnana, Jacopo Jacopo di Paride Parisati da Montagnana	* Montagnana 1440/43 † 1508	Venice/Padua II Venice (A2)	Originated from the Giambellino workshop (Vasari). Clearly influenced by Mantegna, so much so that some of his works were attributed to the latter. Worked in Padua, Cividale, and Belluno (1490).
Montemezzano, Francesco	* Verona 1555 † Verona, after 1602	Verona VII Verona (B3)	Presumably already in Veronese's studio in Venice at the beginning of the eighties. Collaboration with Veronese's son, Benedetto, in Treviso, and in the Villa Giusti alla Magnadola is documented. Otherwise active in Venice and Verona.

Montorfano, Giovanni Donato da	* Montorfano, around 1440 † 1504 (?)	Milan V Lombardy (A1)	Pupil of, and assistant to Foppa. His works include a crucifixion in the refectory of the monastery S. Maria delle Grazie (Milan), on the wall opposite Leonardo's *Last Supper*.
Monverde, Luca also Monteverde	* Udine, around 1491 † 1529	Friuli II Venice (C5)	Assistant to Pellegrino da San Daniele, who, according to Vasari, regarded him highly. Little of his work is preserved.
Morandini, Francesco called il Poppi	* Poppi 1544 † Florence 1597	Florence I Tuscany (B7)	Circle of Vasari, for whom he had also worked in Florence, on the basis of his designs (incl. *The Golden Age* for the Grand Duke). Collaboration with Zucchi (in the "Studiolo"). He was strongly influenced by the Neoparmigininesque style of Fr. Salviati.
Morando, Paolo see Cavazzola			
Moretti, Cristoforo	* Cremona doc. 1451–76	Milan V Lombardy (AB2)	Training under Bonifazio Bembo. Active at the Sforza Court in Milan from 1451 until his expulsion in 1462. Thereafter active in Turin, Casale, and Vercelli. From 1472, back in Milan. Influenced by Foppa. Stylistically allied to G.D. Montorfano.
Moretto da Brescia actually Alessandro Bonvicino *pl. 105*	* Brescia, around 1490 † Brescia 1554	Brescia VIII Brescia (B2)	Pupil of, and assistant to Ferramola. Initially strong formative influences from Romanino, later from Titian. Mainly worked in Brescia, and must be regarded as the most important representative of this School in the first half of the 16th c. Painted important portraits in particular. Moroni was his most gifted pupil.
Moro see Battista del Moro			
Morone, Domenico called Pelacane	* Verona, around 1442 † Verona, after 1518	Verona VII Verona (B2)	From the Squarcione School in Padua. Mainly active in Verona, where, together with Liberale, he may be regarded as one of the most important painters at the end of the 15th c. Later adopted much from Carpaccio. Few of his frescoes are preserved. Father of Francesco M. His best-known work is the *Banishment of Buanaccolsi from Mantua* (Mantua, Ducal Palace).
Morone, Francesco *pl. 98*	* Verona 1471 † Verona 1529	Verona VII Verona (B2)	Together with Girolamo dai Libri, Paolo Morando, and Michele da Verona, the main representative of the Postmantegnesque era at the turn of the 16th c. in Verona. Son and pupil of Domenico M. Other than Venetian influences, demonstrably reminiscent of Foppa.
Moroni, Giovanni Battista *pl. 106*	* Albino (?), 1520/24 † 1578	Brescia VIII Brescia (B2)	Training under Moretto; worked in Brescia and Bergamo. Of his work, his numerous portraits are especially worthy of attention (many of them in London, N.G.). Although he did not work there, he was highly regarded in Venice in his time.
Morto da Feltre Zarotto, Pietro (Zaroto), also Luzzi or Luzio	* Feltre 1467 † near Zara 1512	Venice II Venice (AB4)	Considered a pupil of Giorgione and must also have had close contact with Palma, since M.'s style is clearly influenced by him (Cavalcaselle).

Mottis, Agostino and Jacopino see Mottis, Cristoforo			
Mottis, Cristoforo de	active from 1460 † 1486	Milan V Lombardy (A2)	Member of a large artistic family (glass painters) in Milan. Active for the Milan Cathedral, the Certosa in Pavia, etc. Took ideas from Bramante. Father of Agostino and Jacopino de Mottis.
Murano, Andrea da see Andrea			
Muziano, Girolamo (Musiano) il Cavaliere Giovanni Girolamo, called Girolamo da Brescia	* Acquafredda 1532 † Rome 1592	Brescia / Rome VIII Brescia (B2)	His style developed after initial training under Romanino in Brescia, Padua, and especially in Venice. From 1548, he was in Rome, where he collaborated with Zuccaro and quickly became famous. He brought his talent as a landscapist with him from Venice. Founder of the St Lucas Academy in Rome.
Naldini, Giovanbattista called Battista degli Innocenti	* Fiesole 1537 † Florence 1591	Florence I Tuscany (A7)	As early as the age of twelve, came into Pontormo's workshop, where he remained until the latter's death (1556). Here, he came under the influence of Bronzino in particular. In Florence, Vasari engaged him with the decoration of the Pallazzo Vecchio. In Rome, Sebastiano del Piombo's "luminous sfumato" impressed him. Owing to his worsening gout, his assistants, incl. Balducci and Curradi, had to complete his commissions.
Narvesa, Gaspare	* Porderone 1558 † Spilimbergo 1639	Friuli II Venice (C6)	A Friulian Mannerist; crucial formative influence from Veronese and Montemezzano.
Nebbia, Cesare	* Orvieto, around 1535 † around 1614	Umbro-Roman VIII Brescia (B2)	Assistant to Muziano, with whom he collaborated in Loreto and Rome, and elsewhere.
Nebbia, Galeotto	active btw. 1461 and 1495 † after 1495	Piedmont V Lombardy (C2)	Active in Liguria and Piedmont. Employee of Giov. Mazone. Independent from 1475.
Negretti, Jacopo see Palma Giovane			
Negro, Gaspare also de Nigris	* Venice, around 1475 doc. in Friuli 1503–49	Friuli II Venice (C6)	Son-in-law of Floreano delle Cantinelle. Still very much bound to the style of the late Quattrocento (Cima, Montagna, Marescalco).
Negroponte, Antonio da see Antonio da Negroponte			
Nelli, Ottaviano Ottaviano di Martino, or di Martis	* Gubbio, around 1370 † 1444	Gubbio III Umbria/Marches (A1)	Main representative of the Gubbio School. Worked in Gubbio, Rimini, Foligno, Fano, Perugia, and Urbino. Embodied the original Umbrian School, which was not yet dependent on Florence (Lermolieff).
Nelli di Nello, Tommaso Tommaso di Martino, called Tomasuccio	active in Gubbio, 1st half of the 15th c.	Gubbio III Umbria/Marches (A1)	Brother of Ottaviano.
Nelli, Plautilla Pulisena Nelli, called Sister Plautilla	* Florence 1523 † Florence 1588	Florence I Tuscany (C7)	Sister in the Santa Caterina nunnery, Florence. Influenced by Fra Bartolommeo and Andrea del Sarto. Vasari mentions her great draughtsmanship.

Neri di Bicci see Bicci			
Neroccio de' Landi see Landi			
Neroni, Bartolomeo il Riccio	* Siena 1505/10 † Siena 1571	Siena I Tuscany (C6)	Son-in-law of Sodoma. His first datable works are book illustrations (Antiphonal for the Olivetan monastery of Finalpia) from 1531/32, with reference to Sodoma's compositions. In his frescoes, too, he shows himself to be a successor to Sodoma, and is also influenced by Beccafumi and the Classicist tendencies of B. Peruzzi.
Niccolò da Cremona	active in Cremona, 1st half of the 16th c.	Cremona V Lombardy (C4)	Influenced by Altobello Meloni and Garofalo.
Niccolò da Foligno Niccolò di Liberatore, erroneously called Alunno by Vasari	* Foligno, around 1430 † Foligno 1502	Umbria III Umbria/Marches (AB2)	One of the grand Umbrian masters in the second half of the Quattrocento. Probably a pupil of his father-in-law, Pietro Mazzaforte, and of Benozzo Gozzoli (Morelli). The type of the languishing *Madonnas* and saints, which also characterizes the Umbrian School amongst others, first appears in his work (influence of Taddeo di Bartolo?).
Niccolò del Priore	active 1473–1502 (†)	Umbria III Umbria/Marches (B2)	Under the influence of Bartolomeo Caporale and Pinturicchio.
Niccolò dell'Abbate see Abbate, Nicolò			
Niccolò di Ser Sozzo Nicolò Tegliacci, also Tagliacci	active in Siena † 1363	Siena I Tuscany (A2)	Painter and miniaturist. Pupil of Lippo Memmi. Influence from Simone Martini.
Niccolò di Tommaso	active in Florence 14th/15th c.	Florence I Tuscany (C1)	In Nardo di Cione's sphere of influence. Already caught up in the Neogiottesque stream in Florence.
Niccolò Pisano called dell' Abbruggia	* Pisa 1470 † after 1538	Pisa I Tuscany (C5)	First doc. as painter in 1489. According to Ferretti (1984), in Rome from 1489–93 as an employee of Perugino. Active, e.g., in Pisa (Cathedral), Bologna, and Ferrara, where he collaborated with L. Costa and Niccolò Rossetti.
Nobili, Durante	* Caldarola 1518 † Macerata, after 1578	Marches III Umbria/Marches (A4)	Son of a painter from Lucca. In Caldarola, came to be connected with De Magistri's artist dynasty. Became an assistant to Lotto in the Marches, to whose style he remained true. Active in Caldarola, Ancona, Macerata, Ascoli, and elsewhere.
Nosadella see Bezzi			
Nucci, Benedetto	* Gubbio 1515 † 1596/97	Gubbio III Umbria/Marches (B4)	Pupil and son-in-law of Pietro Paolo Baldinacci. Later under the influence of Raffaelino del Colle.
Nuzi, Alegretto called Nucci di Nuzio, or Gritto da Fabriano	* Fabriano (?), around 1330 † around 1390	Fabriano III Umbria/Marches (A1)	Pupil of B. Daddi, whose style he initially retained. Later approached the realistic interpretation of Orcagna.
Oddone, Pascale	doc. in Piedmont 1523–46	Piedmont / Liguria V Lombardy (A4)	Painter and sculptor, active in the western Piedmont and in Liguria. Collaboration with Gandolfino da Roreto in Savigliano is documented from 1523.

Oggione, Marco d' also Oggiono, Oggionno, Uggioni, or Oglono	* Oggionno, around 1475 † around 1530	Milan V Lombardy (A2)	Counts as one of the more important pupils of Leonardo, from whom he copied numerous works, incl. *The Last Supper*. He tended towards exaggerated gestures in his more independent works.
Oldoni, Boniforte I	* Milan 1412 † Vercelli (?) 1477	Milan V Lombardy (A1)	A painter who moved from Milan to Vercelli. Ancestor of a Lombard dynasty of painters. Father of Ercole, Giosue, and Eleazar.
Oldoni, Boniforte II	active in Milan, † 1579	Milan V Lombardy (A5)	Grandson of Boniforte I. Influenced by Giovenone. Exhibits Mannerist traits.
Oldoni, Eleazar	* Milan 1448 † 1517 (?)	Milan V Lombardy (A3)	Son of Boniforte I. Possibly a pupil of Macrino d'Alba (Lermolieff).
Oldoni, Ercole	active in Vercelli around 1460	Milan V Lombardy (A3)	Son of Boniforte I and brother of Eleazar and Giosue.
Oldoni, Giosue	active in Vercelli, 15th/16th c.	Milan V Lombardy (A3)	Son of Boniforte I and brother of Eleazar and Ercole.
Olivuccio di Ceccarello	active in the Marches, 1488–1539	Marches III Umbria/Marches (A1)	Circle of Carlo da Camerino. According to van Marle (1927), influenced by Alegretto Nuzi and Daddi. Stylistic alliance to Arcangelo di Cola is also verified.
Orcagna Andrea di Cione, called Orcagna	* Florence around 1315 † Florence btw. 1368 and 1377	Florence I Tuscany (C2)	The most important of the three Cione brothers. Painter, sculptor, and architect (Galleria dei Lanzi). Training in the Giotto circle, whose characteristics he further enhanced by a powerful use of colour. His figures have substance and dignity, and seem more full-blooded than those of the Gaddi School. With Orcagna and his school (Spinello Aretino and Nardo di Cione), the Florentine Gothic took a great stride towards the Renaissance.
Organtino di Mariano Organte di Mariani Bisconti	active in Perugia 1529–64	Perugia III Umbria/Marches (B4)	Collaboration with Lattanzio Pagani documented 1547/48.
Orioli, Giovanni degli Giovanni da Faenza, Giovanni di Giuliano Sovoretti	active in Faenza † 1473/79	Verona VII Verona (B1)	Pupil of Pisanello (?).
Orioli, Pietro di Francesco degli	* Siena 1458 † Siena 1496	Siena I Tuscany (A4)	Presumably trained in Matteo di Giovanni's workshop. First documented as a painter in 1474. Active in Siena from 1480–84 and again from 1488–96. Mainly painted religious themes (panel paintings and frescoes). His paintings, with their somewhat elongated figures, are similar to those of G. Pacchiarotti, to whom they were sometimes attributed. Umbrian traits in his painting are indicative of a period in Urbino (with Francesco di Giorgio?).
Orlando da Perugia see Ibi, Sinibaldo			
Orsi, Bernardino	* Collecchio, after 1450 † after 1533	Emilia VI Emilia-Romagna (C3)	Active in Reggio Emilia btw. 1485 and 1533. Stylistically in the tradition of Zaganelli and L. Costa, with whose work he must have had contact during stays in Bologna.

Orsi, Lelio Lelio da Novellara, also 'di Maestri' or 'de Magistris'	* Reggio 1508 (?) † Novellara 1587	Emilia VI Emilia-Romagna (A4)	Painter, draughtsman, and architect, whose early training must be seen in connection with Mantua (Giulio Romano and his frescoes in the Palazzo Te). Probably a pupil of N. Patarazzi. Stylistic influences from Correggio, and also from the adoption of Michelangelesque elements during visits to Rome, through contacts with Perino del Vaga and Daniele da Volterra.
Ortolano, Giovanni Battista Giovanni Battista Benvenuti	* Ferrara, around 1487 † after 1527	Ferrara VI Emilia-Romagna (BC3)	In 1934, R. Longhi first isolated his œuvre from those of Ercole Grandi and Garofalo.
Ottino, Pasquale called il Pasqualotto	* Verona, around 1578 † Verona 1630	Verona VII Verona (A3)	From the workshop of F. Brusasorci, whom he imitated. Much sought after as an engraver.
Pacchia, Girolamo del Identity with Girolamo di Giovanni Pacchiarotti confirmed.	* Siena 1477 † after 1533	I Tuscany (C5)	Temporarily assistant to Neroccio de' Landi. Confusion with the work of Giacomo Pacchiarotto makes a critical appreciation of his œuvre difficult. In the meantime, it is considered verified that two different painters are involved. Probably, however, there was collaboration between Giacomo Pacchiarotto and Girolamo del Pacchia (Sricchia, 1981). Distinctly influenced by Sodoma's works for Monteoliveto.
Pacchiarotto, Giacomo	* Siena 1474 † around 1550	I Tuscany (B5)	For a long time, stylistic similarity to Pietro Orioli led to wrong attributions. Elongated figures are found in the work of both painters. Collaboration with Girolamo del Pacchia (cf. there).
Paccini, Matteo also Matteo di Pacino	active around 1360 in Florence	Florence I Tuscany (BC1)	Son of Pacino di Bonaguida.
Pacino di Bonaguida	ative in the 14th c.	Florence I Tuscany (C1)	Typical of Florentine book illumination of the Trecento, which took its ideas from Giotto. Somewhat clumsy in the forms, with deep colours. In the Accademia (Florence), there is a large-format tree of life from P. which looks like a miniature transferred to a panel picture.
Padovanino, Alessandro see Varotari, Dario			
Paganelli, Niccolò	* Faenza 1538 † Faenza 1620	Romagna VI Emilia-Romagna (A4)	One of Vasari's employees for the decoration of the Palazzo Vecchio in Florence. Even after his leap into Baroque Age, he remained true to the Mannerist tradition.
Pagani, Gregorio	* Florence 1558 † Florence 1605	Florence I Tuscany (C7)	Apprenticeship in Florence, perhaps in the studio of Maso da San Friano. Later in the workshop of Santi di Tito, who had a profound influence on him. On friendly terms with L. Cigoli, who was also interested in Barocci and Venetian art. His later work, which tends towards sentimentality, represents a first step towards the Florentine painting of the 17th c.
Pagani, Lattanzio di Vincenzo Lattanzio della Marca	* Monterubbiano, around 1520 † Monterubbiano, around 1582	Marches III Umbria/Marches (B4)	Son and pupil of Vincenzo P. In Rome, bound to the Mannerism of Giulio Romano and Polidoro da Caravaggio. Mainly active in Umbria and in the Marches, where he collaborated with Cristoforo Gherardi and Raffaelino del Colle, among others.

Pagani, Vincenzo Vincenzo della Marca	* Monterubbiano, around 1490 † 1568	Marches III Umbria / Marches (B4)	One of the most prolific painters in the Marches from the first half of the 16th c. Apprenticeship under Andrea da Salerno. His style represents the balance between the local tradition (with Venetian elements) and the examples of Raphael and Lotto. Father of Lattanzio P.
Palma, il Vecchio Jacopo d'Antonio de' Negretti *pl. 31*	* Serinalta (Bergamo), around 1480 † Venice 1528	Venice II Venice (A4)	Training under Giambellino or Giorgione is not verified; his dependency on the latter, after a somewhat dry phase, to which he perhaps owed the contact with Carpaccio (R. Longhi), is very clear, however. Later approached Titian's style, especially in his portraits of women. One of the great Venetian masters, with a great influence on Veronese's development in particular. Palma Giovane was his grandnephew.
Palma, Antonio	* Serinalta 1511 † Venice 1575	Bergamo II Venice (A5)	Nephew of Palma il Vecchio and father of Palma il Giovane, possibly the grounds for his artistic significance.
Palma, Jacopo called il Giovane	* Venice 1548/50 † Venice 1628	Venice II Venice (B6)	In Rome (from 1567), he came under the influence of the two Zuccari. In 1570, he was back in Venice, where he retained Titian's models. Also borrowed from Tintoretto, after whose death he advanced to become one of the leading painters of Venice. His productive eclecticism is little acknowledged today.
Palmezzano, Marco di Antonio also Palmasanus	* Forlì, around 1458 † 1539	Forlì VI Emilia-Romagna (AB1)	Pupil and employee of many years of Melozzo da Forlì, whose style and technique he retained. Later additional influences from N. Rondinelli.
Pampurino, Alessandro	* Cremona, around 1460 † 1526	Cremona V Lombardy (B2)	First mentioned as a miniaturist in 1482 (Antiphonal for the Cremona Cathedral). Documented collaboration with the elder, but less important Antonio della Corna, who influenced his style. A certain dependency on Ercole Roberti can be attributed to a journey to the Emilia.
Panetti, Domenico	* Ferrara 1470 † Ferrara 1513	Ferrara VI Emilia-Romagna (B1)	Training and stylistic direction under Tura. Bono da Ferrara is regarded as his first tutor. The young Boccaccino also influenced his early work. Collaboration with Mazzolini btw. 1505 and 1507. One of Garofalo's tutors.
Pannonio, Michele	doc. in Ferrara, 1446–64 † 1464 (according to Venturi, 1900)	Ferrara VI Emilia-Romagna (C1)	Important artist at the Court d'Este in Ferrara. His artistic development is nevertheless difficult to reconstruct, since the doc. works have not yet been identified. Stylistically, formatively influenced by Tura.
Paolino, Paolo, Fra Paolino da Pistoia	* Pistoia 1490 † Pistoia 1547	Pistoia I Tuscany (BC6)	Son and pupil of Bernadino del Signoraccio. Later influences from P. Veronese recognizable.
Paolo da San Leocadio "Maestro del Cavaliere di Montesa"(?)	active in Spain, 1472–1520 † after 1520	V Lombardy (C3)	Possibly identical to the "Maestro del Cavaliere di Montesa" (hypothesized by F. Bologna, 1977). From the region of Reggio Emilia, P. worked mainly in Spain (e.g., in Valencia). F. Bologna assumes Ferrarese training. Lombard influences become evident at the end of his œuvre (Andrea Solario).

Paolo da Visso	active in the Marches, 2nd half of the 15th c.	Marches III Umbria/Marches (B2)	Presumably active btw. 1450 and 1481. Various art historians have dealt with P., incl. Gnoli, van Marle, and Zeri. The latter recognizes a strong orientation towards Sassetta, together with stylistic elements from Umbria and the Marches, as with Bartolommeo di Tommaso.
Paolo di Giovanni Fei	* Siena, around 1344 † 1411	Siena I Tuscany (AB2)	Pupil of Andrea Vanni. Bartolo di Fredi and Pietro Lorenzetti also influenced his style. Important painter in the transition from the Trecento to the Quattrocento. Giovanni di Paolo and Sassetta are regarded as his pupils.
Paolo Schiavo Paolo di Stefano Badaloni	* Florence 1397 † Pisa 1478	Florence I Tuscany (B3)	First registered as an independent master in 1429. Vasari names him an assistant to Masolino, which the stylistic alliance appears to confirm.
Paolo Veneziano see Veneziano, Paolo			
Papacello actually Tommaso di Arcangelo Bernabei	* Cortona, around 1500 † Cortona (?) 1559	Umbro-Tuscan III Umbria/Marches (AB4)	Pupil of, and assistant to Luca Signorelli. Later an employee of Giulio Romano.
Parentino, Bernardino also Parenzano	* Parenzo (Istria) around 1450 † Vicenza 1500 (?)	Padua IV Padua (AB2)	Profoundly influenced by Mantegna and a period in Venice. In 1496, appointed to the Gonzaga Court in Mantua (incl. decoration of the Studiolo of the Isabelle d' Este).
Parenzano, Bernardino see Parentino			
Parmigianino actually Girolamo Francesco Maria Mazzola, also called il Parmigiano *plates 74, 75*	* Parma 1503 † Casalmaggiore 1540	Parma V Lombardy (BC5) VI Emilia-Romagna (C3)	Initial training in the Mazzola workshop (Michele and Pier Ilario). Thereafter, distinct influence from Correggio, with whom he had personal contact, as also with Anselmi and Rondani. He gained new inspiration in Rome, where he became acquainted with compositional rules. From these beginnings, he quickly developed a style of refined, occasionally sensual intellectuality, characterized by a complex pictorial design directed towards monumentality. His elongated figures are imbued with a classical, although slightly affected calmness and eschew the obtrusive gestures and mimicry of the Tusco-Roman Mannerists. P. is one of the great masters of the Late Renaissance and had a considerable influence on subsequent generations of painters (e.g., Salviati, Procaccini, Bertoia, and others.).
Parri di Spinello see Spinello, Parri (Gaspari)			
Pasqualino da Venezia	doc. in Venice from 1496 † Venice 1504	Venice II Venice (AB3)	From the circle of Giovanni Bellini and Cima.
Passeri see Andrea de'Passeri			
Passerotti, Bartolomeo also Passarotti or Passarotto *pl. 90*	* Bologna 1529 † Bologna 1592	Bologna VI Emilia-Romagna (BC4)	A pupil of Girolamo Vignola and of T. Zuccaro, in Rome. Back in Bologna, he maintained a large studio. Here, he also came into contact with the

			works of Correggio and Parmigianino. He detached himself somewhat from Roman Mannerism and became open to Venetian use of colour.
Passignano Actually Domenico Cresti	* Passignano 1558 † 1638	I Tuscany (A7)	Training under Macchietti and Naldini in the tradition of the Tuscan Mannerists. Later, a strong orientation towards Veronese. A typical representative of the transition from Mannerism to the Baroque.
Pasti, Matteo di Andrea also Pastis	active in Verona 1446–72 as a miniaturist and medallist	Verona VII Verona (B1)	Pupil of Pisanello, a medallist and miniaturist.
Patarazzi, Nicolò	* Reggio Emilia 1495 † btw. 1552 and 1562	Emilia VI Emilia-Romagna (A3)	Training presumably in the Zacchetti circle (after the latter's contact with the works of Raphael and Michelangelo in Rome).
Pecori, Domenico	* Arezzo, around 1480 † 1527	Arezzo I Tuscany (C5)	Pupil of Bartolommeo della Gatta. Collaboration with Niccolò Soggi around 1506. Active mainly in Arezzo.
Pedrini, Giovanni see Giampetrino			
Pellegrino da San Daniele Martino di Battista, also Martino da Udine	* Udine 1467 † Udine 1547	Friuli II Venice (C3)	One of the most important Friulian painters. Son of Battista Schiavone and partner of Giovanni Martini. His first tutor in Udine was Antonio da Firenze, his second Domenico da Tolmezzo. Thereafter, a thorough continuation of studies may be assumed in Venice, with contacts with the Bellini and Vivarini workshops. Among his pupils and employees were Luca Monverde, Gaspare Negro, Giovanni Greco, and Seb. Florigiorio. P. was also active for the Este in Ferrara on several occasions.
Pellegrino Tibaldi see Tibaldi			
Pellegrino, Francesco di	* around 1500 † France, around 1552	Fontainebleau I Tuscany (C6)	Employee of Rosso Fiorentino in Fontainebleau (1532/34).
Pennacchi, Gerolamo Girolamo da Treviso (the Younger)	* Treviso 1497 † Boulogne-sur-Mer 1544	Treviso II Venice (B4)	Painter, sculptor, and architect. Active in Venice, Bologna, and, from 1538, at the Court of Henry VIII in England.
Pennacchi, Girolamo (the Elder) see Girolamo da Treviso (the Elder)			
Pennacchi, Pier Maria	* Treviso 1464 † Treviso 1514/15	Treviso II Venice (BC3)	Younger brother of Girolamo di Giovanni Pennacchi (whose identity with Girolamo da Treviso is uncertain). Important Venetian master of the 2nd half of the 15th c. Training in his brother's workshop. His initial works originated under the influence of Giovanni Bellini and the Paduan School. Later approached the Vicentines Verla and Fogolino. Domenico Caprioli was one of his employees.
Penni, Gian Francesco called il Fattore	* Florence 1496 (?) † Naples, after 1528 (?)	Umbro-Roman III Umbria/Marches (B3)	Training under Raphael, becoming his close employee and heir (together with Giulio Romano) in Rome. Great talent as a draughtsman and graphic

artist. His drawings in the Albertina (Vienna), which were certainly made after 1530, substantiate doubts concerning the year of death as given by Vasari.

Perino del Vaga (Pierino) Piero di Giovanni Bonaccorsi or Piero de'Ceri (also Perin del Vaga)	* Florence, around 1500 † Rome 1546/47	Tusci-Roman III Umbria/Marches (B3)	From Ridolfo Ghirlandaio's workshop, thereafter in Rome, in the Raphael circle. Work in the Vatican loggias. After commissions in Florence, he returned to Rome, where he collaborated with Giovanni da Udine (Sala dei Pontefici, Vatican). Other than Rome, also active in Genoa and Pisa.
Perugino, Pietro Pietro Vanucci *plates 48, 49*	* Castello della Pieve, around 1450 † Fontignano 1524	Umbria III Umbria/Marches (A2)	After Raphael, the most important Umbrian master. Training (according to Vasari) under a local master in Perugia. He was already an accomplished painter by the time he arrived in Florence (1470). Participation in the Verrocchio workshop is contested. First major commissions in Rome (Sistine Chapel), together with D. Ghirlandaio, Cosimo Roselli, and Botticelli. Productive in Perugia, Florence, and back in Rome (together with Antoniazzo Romano and Pier Matteo Amelia). Died of the plague in 1524. His style, in part characterized by somewhat dreamy and absent-looking *Madonnas* and saints, found numerous imitators, and also influenced his pupil Raphael. Outstanding in the design of space (B. Berenson), and ahead of many contemporaries in his interpretation of landscape. Similarities in the works of Francia cannot be attributed to a direct or indirect influence with any certainty.
Peruzzi, Baldassare Tommaso also Perucci	* Siena 1481 † Rome 1536	Umbro-Tuscan III Umbria/Marches (B4) I Tuscany (B5)	As a painter, and in particular as an architect, he represented early Umbro-Tuscan Mannerism in Rome (work on St Peter's 1520–27, and from 1534). Possibly the pupil of Francesco di Giorgio, of whom he is reminiscent in some respects. Later in the Raphael circle, for whom he was also active in the Vatican Stanze. Other than Rome, also active in Siena and Bologna.
Pesellino actually Francesco di Stefano	* Florence 1422 † Florence 1457	Florence I Tuscany (C3)	Initial training as a painter under Giuliano d' Arrigo (called Pesello). Later in the workshop of Filippo Lippi, whose assistant he also became. A partnership with Piero di Lorenzo and Zanobi di Migliore (1453) has not been completely substantiated. Influences from Domenico Veneziano and Castagno are detectable. First-rate pictorial design, especially in small formats; numerous *cassoni* are preserved from his workshop.
Pesello see Giuochi, Giuliano			
Piazza, Albertino (da Lodi) called Toccagno (Toccagni may be a reference to both brothers, Albertino and Martino)	* Lodi, around 1450 † before 1529	Lodi V Lombardy (A2)	According to the most recent findings (Novasconi and Sciolla, 1971), the works subsumed under "Piazza" are essentially the common work of the brothers Albertino and Martino. Both were influenced by Leonardo and Raphael, and must be regarded as outstanding representatives of the School of Lodi.

Piazza, Bertino	active in Lodi, 15th c.	Lodi V Lombardy (A2)	Father of Albertino and Martino P.
Piazza, Callisto Callisto da Lodi	* Lodi (?), before 1505 active 1524–62 in Lodi	Lodi V Lombardy (B4)	Father of Cesare, Fabio, and Scipione.
Piazza, Cesare	active in the 2nd half of the 16th c.	Lodi V Lombardy (C4)	Son of Callisto P., and brother of Scipione and Fabio.
Piazza, Fabio	active in the 2nd half of the 16th c.	Lodi V Lombardy (B4)	Son of Callisto, and brother of Cesare and Scipione P.
Piazza, Martino	* Lodi † around 1527	Lodi V Lombardy (A2)	See also Albertino Piazza.
Piazza, Paolo Fra Cosimo	* Castelfranco 1537 or 1557 † Venice 1621	Venice II Venice (BC6)	Painter and engraver, with Venetian training and influenced by Titian. Also worked at the Court of Emperor Rudolph II.
Piazza, Scipione	active in the 2nd half of the 16th c.	Lodi V Lombardy (C4)	Son of Callisto, and brother of Fabio and Cesare P.
Picchi, Giorgio	* Urbania 1550/60 † 1605	Tusco-Roman I Tuscany (C7)	Artistic training in the circle of the Roman Late Mannerists (Zuccari and C. Nebbia).
Piccinelli, Andrea Andrea il Brescianino	* Brescia, around 1485 doc. in Siena 1506–25	Tuscany I Tuscany (C6)	Active in Siena, together with his brother, Raffaelo. Influenced by Fra Bartolommeo, Andrea del Sarto, and Raphael.
Piccinelli, Raffaelo Raffaelo del Brescianino	doc. in Siena from 1506 † Florence 1545	Tuscany I Tuscany (C6)	See also Andrea Piccinelli.
Pier Matteo d'Amelia also Piermatteo Lauro de' Manfredi	* Amelia, around 1450 † 1503/08	Tuscany I Tuscany (B3)	Pupil of, and assistant to Filippo Lippi. Influence on lo Spagna (Zeri). Active in Orvieto and Rome (Sistine Chapel), and elsewhere. His significance was recognized only recently (Longhi, 1927, and Zeri, 1953).
Pierfrancesco Fiorentino	* 1444/45 † Florence (?) 1497	Florence I Tuscany (A4)	A master first identified by B. Berenson (1900), to whom numerous Madonna paintings of variable attribution have now been ascribed. Influence from Gozzoli and Baldovinetti. In the case of the so- called "Pseudo Pier Francesco Fiorentino," influences from F. Lippi predominate.
Pieri, Stefano	* 1542 † Florence 1629	Tusco-Roman I Tuscany (A7)	Pupil of, and assistant to Naldini.
Piero della Francesca also Pietro di Benedetto dei Franceschi pl. 10	* Borgo San Sepolcro 1416/17 † Borgo San Sepolcro 1492	Umbro-Tuscan I Tuscany (B3)	One of the most important masters of the Italian Renaissance, whose stylistic influence affected more than just Tuscan painting. Assistant to Do- menico Veneziano, and distinctly influenced by Uccello. He painted little, which is probably why his significance was not properly recognized until the 19th c. His principal work is considered to be the frescoes in St Francesco (Arezzo). His paintings eschew an outward dramatic sense, but instead gain their timeless significance from the monumen- tal interpretation of his solemn figures and from a form of representation in which the narrative elements appear to be cast in an eternally valid form. Piero also showed the way in his command of perspective and treatment of light. He is simi- larly deserving of merit as a mathematician and natural historian. Other than San Sepolcro, he

worked in Rome, Rimini, Arezzo, and Ferrara. Luca Signorelli is considered his most outstanding pupil.

Piero di Cosimo Piero di Lorenzo	* Florence 1461/62 † Florence 1521	Florence I Tuscany (AB5)	Son of the painter Lorenzo di Piero d'Antonio. Later named himself after his tutor, Cosimo Roselli, whom he also accompanied to Rome (frescoes in the Sistine Chapel). Initially painted after Leonardesque motifs in the style of Filippo Lippi. Later adopted ideas from the Flemish School (Hugo van der Goes). In particular, strange and enigmatic representations with mythological scenes (*Death of Procris*, London; *Return from the Hunt*, New York) are associated with his name. The landscapes in these paintings are especially remarkable.
Pieroni, Alessandro	* Florence (?) 1550 † Livorno 1607	Florence I Tuscany (A6)	Training under Bronzino and B. Buontalenti.
Pietro Calzetta Pietro di Benedetto	doc. in Padua from 1450 † 1486	Padua IV Padua (AB1)	Pupil of Pietro da Milano. Contacts with the Squarcione workshop. Cousin of Jacopo da Montagnana, whom he also named as an heir. Most of the frescoes of this master – who was much sought after in his time – have been lost.
Pietro da San Vito Giovanni Pietro di Nicolò Albanese	doc. btw. 1485 and 1529	Friuli II Venice (A3)	Active in Friuli. Dependent on the Venetian painting of the late Quattrocento. Somewhat archaic in his interpretation; occasionally shows a lively narrative talent, however. Stylistically allied to Pietro da Vicenza.
Pietro da Vicenza Fadello	doc. btw. 1492 and 1515 † Mantua 1527	Friuli II Venice (A3)	Documented in Venice and Friuli. In 1492, active in San Vito. Training in Bartolommeo Montagna's circle. Collaboration with Gianfrancesco da Tolmezzo and Pietro Fuluto is verified. His principal work in Friuli is that of the frescoes in St Pietro in Valvasone (strongly influenced by Montagna).
Pietro di Giovanni d' Ambrogio Pietro di Giovanni Pucci	active in Siena, 1410–49	Siena I Tuscany (A3)	Considered a pupil of Sassetta. His work is also distinctly and formatively influenced by the Florentines (Domenico Veneziano?). Collaboration with Vecchietta is documented.
Pinturicchio (Pintoricchio) Bernardino di Betto	* Perugia, around 1454 † Siena 1513	Perugia III Umbria/Marches (A2)	Training in the Perugino circle (Bonfigli, Caporali), and possibly contact with Fiorenzo. Joined the Perugino workshop as an assistant, where (according to Vasari) he was entitled to a third of the takings. Went with Perugino to Rome, where they worked in the Sistine Chapel. Various commissions made him commute between Perugia, Rome, and Orvieto. From 1506, he concentrated his activity in Siena, where he died in December 1513. P. is a great narrator, not always assured in his draughtsmanship, and more imaginative in his landscapes than in his people, who, in their elegant postures and carefully reproduced costuming, became a distinguishing characteristic of his paintings. After Perugino, probably the most important Umbrian master in the second half of the 15th c.

Piombo, Sebastiano del Actually Sebastiano Luciani *pl. 38*	* Venice, around 1485 † Rome 1547	Venice II Venice (AB5)	According to Vasari, Sebastiano worked both in the Giambellino and Giorgione workshops. Training under Cima is more probable. In 1511, he went to Rome, where he came under Raphael's, and later under Michelangelo's influence. With skill, he adopted diverse ideas, without ever becoming an imitator. Towards the end of his creative period, his Giorgionesque blurring of the contours made way for a more marked use of outline. One of the truly great Venetian masters, whose fame was somewhat darkened by his intolerable character.
Pippi see Giulio Romano			
Pisanello Antonio di Puccio di Giovanni; erroneously also Vittore Pisano *pl. 95*	* Pisa, before 1395 † Rome (?) 1455	Verona VII Verona (AB1)	Owing to uncertainty concerning his date of birth, a reconstruction of his artistic training is difficult. It is confirmed (Paccagnini 1972) that he spent a very early period in Venice with Gentile da Fabriano (decoration of the Sala del Maggior Consiglio). Exclusive training under Stefano da Zevio in Verona seems doubtful, however. For that, his contact with the International Gothic is obvious. He must have had many other stimuli on his many travels: Rome (1431/32), Venice, Mantua, Ferrara, Naples (1449), Milan, and, of course, Verona were all his domain. In particular, his activity in Mantua led to considerable trouble with the Veronese, who were on bad terms with Mantua. He probably owed his reputation more to his art as a medal-cutter than to that of his painting, even when it was the latter that showed the way for the Veronese School.
Pisano, Giunta Giunta or Girenta da Pisa	* Pisa, around 1212 (?) † around 1258	Pisa I Tuscany (A1)	In his painting, it is possible to recognize the first efforts to break away from the Byzantine styles. Hence, of significance in connection with the stylistic development of the Tuscan School.
Pisano, Nicola	doc. 1484–1538 btw. 1484 and 1538	Bologna VI Emilia-Romagna (B3)	Active in Pisa, Ferrara, Pietrasanta, and elsewhere. From the Garofalo circle.
Pitati, Bonifazio de' called Bonifazio Veronese or Veneziano	* Verona 1487 † Venice 1553	Venice II Venice (A5)	Pupil and imitator of Palma Vecchio. Formative influences also from Giorgione and Titian, to whom some of his works were long attributed. Had a lasting influence on Tintoretto.
Pizzolo, Nicoletto (Pizolo) Actually Nicolò di Pietro da Villaganzerla	* Villa Ganzerla, around 1421 † Padua 1453	Padua IV Padua (A1)	Painter and sculptor. Towards the end of his œuvre, documented as an employee of Donatello for commissions for the Santo in Padua. Donatello also engaged him as a painter (1449).
Poccetti, Bernardino Bernardino Barbatelli, called Bernardino delle Grottesche	* Florence, around 1542 † Florence 1612	Florence I Tuscany (B6)	Michele Tosini was presumably his first tutor. In 1574, he already maintained his own workshop, which specialized in grotesques and the painting of decorations.
Poggini, Poggio	active at the end of the 15th c.	Tuscany I Tuscany (A5)	Assistant to D. Ghirlandaio and F. Granacci for works in the Cathedral of Pisa. Possibly identical to Zanobi di Poggino.
Poggino, Zanobi di Poggino di Zanobi Poggini	* San Piero a Sieve active in the 16th c.	Tuscany I Tuscany (C6)	Possibly identical to Poggio Poggini.

Polidoro da Caravaggio
see Caldara, Polidoro

Polidoro Veneziano
see Lanzani, Polidoro

Pollaiuolo, Antonio del Antonio di Jacopo d'Antonio Benci	* Florence 1433 † Rome 1498	Florence I Tuscany (B4)	Painter, sculptor, copperplate engraver, and goldsmith. He is considered the more important of the two Pollaiuolo brothers, even when it is not always possible to distinguish between their respective work. Today, it is assumed that it was Antonio in particular who was responsible for the conception and draughting, while Piero was left with the execution. Antonio is an essential link in the stylistic chain of development from Masaccio via Dom. Veneziano, Castagno (his tutor), Verrocchio, and Leonardo. In his painting, there was a swing from a more sober form of representation, grounded in science, to an art in which feeling and humanity are again dominant. The dependence on Castagno remains unmistakable, but the facial features of his saints and mythological figures already tell of a confident individuality and a most personal expression, much as it is found in the works of Leonardo and Botticelli.
Pollaiuolo, Piero Piero di Jacopo Benci	* Florence 1443 † Rome 1496	Florence I Tuscany (AB4)	Younger brother of Antonio P. (cf. there). Vasari still attributes to him most of the paintings which today are considered collaborative works with Antonio. Piero, too, was an assistant to Castagno and, like Antonio, he was interested in Classical excavations, as occasionally expressed in his paintings.

Ponte
see Bassano

Pontormo Jacopo Carucci *pl. 18*	* Pontormo 1494 † Florence 1557	Florence I Tuscany (AB6)	Of all his tutors – Leonardo, Albertinelli, Piero di Cosimo, and Andrea del Sarto – the latter had the most profound influence on P. Later, he came under the influence of Michelangelo, who also draughted cartoons for him (especially evident in the small panel *The Legend of the Ten Thousand Martyrs* in the Pal. Pitti). Pontormo's art is typical of early Florentine Mannerism, even though greater distinctiveness and depth must be conceded to it than to the œuvre of the subsequent generation. An inner tension is expressed by the elongated, ecstatically entwined figures in his paintings, which also justifies the exaggerated gestures and never gives an impression of affectation (as with later Mannerists). P. had a considerable influence on the Tusco-Roman Mannerists. His greatest pupil was Bronzino.
Ponzoni, Giovanni di	active in the 15th c., in Milan	Milan V Lombardy (B1)	In Vincenzo Foppa's sphere of influence.
Ponzoni, Leonardo	active in Milan btw. 1472 and 1477	Milan V Lombardy (A1)	In Vincenzo Foppa's sphere of influence.

Poppi
see Morandini

Porderone Giovanni Antonio de Sacchis	* Porderone 1483/84 † Ferrara 1539	Friuli II Venice (C5)	Nothing is known about his training. His first verifiably documented work shows similarities to that of Montagna. Collaboration with Pellegrino da San Daniele is also held to be possible. Later, the influence of Giorgione and Titian becomes clear, while these are joined by Michelangelesque elements in Rome. Also reminiscent of Correggio and Parmigianino, owing to a period in Emilia. In his time, P. was considered the only serious rival to Titian in Venice. He combined diverse ideas in a talented and imaginative fashion, and achieved impressive effects, in particular with a lively composition and spectacular foreshortening. He could be described as the first Venetian Mannerist.
Porta, Giuseppe called il Salviati (Giovane)	* Castelnuovo 1520/25 † Venice, after 1575	Florence I Tuscany (C7)	Training in Rome under the Florentine Francesco Salviati (1535), whom he followed to Venice in 1539 as an assistant, where he remained until his death. The stays of the two Florentines, and also that of Vasari (1541), represent the entry of Tuscan-Roman Mannerism in Venice. P. specialized in fresco painting and, in time, also adopted Venetian influences.
Portelli, Carlo also Porletti or Portegli	* Loro Ciuffenna † Florence 1574	Florence I Tuscany (B6)	Assistant to Ridolfo Ghirlandaio in Florence (1538). Adopted ideas from Bronzino and Vasari. Trend towards a more lively colourism, possibly going back to the example of Rosso Fiorentino.
Pozzoserrato, Ludovico Lodewijk Toeput	* Antwerp (?), around 1550 † Treviso 1604/05	II Venice (A6)	From 1481 in Italy. Adopted Tuscan influences during a period in Florence. Active in Venice, Vicenza, and Treviso, also for the decoration of villas in Veneto.
Prandino, Ottaviano Ottaviano da Brescia	active in the 15th c.	VIII Brescia (B1)	Fresco executant in Padua and Brescia. Pupil of Altichiero.
Predis, Ambrogio de Giovanni Ambrogio de Predis (Predo)	* Milan around 1455 † after 1508	V Lombardy (A2)	Brother and pupil of the book illuminator Cristoforo de Predis. I. Lermolieff first established the identity of this painter, from Leonardo's circle of pupils. Numerous portraits have been attributed to him in the meantime, in particular the family members of Lodovico Sforza, and also the well-known portrait of the Emperor Maximilian in Vienna. P. completed commissioned copies of some of Leonardo's paintings, but he also deserves attention as an independent artist, even though always dependent on Leonardo.
Predis, Cristoforo de	* Modena † Milan 1486	Milan V Lombardy (A2)	Miniaturist and medallist. Elder brother and tutor of Ambrogio de Predis.
Presutti, Giuliano Giuliano da Fano	* Fano 1465/70 doc. 1490–1554	Marches III Umbria/Marches (A3)	Influence from Perugino and Timoteo Viti. Mainly active in the central Marches (Ancona, Osimo, Jesi). In later works, digestion of Roman impressions (period there doc. 1546).
Previtali, Andrea Andrea Cordelliaghi, or also Cordella	* Brembate Superiore, around 1470 † Bergamo 1528	Venice II Venice (B4)	A Bergamask, who never entirely freed himself from his provincial coarseness, despite his training under Giovanni Bellini and Cima. From around 1515, he showed an increasing interest in L. Lotto, who also must have regarded him highly.

Primaticcio, Francesco also Primadizzi	* Bologna 1504 † Paris 1570	Fontainebleau VI Emilia Bologna (BC4)	According to Vasari, pupil of Giulio Romano, as also shown by his later contribution (1525/26) to the frescoes of the Palazzo del Te (Mantua). His appointment to the French Court was probably also due to Giulio's recommendation. From 1532, he must have been active in Fontainebleau (Chambre de la Reine, 1533–35). His numerous employees in Fontainebleau included Nicolò dell' Abbate. Primaticcio, who was also an outstanding stuccoist and active as an art expert for the French King François I, is one of the founders of the school of Fontainebleau, together with Rosso Fiorentino and Nicolò dell' Abbate.
Procaccini, Camillo	* Bologna 1546 † Milan 1629	Lombardy / Rome V Lombardy (A6)	Eldest son and pupil of Ercole P. In Rome, he trained in accordance with Michelangelo and Raphael. His first paintings identify him as a Late Mannerist. Later, influences from Tibaldi and Zuccari predominate, with the retention of a Corregesque treatment of light. Distinct development towards an "atmospheric" naturalism. The most important, and certainly the most prolific of this artists' dynasty.
Procaccini, Carlantonio	* Bologna 1555 † Milan 1605 (?)	Lombardy V Lombardy (AB6)	The third-eldest son of Ercole P. In particular, he painted landscapes and still-lifes.
Procaccini, Ercole (the Elder)	* Bologna 1515 † Milan 1595	Bologna V Lombardy (A5)	Ancestor of a large family of painters. Mainly active in Bologna, until he went with his sons to Milan in 1585. Training possibly in the circle of the Classicists Girolamo da Carpi and Innocenzo da Imola. Assistant to Prospero Fontana in Rome. Adoption of Parmesan influences may be seen in his works in the Cathedral there.
Procaccini, Giulio Cesare	* Bologna 1570 † Milan 1625	Lombardo-Roman V Lombardy (A6)	Painter, sculptor, and graphic artist. Second-eldest son of Ercole P. Trained in accordance with Raphael and the Venetians.
Pseudo Civerchio		Lombardy V Lombardy (C3)	An anonymous (or hypothetical) master, to whom various paintings are attributed that cannot unequivocally be attributed to either B. Zenale or V. Civerchio.
Pseudo Pier Francesco Fiorent. see under Pier Francesco Fiorentino			
Pseudo-Boccaccino see Giovanni da Lodi (under Lupi)			
Pseudo-Boltraffio		Lombardy V Lombardy (B2)	Hypothetical master, to whom various works have been attributed which are clearly Leonardesque, but which cannot be unequivocally attributed to a painter from the Da Vinci Circle. Some are stylistically allied to Boltraffio, others bear witness to the influence of Zenale or Luini.

Pseudo-Bramantino	active in Cremona, 1500–26	Cremona V Lombardy (A3)	Probably identical to the Spanish painter Pedro Fernandez. The paintings hitherto attributed to Pseudo-Bramantino reveal a certain dependency on Bramantino and Marco D'Oggione, to whom they have been variously attributed.
Pseudo-Giovenone	active in Piedmont in the 2nd quarter of the 16th c.	Piedmont V Lombardy (C4)	In 1970, Giov. Romano collected various paintings under this name from the third and fourth decades of the 16th c. which show an alliance to Giovenone, but which are probably not by him, however. Identity with Eusebio Guidetto is questionable.
Puccinelli, Angelo Angelo di Puccinello	active in Lucca and Siena, 1350–99 † 1407(?)	Lucca I Tuscany (A2)	R. Longhi first identified this painter in 1960 as having painted "one of the ten or fifteen most outstanding panels of the Trecento" (Zeri): *The Archangel Michael with St Antonio Abate and John the Baptist.* (Siena, P.N.) His early work is influenced by Simone Martini and Lorenzetti, and is reminiscent of Lippo Memmi and Lippo Vanni.
Puccio di Simone	active in Florence in the 14th c. † after 1357	Florence I Tuscany (B2)	Pupil of B. Daddi; polyptych in the gallery of Prato.
Puligo, Domenico actually Domenico di Bartolommeo Ubaldini	* Florence 1492 † Florence 1527	Florence I Tuscany (BC6)	According to Vasari, a pupil of Ridolfo Ghirlandaio. Then assistant to Andrea del Sarto for several years, in whose Roman works Domenico's hand is evident. As an independent painter, he used a still softer *sfumato* than Andrea and, by largely dissolving the contours and a preference for a marked *chiaroscuro*, achieved an expressive atmosphere. P. painted numerous *Madonnas*, for which he preferred smaller formats.
Pulzone, Scipione also Polzone, called il Gaetano	* Gaete, before 1550 † Rome 1598	Tusco-Roman I Tuscany (AB7)	Pupil of Jacopino del Conte. Much sought after as a portraitist in Rome, combining impressive Raphaelesque elements with a Venetian style of painting. His painting was, in a certain sense, "Anti-mannerist". Baglione (1642) commented on his portraits that they were "truer" than the original.
Puppini, Biagio also Pipini	active in Bologna, 1530–40	Bologna VI Emilia-Romagna (C2)	Pupil of Francia; later strongly influenced by Raphael.
Quercia, Priamo della	* Siena doc. 1426–67	Siena I Tuscany (A3)	Son of the sculptor Piero d'Angelo and younger brother of the sculptor Jacopo Quercia. Stylistically influenced by Jacopo (plasticity and monumental interpretation), and also by Gentile da Fabriano, Domenico di Bartolo, and in particular Domenico Veneziano.
Raphael Raffaello Santi or Sanzio *plates 41, 50, 51, 52*	* Urbino 1483 † Rome 1520	Umbria III Umbria/Marches (A3)	Probably entered the Perugino workshop even before death of his father, Giovanni (1494). His early genius is verified by the fact that he already bore the title of "magister" at age 17. In 1504, he went to Florence, where he enriched his Peruginesque heritage – which he was never to renounce entirely – with Leonardesque innovations (*sfumato*, composition). Already famous, he went to Rome in 1508, where became familiar with the decoration of the Stanze (*School of Athens, Parnassus, Disputa, Expulsion of Heliodor*). For these works, he engaged

a series of outstanding assistants (Perino del Vaga, Giulio Romano, and others). Influences from Michelangelo are also recognizable in the Vatican frescoes. However, in their composition and especially in the brilliant design of space, they are entirely in Raphael's spirit and count as his principal work. For his numerous *Madonnas*, which initially are still somewhat reminiscent of Perugino, he developed his own type, which was to serve generations of subsequent painters as an model. With his portraits (incl. Popes Julius II and Leo X, and also Baldassare Castiglione), he established himself as one of the great portrait painters. His art represents one of the apogees of the Italian Renaissance and certainly also that of the painting of the occident.

Raffaelino del Colle	* Sansepolcro, end of the 15th c. † Sansepolcro 1566	Umbro-Roman III Umbria/Marches (B4)	Initial training under lo Spagna, then in the workshop of Giulio Romano in Rome. Strongly influenced by his friendship with Rosso Fiorentino, who promoted his development towards a Raphaelesque-influenced Mannerism.
Raffaelino del Garbo Raffaelo Capponi or de' Carli	* Florence, around 1466 † Florence 1524	Florence I Tuscany (B5)	The question of whether Raffaelino de' Carli might in fact have been another painter has not yet been completely answered. R. was an assistant to Filippino Lippi, with whom he also collaborated in Rome. His work exhibits Tuscan and Umbrian influences (Peruginesque in his *Madonnas*). Influences from Piero di Cosimo and L. Credi are also evident. A. Bronzino was his most famous pupil.
Raffaelo da Messina see Alibrando			
Raibolini, Francesco see Francia			
Ramenghi, Bartolomeo (the Elder) called il Bagnacavallo	* Bagnacavallo 1484 † Bologna 1542 (?)	Bologna VI Emilia-Romagna (B3)	Stylistically allied to Costa. Collaboration with Aspertini and Pupini. Considered a protagonist of so-called Bolognese Raphaelism. In 1514, he settled permanently in Bologna, where he produced his principal works between 1520 and 1530. A period in Rome seems fairly certain. Lasting influence on the Bolognese School and on the Roman Mannerists.
Ramenghi, Giovanni Battista	* Bagnacavallo, after 1521 † Bagnacavallo 1601	Bologna VI Emilia-Romagna (B4)	Son of Bartolomeo R.
Reni, Guido	* Calvenzano 1575 † Bologna 1642	Bologna VI Emilia-Romagna (B4)	In both phases of his œuvre, he embodies the transition from Mannerism to the Baroque in exemplary fashion. Initially following the *chiaroscuro* manner of Caravaggio, he later became paler and more cloying. He was more highly regarded during his lifetime than he is today.
Ricchino, Francesco (Ricchini) also Richino	* Bione 1518 † after 1568	Brescia VIII Brescia (B2)	Probably assistant to Agostino Galeazzi (pupil of Moretto). From 1554, active in Saxony (Decoration of the Dresden Palace, 1561).
Ricci, Giovanni Pietro see Giampetrino			

Ricciarelli, Daniele Daniele da Volterra	* Volterra 1509 † Rome 1566	Tuscan-Roman V Lombardy (A4)	Initial training probably under Sodoma in Siena. Mainly active in Rome (from *c.* 1537); there, also assistant to Perino del Vaga. Independent from around 1541. Responsible for alterations to Michelangelos *Last Judgement* in the Sistine Chapel (1565). Important sculptor (incl. busts of Michelangelo and an equestrian statue).
Riccio, Felice see Brusasorci, Felice			
Ridolfi, Claudio	* Verona 1570 † Corinaldo 1644	Verona VII Verona (AB3)	From the workshop of Veronese and his brothers. In Rome, influenced by the painting of Barocci. Temporarily active in Urbino.
Ridolfo del Ghirlandaio see Ghirlandaio, Ridolfo			
Rimini, Lattanzio da see Lattanzio			
Rizo, Francesco see Santacroce			
Rizzi, Stefano	active in Brescia, turn of the 16th c.	Brescia VIII Brescia (AB1)	Probably Romanino's first tutor.
Roberti, Antonio di	active mid-15th c., in Ferrara † before 1479	Ferrara VI Emilia-Romagna (C1)	Father of Ercole Roberti.
Roberti, Ercole Ercole d'Antonio dei Roberti Grandi *pl. 82*	* Ferrara, around 1450 † 1496	Ferrara VI Emilia-Romagna (C1)	Court Painter for the Dukes of Ferrara and one of the grand masters of this School. Probably a pupil of Cosme Tura, who formatively influenced his style. Influences also from Fr. Cossa. His combined his dramatic narrative art and an ascetic, strict interpretation with a remarkable naturalistic tendency. Occasionally also borrowed from Mantegna and Bellini. His pupils included Lodovico Mazzolino and possibly L. Costa.
Robusti, Domenico also Domenico Tintoretto	* Venice 1560 † Venice 1635	Venice II Venice (A6)	Son and pupil of Jacopo Tintoretto. Outstanding portraitist. Active almost exclusively in Venice. (Only brief stays in Ferrara and Mantua are documented.)
Robusti, Jacopo see Tintoretto			
Romanino (the Elder)	active around 1500	Brescia VIII Brescia (AB1)	Father of Alessandro, Antonio, and Girolamo.
Romanino, Alessandro	* Brescia 1490	Brescia VIII Brescia (A1)	Brother of Girolamo.
Romanino, Antonio	active at the turn of the 16th c. in Brescia	Brescia VIII Brescia (B1)	Brother of Girolamo.
Romanino, Girolamo Girolamo da Brescia *plates 103, 104*	* Brescia 1484/87 † after 1562	Brescia VIII Brescia (AB1)	Together with Moretto and Savoldo, one of the grand masters of the Brescia School. His style developed between native tradition and Venetian examples (Giorgione, Titian). Adoption of Lombard elements through contacts with Altobello Melone. After works in Padua (1513) and Cremona (1517), active in Brescia, where he also collaborated with Moretto. 1531/32 in Trent, with Dosso Dossi

and Fogolino for the fresco painting of the Palazzo Cles. He painted other frescoes in Brescia (after 1550) in collaboration with Lattanzo Gambara. Also active in Modena and Verona, and elsewhere, R. was an industrious, important master, who countered the oncoming Classicist tendencies (e.g., Moretto) with his Nordic-influenced art, which was more dramatically inclined.

Romano, Antoniazzo see Antoniazzo			
Romano, Giulio Giulio di Pietro de' Gianuzzi Pippi *pl. 53*	* Rome 1499 † Mantua 1546	Umbro-Roman III Umbria/Marches (A4)	Closest employee and friend of Raphael, and one of his heirs (together with Penni). Raphael also had a strong influence on his painting. Also worked as an architect from 1524, in Mantua. Of great influence on the Mannerists were his frescoes in the Palazzo Te (Mantua), which are characterized by painterly verve and an inventive spirit, but are not always satisfactory in their execution, however.
Rondani, Francesco Maria also Rondono	* Parma 1490 † Parma 1548	Parma V Lombardy (C5)	Outstanding pupil and employee of Correggio. Many of his works have been attributed to the latter.
Rondinelli, Nicolò also Rondinelo	* Ravenna, around 1470 doc. btw. 1495 and 1502	Venice VI Emilia-Romagna (B1)	Employee (1495) and imitator of Giov. Bellini. Active in Forlì and Ravenna, and elsewhere. Despite little documentary evidence of his career, there are numerous paintings that can be attributed to him with certainty.
Rosa, Pietro	* Brescia 1541 doc. in Venice 1563	Brescia VIII Brescia (A2)	Pupil of Titian. Active in Brescia and Tyrol, and elsewhere.
Roselli, Cosimo	* Florence 1439 † Florence 1507	Florence I Tuscany (A4)	Most important representative of a widely ramified Florentine artistic family. Pupil of Neri di Bicci (1453–56), and tutor of Piero di Cosimo and Fra Bartolommeo, who later far surpassed him in significance. Cosimo adopted ideas from Benozzo Gozzoli and A. Baldovinetti early on, but also exhibits naturalistic tendencies that possibly go back to Flemish examples.
Roselli, Niccolò also Rosselli	* Ferrara † Ferrara 1580	Ferrara Emilia-Romagna (A3)	Father of Giovanni Battista Roselli, active btw. 1550 and 1600 in Ferrara. Dosso School.
Rosello di Jacopo Franchi see Franchi			
Rosetti, Giovanni Battista	* Forlì doc. 1495–1545	Forlì VI Emilia-Romagna (A2)	Frequently documented, but few verified works, incl. *Madonna with Child* in Faenza (Pinacoteca Civica).
Rossi, Francesco de' see Salviati			
Rosso, Antonio (the Elder)	* Vissa di Tai di Cadore 1455/60 † Mel around 1510	Venice II Venice (C4)	Considered one of Titian's early tutors. In 1488, he moved to Belluno, and settled in Mel in 1494.
Rosso, Fiorentino Giovan Battista di Jacopo di Guasparre, in France "Maître Roux" *pl. 15*	* Florence 1495 † Paris 1540	Fontainebleau I Tuscany (B6)	One of the main representatives of Mannerism. Strongly influenced by Michelangelo and Andrea del Sarto, in whose workshop he also collaborated with Pontormo. His art shows, in exemplary fashion, the characteristics that define Mannerism:

ecstatic movement, elongation of the figures, sentimental exuberance, and a decentralization of the composition. In 1530, he emigrated to France, where he became official Court Painter and, together with Primaticcio, decorated the Galerie de François I in Fontainebleau. This work showed the way for later representatives of the Fontainebleau School.

Rusconi, Benedetto see Diana			
Sabatini, Andrea Andrea da Salerno	* Salerno, around 1480 † Gaeta 1530	Umbro-Lombardy III Umbria/Marches (B3)	Influenced by Lombardy (C. da Sesto) and Umbria (Perugino and Raphael).
Sabatini, Lorenzo Lorenzo da Bologna	* Bologna, around 1530 † Rome 1576	Bologna VI Emilia-Romagna (AB4)	Employee of Vasari for the decoration of the Palazzo Vecchio in Florence.
Sacchi, Battista	† Genoa 1528 (?)	Genoa V Lombardy (C4)	Brother of Pier Francesco.
Sacchi, Gaspare	doc. in Imola 1517–36	Romagna VI Emilia-Romagna (A3)	Similarities to Girolamo Genga.
Sacchi, Pietro Francesco Pietro da Pavia	* Pavia, around 1485 † Genoa/Albaro 1528	Genoa V Lombardy (C4)	Flemish influences. His younger brother, Battista, was his pupil and assistant.
Sacchis see Porderone			
Sacco, Scipione	* Cesena or Sogliano 1495 † Cesena 1558	Romagna VI Emilia-Romagna (C4)	Influences from Lotto in his later works.
Salaino, Andrea also Salai or Salario	* Milan, around 1480 † Milan 1540	Milan V Lombardy (AB4)	One of Leonardo's most remarkable pupils; in 1514, he went with Leonardo to Rome, but did not follow him to France, however.
Salerno, Andrea da see Sabatini, Andrea			
Saliba, Antonello de also Antonello de Saliba (also Resaliba) Messanensis	* Messina, around 1466 † Sicily 1535	Venice/Sicily II Venice (C1)	Son of the wood-carver Giovanni de Saliba (the brother-in-law of Antonello da Messina), and younger brother of Pietro de Saliba. Brother of the pupil of Jacobello di Antonio. After his training in Venice, he worked in Sicily.
Salimbeni, Arcangelo Arcangelo di Leonardo	* Siena, doc. from 1561 † Siena, around 1580	Siena I Tuscany (AB6)	Father of Ventura and father-in-law of Fr. Vanni. On friendly terms with Federico Zaccaro. Stylistically, he orientated himself towards Sodoma and Beccafumi.
Salimbeni, Jacopo	* San Severino † after 1427	Marches III Umbria/Marches (B1)	Brother and employee of Lorenzo S.
Salimbeni, Lorenzo	* San Severino, around 1374 † before 1420	Marches III Umbria/Marches (B1)	Brother and employee of Jacopo S. There is little documentary material on the two brothers. Their training appears to correspond to that of Gentile da Fabriano, who also influenced their style.
Salimbeni, Ventura di Arcangelo called Bevilacqua	* Siena 1568 † Siena 1613	Siena I Tuscany (A7)	Son of Arcangelo, half-brother of Francesco Vanni. One of the protagonists of Sienese Mannerism.
Salviati (il Giovane) see Porta, Giuseppe			

Salviati, Cecchino del Francesco de' Rossi	* Florence 1510 † Rome 1563	Tusco-Roman I Tuscany (B6)	Mannerist influenced by Pontormo and Parmigianino. Remarkable portraits. Mainly active in Rome.
Samacchini, Orazio	* Bologna 1532 † Bologna 1577	Bologna V Lombardy (A6)	According to Winkelmann (1986), Samacchini ended his training in Bologna, and not under E. Procaccini in Milan, as Lomazzo claims.
San Daniele, Leonardo da see Leonardo da San Daniele			
San Daniele, Pellegrino da see Pellegrino			
Sangallo, Sebastiano da called Aristotile	* Florence 1481 † Florence 1551	Florence I Tuscany (A6)	Employee and imitator of Michelangelo. Later a friend of Raphael.
Sano di Pietro Ansano di Pietro di Mencio	* Siena 1406 † Siena 1481	Siena I Tuscany (AB2)	Left one of the most extensive bodies of work of all Sienese painters. B. Berenson had still regarded him as the "Master of the Osservanza," which in the meantime appears to have been refuted, however (Torriti, 1977 and Boskovits, 1983). Training in the circle or workshop of Sassetta.
Sanseverino, G. and L.	active 1st half of the 15th c. in the Marches	Camerino III Umbria/Marches (A1)	Circle of Girolamo da Camerino.
Santacroce, Francesco I da Francesco di Simone	* 1440/45 † Venice 1508	Venice II Venice (B2)	Master in the workshop of Giov. Bellini. Tutor of Francesco Rizzo da S.
Santacroce, Francesco Rizzo da Francesco II di Bernardo Vecchi, or Francesco de' Galizzi	active in Venice, 1st half of the 16th c.	Venice II Venice (C3)	Pupil of Francesco di Simone da S. Following a Bellinesque, Mantegnesque phase, he came under the influence of Palma.
Santacroce, Girolamo I da	* Santa Croce, turn of the 16th c. † after 1556	Venice II Venice (A5)	Son of Bernardino Sartor and father of Francesco Rizzo da Santacroce. Assistant to Gentile, later to Giovanni Bellini. One of the more important representatives of this large family of painters. The examples of Palma and Lotto are to be found in his landscapes.
Santacroce, Pietro Paolo	active until *c.* 1600	Venice II Venice (AB6)	Nephew of Girolamo da S.
Santi di Tito	* Sansepolcro 1536 † Florence 1603	Florence I Tuscany (A7)	Initial training under Bastiano da Montecarlo, later under Bronzino and the sculptor Bandinelli. 1558–64 in Rome as an assistant to T. Zuccari. Resisted (to an extent) the Mannerist tendencies of his contemporaries and orientated himself more towards the Classicist examples of the early Cinquecento.
Santi, Giovanni	* Colbordolo, around 1440 † Urbino 1494	Urbino III Umbria/Marches (A3)	Father of Raphael. Trained in the artist and scholarly circle at the Court of Federico da Montefeltre. Painter, writer, and poet. Probably had only a minor influence on the painterly training of his son, who was only 12 at the time of S.'s death.
Sarto, Andrea del Andrea d'Angelo di Francesco *pl. 16*	* Florence 1486 † Florence 1531	Florence I Tuscany (B5)	Artistic training was in fact under Piero di Cosimo, who, together with Raffaelino del Garbo, influenced Andrea's early style. Workshop together with Franciabigio, which produced the Mannerists

Pontormo and Rosso Fiorentino. His style also exhibits a distinct formative influence from Fra Bartolomeo and Leonardo, whose *sfumato* he adopted. Andrea worked mainly in Florence, but was also in Rome, and received commissions from the French king François I. He was one of the greatest Florentine masters in the first half of the 16th c. He died of the plague in 1531.

Sassetta, il actually Stefano di Giovanni di Consolo	* Cortona (?) 1392 † Siena 1450	Siena I Tuscany (A2)	Siena's most important painter in the 15th c. Possibly came from the workshop of Benedetto di Bindo. Berenson presumes training in the circle of G. Fei. Active as a painter, mosaicist, and designer of glass windows. Thoroughly bound to the tradition of the Trecento, S. nevertheless counts as one of the Sienese who adopted numerous ideas from Florence, e.g., from Ghiberti, Masaccio, and Fra Angelico.
Savoldo, Giovan Girolamo	* Brescia 1480/85 † Venice, after 1548	Brescia VIII Brescia (A2)	Active in Parma 1506, in Florence 1508, and in Venice from 1520. Early Tuscan training is later distinctly overlaid with Venetian influences (in particular Giorgione). His best-known painting, the *Maria Magdalena* (several variations in the Pitti Pal., in London, and elsewhere), is indicative of his preference for dusky scenes and soft light. A great painter, about whom we still know little.
Scaletti, Leonardo (the Elder)	* Faenza, † before 1487	Faenza VI Emilia-Romagna (A1)	The most important representative of a large artistic family and one of the most important masters of the local School of Faenza. His son, Gaspare S., lived from 1477 until 1529, and was mainly active as a chest painter.
Scannabecchi, Dalmasio see Lippo di Dalmasio			
Scarsella, Sigismondo called Mondino	* Ferrara 1530 † Ferrara 1614	Ferrara VI Emilia-Romagna (A4)	Father of Ippolito S.
Scarsellino, Ippolito da Ferrara also Scarcellino, Scarsella, or Scarcellini	* Ferrara 1551 † Ferrara 1620	Ferrara VI Emilia-Romagna (A4)	Son and pupil of Sigismondo Scarsella. Trained in the style of the local Mannerists. Later influenced by Veronese and Bassano. Mainly active as architect.
Schedone, Bartolommeo also Schidone or Schedoni	* Formigine, around 1570 † Parma 1615	V Lombardy (C6)	Training under the Caracci is not verified. Imitator of Correggio. Distinct Venetian influences.
Schiavone, Andrea il Andrea Medulla or Meldolla	* 1522 † Venice 1563	Venice II Venice (C6)	Trained in the style of Giorgione and Titian. Later influenced by Parmigianino and also by the Dutch (?).
Schiavone, Battista called di Zagabria, or di Dalmazia	doc. in Friuli 1468–84	Friuli II Venice (BC2)	Father of Martino da Udine (Pellegrino da San Daniele). Can only have had only a minor influence on Pellegrino's artistic development.
Schiavone, Giorgio (Gregorio) Giorgio di Tommaso or Giorgio Chiulinovic *pl. 61*	* Scardona 1436/37 † Sebenico 1504	Padua IV Padua (B2)	In 1458, became an assistant in Squarcione's workshop. In 1462, he was back in Dalmatia, where he opened a workshop in Zara. In 1476, again documented in Padua. His painting style is influenced by Mantegna, Zoppo and Donatello, and in some works shows a strong similarity to the style of C. Crivelli, with whom he probably also collaborated.

Scipioni, Jacopino de'	* Averara † 1532/43	Bergamo VIII Brescia (A2)	Mediocre representative of the Bergamasque painting of the early Cinquecento. His style is reminiscent of Montorfano and Giovan Pietro da Cemmo (Caylina).
Scotti, Gottardo also de Scotis, Schotis or Scoto	* Piacenza active in Milan, 1454–85	Milan V Lombardy (C1)	Probably the father of Stefano S. In his time, a highly regarded and much engaged painter in Milan. Active in the Cathedral and in the Castello, where he collaborated with Bonifazio Bembo and Costantino da Vaprio. In Pavia, he was the partner of P. Marchesi, Stefano de' Fedeli, and others.
Scotto, Stefano	active in Milan end of the 15th c.	Milan V Lombardy (BC2)	Son of Gottardo S. Tutor of Gaudenzio Ferrari and Luini. Specialist in grotesques.
Sebastiani, Lazzaro also Bastiani	* around 1425 † 1512	Venice II Venice (A1)	A highly regarded painter in Venice in his time. Little is known of his artistic development. Contacts with Bart. Vivarini and the Bellini are possible. Diana, Carpaccio, and J. Bello came from his workshop.
Sebastiano del Piombo see Piombo			
Sebastiano di Niccolò or Bastiano di Niccolò di Bastiano da Montecarlo	active in Pescia and Florence † 1563	Florence I Tuscany (B6)	Pupil of Raffaelino del Garbo.
Sebastiano Florigiorio see Conegliano			
Seccante, Giacomo called Trombon	active mid-16th c. † Udine 1585	Friuli II Venice (C5)	Brother of Sebastiano (the Elder). Active in Udine, Moruzzo, Nogaro, Asio, Folignano, and elsewhere.
Seccante, Sebastiano (the Elder) also Secante	active in Udine, mid-16th c. † Udine 1581	Friuli II Venice (C5)	From a large family of painters of the Friuli. Brother of Giacomo S. and brother-in-law of Pomponio Amalteo, who also influenced his style. Active in Udine and Cividale.
Seccante, Sebastiano (the Younger)	* Udine active in Friuli, 16th c.	Friuli II Venice (C6)	Pupil and relation of Pomponio Amalteo.
Segna di Bonaventura actually Nicolò di Segna di Bonaventura	active in Siena, 1298–1326	Siena I Tuscany (A1)	Pupil of Duccio di Buoninsegna. Stylistically allied to Pietro Lorenzetti.
Sellaio, Jacopo del	* Florence 1441/42 † Florence 1493	Florence I Tuscany (B5)	Trained in accordance with Botticelli and Ghirlandaio.
Sellari, Girolamo see Carpi			
Semino, Andrea	* Genoa, around 1526 † Genoa 1594	Genoa V Lombardy (A5)	Son of Antonio St. and brother of Ottavio. Early collaboration with Perin del Vaga in Rome.
Semino, Antonio	* Genoa, around 1485 † Genoa 1554/55	Genoa V Lombardy (A4)	Collaboration with Battista da Como documented from 1520; with Bern from 1521. Fasolo. In total, bound to the Lomb. art of the Quattrocento.
Semino, Ottavio	* Genoa 1520 (?) † Milan 1604	Genoa V Lombardy (A5)	Brother of Andrea S.
Serfolio, Giacomo	active in Liguria, 2nd half of the 15th c.	Liguria V Lombardy (C2)	Documented in Genoa, 1498. His œuvre is in the Ligurian tradition with noticeable influences from the north. Similarities to Mazone and Giusto d' Alemagna.

Sesto, Cesare da called il Milanese	* Sesto Callende 1477 † Milan 1523	Milan V Lombardy (A3)	Pupil of Leonardo. Influenced by Raphael during a period in Rome. Also reminiscent of Dosso Dossi.
Signoracci, Bernardino d'Antonio	* Pistoia 1460 † Pistoia after 1532	Pistoia I Tuscany (B5)	Father of Fra Paolino.
Signorelli, Francesco	* Cortona active first half of the 16th c.	Umbro-Tuscan I Tuscany (A5)	Nephew of Luca Signorelli. Active in Gubbio and elsewhere.
Signorelli, Luca *pl. 11*	* Cortona 1441 (?) † Cortona 1523	I Tuscany (B5)	Umbro-Tuscan influence from his tutor Piero della Francesca, the Pollaiuoli brothers, and Verrocchio. One of the great master at the close of the 15th c. with repercussions for Michelangelo and Raphael. Frescoes in the Sistine Chapel (Rome) and in the Cathedral of Orvieto. A distinct aspiration towards plasticity and a preference for the representation of naked, anatomically meticulously treated bodies are the distinguishing characteristics of his style.
Simone da Corbetta	* Corbetta active in Milan until 1382	V Lombardy (A1)	In Giotto's sphere of influence.
Simone di Filippo dei Crocefissi called Crocefissaio	active in Bologna, 1355–99	Bologna VI Emilia-Romagna (B1)	School of Vitale da Bologna. Sienese influence.
Sinibaldo Ibi see Ibi			
Smeraldo di Giovanni	* 1366 * Florence (?) 1444	Florence I Tuscany (B1)	Painter of chests and frescoes in Florence; assistant to Giov. del Ponte.
Sodoma, il Giovanni Antonio Bazzi *pl. 72*	* Vercelli † Siena 1549	Milan/Siena V Lombardy (A3)	One of the great Northern Italian masters at the turn of the 16th c. Despite unmistakable influence, an apprenticeship under Leonardo in Milan is not documented. Worked for some years in Rome before settling in Siena and influencing the local School. From Leonardo, he adopted the *sfumato*; from Perugino and Raphael, he took ideas for his picture composition. Baldassare Peruzzi and Beccafumi trained under him.
Soggi, Niccolò	* Arezzo 1479 † Arezzo, around 1551	Arezzo III Umbria/Marches (B3)	Vasari counts him as one of Perugino's pupils. Collaboration with Dom. Pecori around 1506. Active in Arezzo, Prato, and Milan (around 1446), and elsewhere.
Sogliani, Giovanni Antonio also Sogliari	* Florence 1492 † 1544	Florence I Tuscany (BC6)	"Most loyal" (Vasari) assistant to L. Credi. Kept his own workshop from 1515. Influences from Fra Bartolommeo and Albertinelli.
Solario, Alberto see Solario, Andrea			
Solario, Andrea also Solari *pl. 70*	* Solario or Milan, around 1465 † Milan 1524	Milan V Lombardy (BC3)	From a family of sculptors and architects (Lugano). Collaborated with the Alberto brothers, Giacomo, Pietro, and Cristoforo (il Gobbo). Influenced by a period in Venice (around 1492). Cardinal Georges d'Amboise commissioned him with the decoration of a chapel in Gaillon near Rouen (1507). Until 1509, he acted as artistisc advisor to the French king Louis XII. Around 1513, closer contacts with Leonardo, to whom he owes much stylistically. His

best-known painting is the *Madonna of the Green Cushion* in the Louvre, with a distinct Leonardesque influence.

Solario, Antonio di Giovanni also Solari, called lo Zingaro	active in the 1st quarter of the 16th c. doc. from 1502	Venice II Venice (A3)	Presumably from the Veneto. Worked in Naples and in the Marches. Influences from Giambellino and Bramante. Indications of a period in England.
Solario, Cristoforo (il Gobbo) see Solario, Andrea			
Solario, Giacomo see Solario, Andrea			
Solario, Pietro see Solario, Andrea			
Soleri, Giorgio	* Alessandria † Turin 1587	Piedmont V Lombardy (A3)	Brother-in-law of Bern. Lanino. Active at the Court of Emanuele Filiberto in Turin. Period in Spain (1584).
Soleri, Raffaele Angelo	active in the 2nd half of the 16th c.	Piedmont V Lombardy (A4)	Son of Giorgio S., but more bound to local tradition.
Spagna, Giovanni di Pietro called lo Spagna	* after 1450 † Spoleto 1528	Perugia III Umbria/Marches (B2)	Companion of Raphael in Perugia. Influences from Piermatteo d'Amelia and B. Caporali. Left an extensive body of work with a considerable impact on the Umbrian School.
Spanzotti, Francesco	doc. in Casale, 1483–1528	Piedmont V Lombardy (B2)	Son of Pietro and brother of Giov. Martino S. Father-in-law and tutor of Pietro Grammorseo.
Spanzotti, Giovanni Martino	* Casale, around 1456 † 1526/28	Piedmont V Lombardy (B2)	From a family of painters in Varese. In 1481, he moved to Vercelli. Tutor of the most important Piedmont painters (Sodoma, Deffendente Ferrari, and others). Last recorded in Vercelli in 1498. Active (among other places) in Casale and Turin, where received citizenship in 1513.
Spanzotti, Pietro	* Varese (?) doc. 1470–1506	Piedmont V Lombardy (B1)	Active in Casale Monferrato. Father of Giovanni Martino and Francesco S. Both he and Francesco are brought into connection with the so-called "Maestro di Crea", whose identity is still unclear.
Speranza, Giovanni called Vaienti	* Vicenza, around 1470 † Vicenza, before 1536 (?)	Vicenza II Venice (A4)	In 1488, doc. in the workshop of Montagna. Later influences from M. Fogolino and Francesco Verla.
Spinello, Luca called Spinello Aretino	* Arezzo around 1350 † Arezzo 1411	Florence I Tuscany (C2)	His tutor was Jacopo del Casentino. For the Trecento, he already represented a remarkable realism. He worked in Florence (works in the cathedral tog. with Lorenzo di Bicci and Agnolo Gaddi), Arezzo, Lucca, Monte Oliveto, Pisa (Campo Santo), and Siena. Father and tutor of Parri Spinello.
Spinello, Parri (Gaspari)	* Arezzo 1387 † Arezzo 1453	Florence I Tuscany (C2)	Son and pupil of Spinello Aretino. Worked in Florence with Ghiberti. Efforts towards movement and dramatized representation.
Squarcione, Francesco also Squarzon or Squarzioni pl. 56	* Padua 1394 † Padua 1468	Padua IV Padua (A1)	Worked little as a painter, but as a tutor influenced an entire generation of painters in Northern Italy. The efforts towards a revival of the "Classical" style and the search for models in the Greek and Roman plastic arts are essentially due to S. Dona-

tello also had a crucial influence on him and his pupils. Even though hardly anything of his work is preserved, he must have been more important as a painter than many would believe. According to Vasari, he trained 137 painters in his workshop, including the Bellini, Vivarini and, in particular, Mantegna. In Berlin, there is a *Virgin and Child* by him.

Starnina, Gherardo di Jacopo also Starna	* Florence 1354 † Florence, btw. 1409 and 1413	Florence I Tuscany (B2)	Registered as a painter in 1487. Pupil of Antonio Veneziano. Masolino is considered his pupil. Documented in Valencia and Toledo btw. 1395 and 1401. Active in Florence and Empoli after his return from Spain.
Stefano da Ferrara Stefano Falzagalloni	* Ferrara before 1430 † Padua 1500	Ferrara VI Emilia-Romagna (B1)	Friend of Mantegna. Retained the painting style of Giov. Bellini.
Stefano da Zevio Stefano di Giovanni da Verona	* Verona 1374 † Verona 1450/51	Verona VII Verona (A1)	Active in Verona, Mantua, and Castel Romano. More subject to Florentine and Nordic influences than from Altichiero. Pisanello was probably his pupil.
Stefano Veneziano see Veneziano			
Stella, Fermo da Caravaggio	active 1510–62 in Piedmont	Piedmont V Lombardy (BC4)	Painter and wood-carver, probably from the Netherlands. Influenced by Gaudenzio Ferrari.
Stradano, Giovanni also Strada, or Jan van der Straet	* Bruges 1523 † Florence 1605	I Tuscany (C6)	Trained under Pieter Aertsen in Antwerp, among others. From 1545 in Italy (Venice and Florence). Here, crucially influenced by Vasari.
Strozzi, Zanobi di Benedetto	* Florence 1412 † Florence 1468	Florence I Tuscany (C2)	Came from a side-branch of one of the most important Florentine families. Pupil and employee of many years of Fra Angelico, on whom he was stylistically dependent. Mainly active as book illuminator.
Suardi, Bartolomeo called Bramantino *pl. 67*	* Milan around 1465 † Milan 1530	Milan V Lombardy (A3)	One of the grand masters of the Milanese School. Initial training under B. Butinone, later from Bramante, also as a master-builder (incl. a mausoleum of the Trivulzio family). Also adopted Ferrarese ideas related to composition and the design of space. Bramante's example is especially evident in his frescoes, in which his approach to Classical monumentality was the most successful. Architecture and Classical ruins played a major role in his panel paintings. The use of colour is subdued and very harmonious.
Taddeo di Bartolo	* Siena (?) 1363 † 1422	Siena I Tuscany (A2)	One of the most important Sienese masters in the transition from the Trecento to the Quattrocento. Pupil of Bartolo di Fredi. Worked in Perugia and Pisa. Already takes paths that lead out of the Gothic, especially in his *predelle* with their many figures, in which he aims for a realistic representation with clear gestures, atmospheric landscape, and depth.
Tamagni, Vincenzo	* San Gimignano 1492 † San Gimignano, around 1530	III Umbria / Marches (A4)	Frescoes in Montalcino (1510–12). Training probably in the Sodoma circle (Siena). Influence from Raphael and Peruzzi.

Tamarozzo, Cesare also Tamaroccio	* Bologna, turn of the 16th c.	Bologna VI Emilia Bologna (B3)	Pupil of Francia and Costa.
Tegliacci (Tagliacci) see Nicolò di Ser Sozzo			
Tessari, Girolamo called Girolamo del Santo	* Padua, around 1490 † after 1561	Padua IV Padua (B2)	Son of the painter Battista Tessari. Only in our century have several art historians been able to identify the master and gain an impression of his work (Pietrogrande, Rigoni, Grossato, Lucco). Initially true to the style of Bellini and Carpaccio; later reminiscent of Romanino and D. Campagnola. He mainly worked in Padua (Cathedral, Sta. Giustina).
Tibaldi, Pellegrino Pellegrino da Bologna	* Puria (Valsolda) 1527 † Milan 1596	Bologna VI Emilia-Romagna (C4)	Influenced by Perin del Vaga during a stay in Rome in 1547 (decoration of the Castel Sant' Angelo). Later, orientation towards Michelangelo.
Tiberio d'Assisi see Tiberio di Diotallevi			
Tiberio di Diotallevi Tiberio d'Assisi	* Assisi 1460/70 † 1524	Umbria III Umbria/Marches (A3)	Pupil and imitator of Perugino. Also worked in the workshop of Pinturicchio, whom he followed to Rome.
Tinghi, Luigi di Francesco	* Florence † before 1411	Florence I Tuscany (C1)	In the sphere of influence of T. Gaddi. Worked in Perugia, and elsewhere.
Tintoretto Jacopo Robusti *plates 33, 34*	* Venice 1519 † Venice 1594	Venice II Venice (AB6)	One of the grand masters of the Venetian School. After a brief apprenticeship under Titian (?), training under Bordone and possibly Bonifazio Veronese, whom he resembles stylistically. Later, lasting influences from Parmigianino and Michelangelo. Even in his early œuvre, he displayed creativity and narrative momentum. With his perspective-dominated architectural rows, his luminous figures, and his expressive gestures, he developed a Mannerism to which he gave a completely distinctive character through mystical light effects. With his *Paradise* in the Doges' Palace, he created one of the greatest wall paintings in the world. His principal works also include the paintings in the Scuola San Rocco (Venice). His pupil, El Greco, continued his œuvre in the style of the Baroque. Had a great influence on Veronese. Father of Domenico Robusti.
Tisi (Tisio) see Garofalo			
Titian Tiziano Vecellio da Cadore *plates 21, 29, 30*	* Pieve di Cadore 1486/89 † Venice 1576	Venice II Venice (B4)	A grand master of Venetian painting, and one of the greatest painters in the world. Came from the school of Giambellino and Giorgione, whom he followed stylistically, particularly in the painterly landscape interpretation. After a Giorgionesque phase, he painted the *Assumption of the Virgin* in 1516, which in many respects can already be regarded as a Baroque work. Apart from his numerous portraits of women, he revealed his genius as a portraitist in the paintings of Emperor Charles V in particular (Prado, Munich, etc.) In his late paintings, he went far beyond the Mannerism of his contemporaries and, by a reduction of means

and an accentuation of the effects of colour and light, created works of moving drama (*Christ Crowned with Thorns*, Paris and Munich). Had a great influence on the painting of the Cinquecento, not just in Northern Italy.

Tolmezzo see Gianfrancesco da T.			
Tommaso Giovanni Cianfanini (?)	active in Florence, around 1500–10	Florence I Tuscany (C5)	A fictitious name (I. Lermolieff), used to designate a painter from the circle of L. Credi. Later (1966) associated by G. Dalli Regoli with Giovanni Cianfanini.
Tommaso da Bologna see Vincidore			
Tommaso da Modena Tommaso da Barisino, also Barisino da Modena or Rabisino	* Modena 1325/26 † 1379	Modena VI Emilia-Romagna (C1)	Son of Barisino di Barisini.
Tonducci, Giulio	* Faenza around 1513 † Faenza btw. 1582 and 1598	Faenza VI Emilia-Romagna (A3)	An important Mannerist of the local School of Faenza, from whom little is preserved. Stylistically similar to Vasari, but probably also influenced by Girolamo da Treviso, who left one of his principal works in Faenza.
Torbido, Francesco di Marco called il Moro	* Venice 1482/85 † Verona 1551	Verona VII Verona (B2)	Important representative of the Verona School. Pupil and foster-son of Liberale. During his stay in Venice, he came under the influence of Giorgione. Reminiscent of Lotto in his later work, which in its use of colour also borrowed from Titian.
Toscani, Giovanni Francesco also Tossicani or Toschani	* Florence, around 1370 † Florence 1430	Florence I Tuscany (C2)	Pupil of Giottino, whose style he imitated.
Tosini, Michele called Michele di Ridolfo Ghirlandaio	* Florence 1503 † Florence 1577	Florence I Tuscany (A6)	Pupil of, and assistant to Ridolfo Ghirlandaio. Later maintained a large studio in Florence. After an initial dependency on Ridolfo and Andrea del Sarto, he later leaned stylistically towards Vasari and Bronzino. Girolamo Macchietti and B. Traballesi were among his pupils.
Toto del Nuciata Antonio del Nunziator	* Florence 1498 † England 1556	Florence I Tuscany (A6)	Painter and architect from the Ghirlandaio School. In 1531, he went to England, at the Court of Henry VIII.
Traballesi, Bartolomeo	* Florence, around 1540 † Florence 1585	Florence I Tuscany (BC6)	Assistant to Michele Tosini. Influences from Vasari.
Traini, Francesco	* Pisa active 1321–69	Pisa I Tuscany (A1)	Important representative of the Pisan painting of the Trecento. Pupil of Andrea Orcagna. Influences from P. Lorenzetti und Giotto.
Treviso, Dario da see Dario da Treviso			
Tucci, Biagio d'Antonio also Tuccio	* Florence 1446 † 1515	Florence I Tuscany (C6)	Assistant to Perugino for the decoration of the Palazzo della Signoria in Florence. Initially influenced by Filippo Lippi, later by Botticini and Verrocchio.
Tucci, Giovanni Maria	* Piombino doc. btw. 1542 and 1549	Siena I Tuscany (C6)	Pupil of Sodoma, with whom he worked in Pisa. Later active in Siena and environs.

Tura, Cosimo (Cosmé) *plates 79, 80*	* around 1430 † Ferrara 1495	Ferrara VI Emilia-Romagna (B1)	One of the grand masters of the Ferrarese School. Strongly influenced by Padua, although personal contact with Squarcione is not documented. Activity as a painter recorded from 1451. Many of his frescoes are lost. The panel paintings are informed with a deep earnest and ascetic rigor; they are, however, monumental in their interpretation and exquisite in their use of colour. His style influenced the œuvre of many Ferrarese artists (incl. L. Costa and Ercole Roberti).
Turchi, Alessandro called Orbetto	* Verona 1578 † Rome 1648	Verona VII Verona (A3)	A dull close to the Veronese School in Rome. Hardly anything remains of Brusasorci; the panel paintings are evidence of an encounter with Reni and the Carracci, however.
Turoni (Turone)	active in Verona in the 14th c.	Verona VII Verona (A1)	Imparted the Giottesque styles to the Veronese School.
Ubertini, Francesco called Bachiacca	* Borgo San Lorenzo 1494 † Florence 1557	Florence I Tuscany (A6)	Initially influenced by Perugino, then by Andrea del Sarto and Franciabigio. The cartoons for the wall tapestries with the *Twelve Months* (Uffizi) are by him, documenting the elegance and richness of detail of the Florentine Mannerism in exemplary fashion.
Uccello, Paolo Paolo di Dono	* Florence 1397 † Florence 1475	Florence I Tuscany (C2)	Early apprenticeship under the Florentine sculptor L. Ghiberti (1407–12). On friendly terms with Donatello. Periods in Venice (1424–30), Padua, and Urbino (1457). Showed enthusiasm for the problems of perspective and was stylistically influential for all Tuscan painting (especially Piero della Francesca). Few of his works are preserved, and there is little certainty with respect to the attribution of various frescoes in Florence and Prato. His best-known work, *Battle*, is now separately in London, in the Louvre, and in the Uffizi.
Udine, Giovanni da see Giovanni da Udine			
Udine, Girolamo da see Girolamo da Udine			
Ugolino da Siena Ugolino di Neri (Nerio)	* Siena before 1295 † 1339 (?)	Siena I Tuscany (A1)	Doc. btw. 1317 and 1327. Close employee of Duccio di Buoninsegna. In some works, he shows an alliance to P. Lorenzetti (plasticity). A third artist has been hypothesized, for whom the name of Ugolino Lorenzetti has been given (Berenson).
Ungiano, Girolamo	active in Brescia, 1st half of the 16th c.	Brescia VIII Brescia (A2)	Pupil of Romanino.
Urbani, Ludovico Ludovico da San Severino	* San Severino doc. in the Marches 1460–93	Marches III Umbria / Marches (B1)	Active in Recanati, Macerata, Matelica, Potenza Picena, and elsewhere. His frescoes reveal knowledge of the painting of Piero della Francesca, but remain provincial in their interpretation.
Urbino, Carlo	* Crema 1510/20 † after 1585	Crema V Lombardy (BC5)	One of the more gifted Lombard Mannerists (a great draughtsman). Close collaboration with B. Campi, and later with Aurelio Luini.
Vaga, Perino del see Perino			

Valenza, Jacopo da see Jacopo			
Vanni, Andrea di see Andrea			
Vanni, Francesco	active in Siena from 1580/82 † 1610 (?)	Siena I Tuscany (AB7)	There is uncertainty concerning his date of birth (1563?). One of the central figures in the Ital. painting of the Counter-Reformation. Stepson, and presumably pupil of Arcangelo Salimbeni. A period in Rome btw. 1580 and 1584 is assumed. There, he adopted the notions of Tusco-Roman Mannerism and further adopted Nordic ideas. A later phase reveals distinct influences from Baroccio and the Carracci. Vanni was very pious and maintained close contacts with various brotherhoods. With zeal, he artistically executed the requirements of the Council of Trent, after emphasis on the religious content. The Sienese nobility adopted him in recognition of his art.
Vaprio see Costantino da Vaprio			
Varotari, Dario (the Elder)	* Verona 1539 † Padua 1596	Verona VII Verona (B3)	From a family of German origin (Weyrother). Very early on, a pupil under P. Caliari. Later settled in Padua. Father of Alessandro Varotari (il Padovanino).
Vasari, Giorgio	* Arezzo 1511 † Florence 1574	Florence I Tuscany (A6)	Architect (Uffizi), painter and art historian. Diverse training and a great impact on the Tuscan and Roman Mannerists. Played a crucial role in the highly educated artistic and scholarly circle at the Medici Court of Cosimo I in Florence. Despite many inaccuracies, his artist biographies ("Le vite de' più eccelenti pittori, scultori e architettori," Florence, 1550 and 1568) still form the basis of all research on the Italian Renaissance today. His painterly and organizational achievements are easily forgotten, however.
Vassilacchi, Antonio called Aliense	* Milo 1556 † Venice 1629	Venice II Venice (B6)	Of Greek origin. Came to Venice in 1571 and trained in accordance with Veronese. Collaboration with Benedetto Caliari.
Vecchi, Giovanni de'	* San Sepolcro 1537 † Rome 1615	I Tuscany (A7)	Circle of Santi di Tito in Rome. Influences from Perin del Vaga and Salviati.
Vecchietta Lorenzo di Pietro	* Siena 1410 † Siena 1480	Siena I Tuscany (BC3)	Initial training probably in the workshop of Taddeo di Bartolo and outside of Siena in the circle of Masolino di Panicale, with whom he worked in Castiglione Olana. He identifies himself to be a mature artist in later collaboration with Paolo Schiavo (Longhi 1928). In Siena, he worked together with Sano di Pietro in the Chiesa dello Spedale di Santa Maria della Scala. After Sassetta's death, he became the leading artist in Siena. His style was a point of departure for the artistic development of Benvenuto di Giovanni, Matteo di Giovanni, and Francesco di Giorgio.

Vecellio, Cesare	* Pieve di Cadore, around 1521 † Venice 1601	Venice II Venice (C5)	Relation of, and assistant to Titian.
Vecellio, Francesco	* Pieve di Cadore 1475 † Pieve di Cadore 1559	Venice II Venice (C4)	Elder brother of Titian, likewise from the Bellini School. Later in the workshop of Seb. Zuccato.
Vecellio, Marco called Marco di Titiano	* Venice 1545 † Venice 1611	Venice II Venice (C6)	Nephew of Titian and probably the son of Francesco. A favourite pupil of Titian, whom he accompanied on trips to Rome and Germany. An important painter.
Vecellio, Orazio	* Venice, before 1525 † Venice 1576	Venice II Venice (B5)	Son and pupil of, and assistant to Titian.
Vecellio, Tiziano (Tizianello)	* Venice, around 1570 † Venice 1650	Venice II Venice (C6)	Son of Marco Vecellio. Outstanding portraitist on the threshold of the Baroque.
Vendri, Angelo da	active in Verona mid-16th c.	Verona VII Verona (B3)	Pupil and stepson of Antonio da V.
Vendri, Antonio da	* Verona 1485/89 † after 1545	Verona VII Verona (B2)	From the circle of Paolo Cavazzola.
Veneto, Bartolomeo see Bartolomeo Veneto			
Veneziano, Domenico	* Veneto (?), around 1410 † Florence 1461	Florence I Tuscany (A3)	One of the great masters of the Quattrocento. No Venetian heritage, as might otherwise be presumed from his name. Mediator between Fra Angelico and Piero della Francesc. In particular, had a lasting effect on the latter, Antonio Pollaiuolo, and Baldovinetti. One of his most beautiful portraits of women is in Berlin (variously attributed to Piero del Pollaiuolo).
Veneziano, Giovanni see Paolo Veneziano			
Veneziano, Jacopo see Paolo Veneziano			
Veneziano, Lorenzo	active in Venice btw. 1357 and 1379	Venice VII Venice (BC1)	Pupil of Paolo Veneziano.
Veneziano, Paolo Maestro Paolo	* Venice or Vicenza † before 1362	Venice VII Venice (B1)	Active btw. 1333 and 1358. In Paolo's work there is a mixture of influences from the West with the Byzantine tradition, which in the case of his pupil Lorenzo is already more strongly overlaid with Late Gothic elements. Giovanni and Jacopo were his sons.
Veneziano, Polidoro see Lanzani, Polidoro			
Veneziano, Stefano Stefano Pievano di Sant' Agnese	active in Venice btw. 1353 and 1381	Venice VII Venice (B1)	Circle of Paolo Veneziano.
Venusti, Marcello	* Como, around 1512 † Rome 1579	III Umbria/Marches (B3)	Of Lombard origin; mainly worked in Rome (from the mid-16th c.). There, he initially trained under the Umbrian Perino del Vaga; later came under the influence of Michelangelo and Piombo.
Verla, Francesco also Verlo	* Vicenza (?) 1470/75 † after 1520	Vicenza II Venice (C3)	Early Paduan training; later influences from Montagna and Carpaccio verifiable.

Verona, Michele da
see Michele

Veronese, Bonifazio
see Pitati, Bonifazio

Veronese, Paolo Paolo Caliari *plates 93, 101*	* Verona 1528 † Venice 1588	Verona VII Verona (B3)	Early apprenticeship under Antonio Badile, where he came into contact with Mantuan-Emilian Mannerism (Giulio Romano). In Venice (from 1563), he came under the influence of Titian und Tintoretto. His large paintings with many figures convey the impression of magnificent theatrical scenes (incl. *Feast in the House of the Levi* in the Accademia and the *Triumph of Venice* in the Doges' Palace). He proved to be a master second to none in his painterly treatment of precious materials. Had a considerable influence on all Baroque painting, and on Tiepolo in particular.
Verrocchio, Andrea Andrea di Michele Cioni	* Florence 1436 † Venice 1488	Florence I Tuscany (C4)	Son of Michele di Francesco di Cione. Initial apprenticeship under the goldsmith Antonio di Giovanni Dei, then partner of Francesco di Luca Verrocchio, whose name he adopted. Thereafter he opened a large sculptors' and painters' workshop in Florence, which produced many great and different artists (Perugino, Leonardo, Botticelli, Botticini, and others). His qualities as a tutor were especially due to his versatility as a painter, sculptor, goldsmith, and musician. The influence of A. Pollaiuolo can be seen the most clearly in his paintings. His produced his principal work as a sculptor with the equestrian statue of Colleoni in Venice.

Veruzio, Francesco
erroneously for Francesco
Verla

Vicenza, Girolamo da
see Girolamo da Vicenza

Vignola, Girolamo
see Passerotti, Bartolomeo

Vincenzo da San Gimignano
see Tamagni, Vincenzo di Benedetto

Vincenzo da Treviso
see Vincenzo dalle Destre

Vincenzo da Verona
see Vincenzo di Stefano

Vincenzo dalle Destre called Vincenzo da Treviso	* Treviso, around 1488 † 1557 (?)	Venice II Venice (C3)	Pupil and imitator of Giovanni Bellini. Worked in Verona and Venice.
Vincenzo di Stefano da Verona Vincenzo da Verona	active in Verona in the 15th c.	Verona VII Verona (AB1)	Tutor of Liberale da Verona.

Vinci, Leonardo da
see Leonardo

Vincidore, Tommaso di Andrea Tommaso da Bologna	active in Rome † Breda (?) 1536	Umbrian-Roman III Umbria/Marches (A4)	Pupil of, and assistant to Raphael in Rome. Assisted in work on the cartoons for the wall tapestries of the Vatican, among other things.
Vitale da Bologna Vitale d' Aimo de' Cavalli, also Vidolini or Vitale delle Madonne	* Bologna, btw. 1289 and 1309 † btw. 1359 and 1369	Bologna VI Emilia-Romagna (B1)	Founder of the School of Bologna. Sienese influenced.
Viti, Timoteo also Vite	* Urbino 1469 † Urbino 1523	Umbria III Umbria/Marches (B3)	Probably a pupil of Giovanni Santi. From 1490–95 in the Francia workshop. Later settled permanently in Urbino. Strongly influenced by the Ferrarese.
Vittore di Matteo Probably identical to Vittore Belliniano	* 2nd half of the 15th c. † Venice (?), before 1529	Venice VII Venice (B3)	Assistant to Giambellini for the decoration of the Sala del Gran Consiglio.
Vivarini, Alvise (Luigi)	* Venice, btw. 1442 and 1453 † Venice 1503/05	Venice II Venice (C2)	Son of Antonio V. Mainly trained by his uncle, Bartolommeo. Distinct formative influences from Giovanni Bellini, Antonello, and Cima. Together with Giambellini, he was a stylistic leader in the Venetian painting of the Cinquecento, in addition to having many pupils and assistants, incl. Moceto, Basaiti, Catena, and Lotto. In contrast to his father, he also painted various portraits.
Vivarini, Antonio Antonio da Murano	* Murano, around 1415 † Venice btw. 1476 and 1484	Murano II Venice (B1)	The transition from the Byzantine-influenced style to the Early Renaissance is complete in his work. Elder brother of Bartolommeo V. and father of Alvise V. Brother-in-law of Giovanni d'Alemagna, with whom he also collaborated. Antonio painted numerous multipartite altarpieces, in a Gothic style, with decorated frames with inlays and a gilded background. Commissions came from Bologna, Brescia, the Marches, Istrien, Dalmatien, Pesaro, and elsewhere. The contribution of Antonio's partner, Giovanni d' Alemagna, to his works still leaves many questions open.
Vivarini, Bartolommeo Bartolommeo da Murano *pl. 22*	* Murano, around 1432 † around 1499	Murano II Venice (B1)	With his brother, Antonio, a grand master of the Murano School with repercussions for all painting of the Veneto. More clearly detached from the Byzantine style than Antonio, to whom he was initially an assistant. Also had an influence on Giovanni Bellini. Bartolommeo, too, received commissions from all parts of Northern Italy (Padua, Dalmatia, Marches) and even from Calabria. His produced his most important works in Venice for the Frari Church, S. Giovanni e Paolo, Santa Maria Formosa, and other churches. His stylistic development – in the sixties, he could still be called progressive – was unable to keep pace with Giambellino and or Antonello, so that his work already seemed somewhat antiquated towards the end of his creative period.
Viviani, Antonio called il Sordo di Urbino	* Urbino 1560 † 1620	III Umbria/Marches (AB4)	Assistant to Barocci in Rome. Combined Umbrian tradition with late Roman Mannerism.
Volpi, Aimo and Balzarino	active in Casale Monferrato doc. btw. 1491 and 1555	Piedmont V Lombardy (B4)	From the circle of Martino Spanzotti. Influences from Grammorseo.

Volponi, Giovanni Battista called Scalabrino	* Pistoia 1489 † Pistoia 1553	Pistoia I Tuscany (AB5)	Under the influence of D.Ghirlandaio, Perugino, and Fra Bartolommeo. Employee of Michelangelo. Father of Piero V., likewise mainly active in Pistoia.
Volponi, Piero see Volponi, Giovanni Battista			
Volterra, Daniele da see Ricciarelli, Daniele			
Volterra, Francesco da see Francesco da Volterra			
Zacchetti, Bernardino	* Reggio Emilia 1472 † after 1525	VI Emilia-Romagna (C3)	In 1510, employee of Michelangelo in Rome. In 1517, documented in Piancenza. Tutor of Nicolò Patarazzi.
Zacchia il Vecchio (da Vezzano)	* Lucca or Vezzano around 1496 † after1561	Lucca I Tuscany (C7)	Trained in the workshop of Agostino Marti (Lucchesian family of painters). Later influenced by Fra Bartolommeo and A. Aspertini. Elder cousin of Lorenzo Z.
Zacchia, Lorenzo (the Younger) il Giovane	* Lucca 1524 doc. until 1587	Lucca I Tuscany (C6)	Cousin of Zacchia (Vecchio) da Vezzano. The most important representative of Lucchesian School in connection with the Counter-Reformation.
Zaffoni, Giovanni Maria called il Calderari	* Porderone 1490/95 † 1563	Friuli II Venice (BC5)	Pupil of, and assistant to Porderone. Active in Porderone and environs.
Zaganelli, Bernardino Bernardino da Cotignola	* Cotignola 1460/70 † Cotignola around 1510	Ravenna VI Emilia-Romagna (C1)	Collaboration with his brother Francesco. It is difficult to distinguish between their respective individual achievements (Longhi mentions the "Siamese twins").
Zaganelli, Francesco Francesco da Cotignola	* Cotignola 1460/70 † Ravenna 1532	Ravenna VI Emilia-Romagna (C1)	Mainly active in Ravenna. Pupil of Rondinelli. Later adoption of Venetian elements (Montagna, Bellini). Close collaboration with his brother Bernardino.
Zampieri, Domenico called Domenichino	* Bologna 1581 † Naples 1641	Bologna VI Emilia-Romagna (C4)	Main representative of the Bolognese Baroque, formative influences from Calvaert and the Carracci. Worked in Rome and, for a long time, in Naples. Still preserved Classical elements of the Renaissance style and eschewed the Baroque excesses of his contemporaries.
Zanguidi, Jacopo see Bertoia, Jacopo Zanguidi			
Zanino di Pietro Giovanni di Pietro Charlier di Francia	doc. 1389–1448	Venice II Venice (A1)	Active in Veneto, Bologna and Central Italy. In 1985, various art historians (especially Serena Padovani and M. Boskovits) were able to verify the identity between Zanino di Pietro and Giovanni di Pietro Charlier. He is considered an important master in Veneto at the turn of the Quattrocento, and also must have been in contact with Gentile da Fabriano. The problems concerning his identification were due to stylistic divergences between the early and later periods of his œuvre, which led to an assumption of two different painters.

Zanobi di Poggino see Poggini			
Zanoni, Costantino degli Costantino da Vaprio, also da Zenoni	* Vaprio (?) active in Milan, 1453–82	Milan V Lombardy (A1)	Son of Giovanni Z. and founder of a large dynasty of painters in Milan. In the service of Francesco Sforza, Galeazzo Maria, and Lodovico il Moro. Collaboration with Foppa for works in the Castel of Milan. In a ducal decree of 1481, the painter was formally "ennobled" into the ducal family, with all associated rights and privileges.
Zappi, Lavinia see Fontana, Lavinia			
Zavattari, Ambrogio also Zavatteri or Zavatari	* Milan active around 1450	Milan V Lombardy (B1)	Son of Francesco I and brother of Gregorio Z.
Zavattari, Francesco I	doc. in Milan 1417–53	Milan V Lombardy (B1)	Father of Ambrogio and Gregorio (perhaps also of Giovanni). Circle of Michelino da Besozzo. The most important representative of a large artistic family in Milan; first documented in 1404 in connection with the Milan Cathedral (according to Cristoforo Zavattari).
Zavattari, Francesco II il Giovane	active in Milan in the 15th c.	Milan V Lombardy (BC1)	Documented from 1479 as an employee of Gregorio Z. Son of Giovanni Z.
Zavattari, Giovanni	15th c.	Milan V Lombardy (BC1)	Probably the son of Francesco I. Father of Francesco il Giovane.
Zavattari, Gregorio	* Milan active in the 15th c.	Milan V Lombardy (BC1)	Brother of Ambrogio, Son and employee of Francesco I. Work on frescoes in the certosa of Pavia and in Caravaggio.
Zelotti, Giambattista Battista da Verona (Vasari)	* Verona 1526 † Mantua 1578	Verona VII Verona (A3)	Training under A. Badile. Initial collaboration with Paolo Caliari, later with Fasolo. Last worked in Mantua. Paolo Farinati was his uncle.
Zenale, Bernardo **(Bernardino)** Zenale da Treviglio *pl. 65*	* Treviglio, around 1450 † Milan 1526	Milan V Lombardy (C1)	One of the grand masters of the Lombardy School of the 15th c. Under the influence of Mantegna and Leonardo, with whom he was on friendly terms. Close contacts with V Civerchio. Highly regarded artist at the Court of Lodovico il Moro. Also worked as an engineer and architect. His produced his first documented work in collaboration with his partner of many years, B. Butinone (1485). After 1507, he approached Foppa and Borgognone stylistically. In 1522, he was appointed Cathedral Masterbuilder. Also documented in Bergamo as an architect.
Zeno da Verona also Zenone	* Beverara 1484 † 1552/54	Verona VII Verona (B2)	Worked in Salo, Desenzano, Volciano, and Spoleto, and elsewhere.
Zenobio di Jacopo see Macchiavelli, Zenobio			
Zevio see Altichiero			
Zevio, Stefano da see Stefano da Zevio			
Zingaro (also lo Zungaro) see Solario, Antonio			

Zoppo, Marco il Actually Marco di Antonio di Ruggero *pl. 60*	* Cento 1433 † Venice 1478	Padua IV Padua (A1) VI Emilia-Romagna (A1)	Around 1453, an assistant in Squarcione's workshop in Padua. In 1455 in Venice, and 1460–61 in Bologna. Painted in the style of Mantegna and Giambellino. In a decorative sense, his works also show similarities to the paintings of Carlo Crivelli. According to Volpe (1979), the great *Crucifixion* in S. Giuseppe in Bologna reveals a new example: that of Piero della Francesca.
Zuccari, Federico also Zucchero or Sucarus	* Sant'Angelo in Vado 1540 / 41 † Ancona 1609	III Umbria / Marches (B4)	Younger brother of Taddeo, who took him into his care in Rome, from 1550. Trained in the style of the Roman Mannerists (Polidoro da Caravaggio) and in the Michelangesque traditionan imparted by Taddeo. In 1603, he left Rome for good and worked in Venice, Pavia, Parma, and Turin. Influence on Salimbeni and Cigoli. Close contact with F. Barocci. Considered to be one of the great Mannerists, and also attained significance as an architect and art theoretician.
Zuccari, Taddeo also Zuccaro	* Sant'Angelo in Vado 1529 † Rome 1566	III Umbria / Marches (B3)	Elder brother of Federigo Z. Born in the Marches, came early into the Roman circle of Vasari, however. Here, influenced by Polidoro da Caravaggio amongst others, especially however by Perin del Vaga, whose stylistic heritage he adopted.
Zuccati, Francesco also Zuccato	active in Venice, 1st half of the 16th c. † Venice btw. 1572 and 1577	Venice II Venice (BC4)	Painter and mosaicist. Son and pupil (?) of Sebastiano Z. Brother of Valerio Z.; it is difficult to distinguish between their respective works.
Zuccati, Valerio see Francesco Zuccati			
Zuccato, Sebastiano also Zuccati	* Cadore (?) † Venice 1527	Venice VII Venice (B4)	Mosaicist. Titian may have had his initial training as a draughtsman under him.
Zucchi, Jacopo	* Florence, around 1542 † Rome 1596	Florence I Tuscany (A7)	Assistant to Vasari, whose style he initially copied. In Rome, the light-dark painting of Caravaggio impressed him, while compositional solutions can in part be traced to Bart. Spranger, who was resident in Rome.

Chronological Table

Milan · Genoa · Mantua · Bologna · Ferrara

1162	Destruction of Milan by Frederick I (Barbarossa)	1120–1200	Basilica, *San Pietro in Ciel d'Oro* (Pavia)
1248	Battle of Parma – victory of the Lombard league over the Emperor	1228–33	Construction of the *Palazzo della Ragione,* Milan (Broletto Nuovo)
1250	† Frederick II	c. 1250	Laying of the foundation stone of the *Cathedral of Monza* (San Giovanni Battista) – completed in 1310 – one of the most important ecclesiastical buildings in Northern Italy
1257	End of the consular constitution in Milan		
1261	Genoa effects the end of the Latin Empire in Constantinople (established by Venice)	from 1250	Cremona: construction of the *Torrazzo* begins (at 111 m the highest campanile in Italy)
1262	Ottone Visconti is appointed Archbishop of Milan		
from 1264	The Este family governs in Ferrara		
1277	Battle of Desio – Ottone Visconti defeats Napo Torriani and becomes city ruler for life		
1284	After 100 years of war, Genoa conquers Pisa and gains Corsica, Sardinia, and Elba by 1300	1287	Construction begins on the *Palazzo Communale,* Bologna
1311–28	Milanese conquests: Como, Bergamo, Piancenza, Cremona, Vercelli, Tortoni and Alessandria	1307	Commencement of the Gothic conversion of the *Cathedral of Genoa*
		1308	*Palazzo del Capitano,* Mantua (converted by the Gonzaga in 1328)
from 1328	The Gonzaga family governs in Mantua (until 1707)		
1339	The title of Doge becomes hereditary	1340–96	*Cathedral of Monza:* extension in the Gothic style
from 1353	Genoa is alternately dependent on Milan and France	1360	Construction begins on the *Castel of Pavia* (completed under Giangaleazzo Visconti)
1359	The Visconti subjugate Pavia		
1361	Foundation of the University of Pavia	1362	Giovanni di Balduccio: *Arca di San Agostino* (tomb of St Augustine in *San Pietro in Ciel d'Oro,* Pavia)
1379	Venice defeats Genoa in the Battle of Chioggia	1368–70	Petrarca resides in Pavia as the guest of Galeazzo ii

1381	Definitive victory of Venice over Genoa – end of the Hundred Years' War	1384–91	*Palazzo della Merganzia* (Bologna)
		1386	Laying of the foundation stone of the *Cathedral of Milan*
1390–94	Revolutions in Genoa	1390	Laying of the foundation stone of *San Petronio* (Bologna)
1395	Giangaleazzeo Visconti acquires the title of Duke	1396	*Certosa of Pavia* (construction begins)
1402	† Giangaleazzeo Visconti	1396	Construction begins on the *Cathedral in Como*. The *facade* is an outstanding example of the decorative style of the Early Renaissance in Lombardy
1405/06	Venice claims Verona, Vicenza and Padua		
		1413/14	Bell tower (Late Gothic) of *San Andrea* in Mantua
1421	Genoa unites with Milan		
1428	Milan loses Brescia and Bergamo to Venice	after 1427	Michele di Matteo: *polyptych of the Virgin and Child with Saints and Scenes from the Cross* (Accademia, Venice)
1433	Mantua becomes a margravate		
1435	Re-establishment of the Republic in Genoa	1431	* Andrea Mantegna († 1506 in Mantua)
1441	Francesco Sforza marries Bianca Visconti	1435	Masolino: *frescoes in the Baptistry of Castiglione Olona*
1447	Filippo Maria Visconti dies, leaving no heirs – proclamation of the Ambrosian Republic (in existence for three years)	1440/44 ?	Pisanello: *fresco cycle in the Castel of Mantua*
		c. 1450	Donato d' Bardi: *Crucifixion* (Savona)
c. 1451	* Christopher Columbus is born in Genoa	1450	Vincenzo Foppa returns to Brescia
1453	Conquest of Constantinople by the Turks	1454–59	Mantegna: *frescoes in the Eremitani Church, Padua* (early work)
1454	Peace of Lodi: creation of the balance between the leading Italian states (Milan, Venice, Florence, Papal States and Naples) – forty years of peace with cultural and economic development	1455	Marco Zoppo: *Virgin and Child* (Louvre)
		1457/60	Mantegna: *Crucifixion*, from the *Church of St Zeno* in Verona (copy in situ; original in the Louvre)
		c. 1460	Squarcione: *Virgin and Child* (Berlin)
1459–60	Pius II in Mantua (Congress)	1463	Laying of the foundation stone of *S. Maria delle Grazie* (from 1464, construction supervised by Guiniforte Solari [Milan])
1464	Genoa (from 1458 under French sovereignty) is returned to Milan		
		1465–68	Foppa: *frescoes in the Portinari Chapel* (Milan)
		1465–74	Mantegna: *frescoes in the Camera degli Sposi* in the *Castello San Giorgio* (Mantua)
		1467	Mantegna in Florence: *Portrait of*

			Cardinal Carlo de' Medici (Uffizi), among others
		1469	First printing office in Milan
		from 1470	Francesco Cossa: *frescoes* in the *Palazzo Schifanoia* (Ferrara)
1471	The Pope raises the status of Ferrara to that of duchy	1470/72	Cossa: *Annunciation* (Dresden)
1471–1505	Ercole I Duke of Ferrara	from 1472	I.B. Alberti: construction of *San Andrea* (Mantua)
1473	Ercole I d'Este marries Leonora of Aragon (parents of Isabella and Beatrice)	1472–76	Giov. Antonio Amadeo: construction of the *Colleoni Chapel* (Bergamo)
		1474	Cossa: *Virgin and Child with Sts Petronius, John the Evangelist, and A Donor* (Pinacoteca, Bologna)
		c. 1475	Cosimo Tura: *The Body of Christ supported by two Angels* (Kunsthistorisches Museum, Vienna)
1476	Galeazzo Maria Sforza murdered – disorder in Milan – Genoa becomes independent	c. 1480	Melozzo de Forlì: *Music-making Angel* (Pinacoteca Vaticana)
		c. 1480	Ercole Roberti: *Portrait of Giovanni II Bentivoglio* (Washington, N.G.)
		from 1480	Luca Fancelli: construction of the *Domus Nova, Mantua* (one of the most impressive Renaissance buildings in Lombardy)
1481	Ludovico Sforza (il Moro) is appointed Regent in Milan (1494 Duke)	c. 1480	Mantegna: *Dead Christ* (Brera, Milan)
		c. 1480	Tura: *Pietà* (Louvre)
		1482	Leonardo da Vinci comes to Milan and remains there, with interruptions, until 1499
		1485–88	Leonardo: *Last Supper* (Santa Maria delle Grazie, Milan)
		1488–94	Borgognone: works in the Certosa di Pavia (incl. *St Ambrosius with four Saints*)
		1490	Bramantino: *Adoration of the Magi* (London, N.G.)
		1490/94	Donato Bramante: *Christ at the Column* (Milan, Brera)
		1490/1500	Foppa: *Altar of Miracles* (polyptych, Brera, Milan)
		1492–1497	D. Bramante: east wing of *Santa Maria delle Grazie* (Milan)

1490	Francesco II Gonzaga marries Isabella d'Este	1492–1514	Conversion of the *Palazzo del Podesta*, Bologna, by Giov. di Pietro da Brensa and Francesco Fossi
1491	Ludovico il Moro marries Beatrice d'Este	1493	Leonardo completes the *model of the equestrian statue of Francesco Sforza*
1492	Columbus discovers America		
1494	Ludovico Sforza summons the French into the Milanese realm	1494	Francia: *Felincini Altarpiece* (Pinacoteca Nazionale, Bologna)
1495	Battle of Fornovo – Milan victorious over the French	1495/96	Mantegna: *Madonna della Vittoria* – commemorating the Battle of Fornovo (Louvre)
1497	† Beatrice d'Este	1498–1506	Pietro Bembo (the Humanist) resides in Ferrara
1499	Ludwig XII conquers Milan and Genoa	1499	Leonardo in Mantua: portrait sketch of *Isabella d'Este* (Louvre)
		c. 1500	Gian Martino Spanzotti: *St Catherine of Siena* (Castel, Verona)
1500	Battle of Novara – Ludovico Sforza is taken captive and dies in France in 1508	1500	Giov. Antonio Boltraffio: *Virgin and Child with Sts John the Baptist and Sebastian and Two Donors* (Louvre)
		1500	Ludwig XII abducts the library from the Castel of Pavia
		1502	Ambrogio de' Predis: portrait of *Emperor Maximilian* I (Kunsthistorisches Museum, Vienna)
		c. 1505	Lorenzo Costa: *Allegory for the Court of Isabella d'Este* (Louvre)
		c. 1505	Boccaccio Boccacino: *Gypsy Girl* (Uffizi)
		1505–16	L. Ariosto: *Orlando furioso*
1506	Siege of Bologna by Pope Julius II – expulsion of the Bentivogli (Giovanni II) – Bologna remains under Roman rule for more than 300 years	1506	† Mantegna
		c. 1506	Francia: *Madonna and Child Enthroned with Saints and Angels* (Basilica di San Martino, Bologna)
		1506–16	Leonardo, with interruptions, back in Milan in the service of Charles VIII of France
		c. 1507	Bernardo Luini: *Head of the Baptist* and *Salome with the Head of the Baptist*
		c. 1507	Leonardo completes the *Virgin of the Rocks* (Louvre)
		1507–10	Andrea Solario in France: *Madonna of the Green Cushion* (Louvre)

		1510–13	Sodoma: *Holy Family* (Alte Pinakothek, Munich)
1512	The Swiss drive the French back over the Alps	c. 1511	Francia: *Virgin and Child with St Anne and Saints* (London, N.G.)
1515	Francis I of France victorious in the Battle of Marignano	1515/20	Bramantino: *Crucifixion* (Brera, Milan)
		1516	G.A. Boltraffio: *Portrait of a Youth* (Washington, N.G.)
		1520–24	Correggio: *Assumption of the Virgin* (cupola fresco in the *Cathedral of Parma*)
1519	† Lucrezia Borgia	c. 1520	Dosso Dossi: *Departure of the Argonauts* (Kress Collection, Washington)
1521	Federigo II Gonzaga takes Parma and Milan	1522/23	L. Mazzolino: *Anna Selbdritt* (Uffizi)
		c. 1523	Borgognone: *Assumption of the Virgin* (Brera, Milan)
		1524	Giulio Romano moves to Mantua
		1524/25	Correggio: *Venus and Cupid with a Satyr* (Louvre)
1525	Definitive expulsion of the French from Italy by Emperor Charles V	1525	Pietro Aretino in Mantua
		1526–34	Giulio Romano builds and decorates the *Palazzo del Te* in Mantua (incl. frescoes in the *Sala dei Giganti*)
1527	Sack of Rome by imperial troops	1527	B. Luini: *St Catharine* (Eremitage, St Petersburg)
1528	Andrea Doria frees Genoa from French rule – Genoa receives a republican constitution and keeps its independence until 1797	1527	Parmigianino: *Virgin and Child with Sts John the Baptist and Jerome (Vision of St Jerome)* (London, N.G.)
		1527/31	Parmigianino: *Virgin of the Rose* (Dresden)
1529	Francesco II Sforza is appointed Duke of Milan	1529/32	Gerolamo da Carpi: *Adoration of the Magi* (San Martino, Bologna)
1530	Charles V is crowned Emperor in Bologna	1530/32	Correggio: *Virgin of St George* (Dresden)
1530	Mantua becomes a duchy	1530/35	Correggio: *Adoration of the Child* (Uffizi)
		1531	Correggio: *Ganymede* (Kunsthistorisches Museum, Vienna)
1535	Milan confiscated as a settled feudal kingdom and comes under Habsburg rule – economic decline	1534/40	Parmagianino: *Madonna of the Long Neck* (Uffizi)
		from 1540	Renewed artistic revival under Carlo Borromeo

1538–84	Carlo Borromeo becomes Archbishop of Milan – Milan becomes a bulwark of the Counter Reformation
1546–63	Council of Trent
1547	Conspiracy in Genoa of the Fiesco against Gianettino Doria
1547	The Council of Trent sits in Bologna
1576/77	Plague in Milan
1598	Ferrara is confiscated as a settled feudal kingdom by the Pope

c. 1540	Garofalo: *Annunciation* (Uffizi)
c. 1540	Nicolò del' Abate: *fresco cycle in the Castello di Scaniano* (Modena)
1542	Dosso Dossi: *Stregoneria* (Sorcery), (Uffizi)
1550/52	del' Abate: *Wild Boar Hunt* (Galeria Spada, Rome)
1558	Galeazzo Alessi: *Palazzo Marino* (Milan); Roman Mannerism
1565/66	Prospero Fontana: *Portrait of a Lady* (Museo D. Bargellini, Bologna)
1571	del' Abate: *The Magnaminity of Scipio* (Louvre): a remarkable example of the Fontainebleau style
1584/85	Bart. Cesi: *Crucifixion* (S. Martino, Bologna)
c. 1584	Bart. Passarotti: *Old Lady* (Vienna)
1584	Bernadino Campi: *Christ on the Cross* (Pinacoteca di Castello, Milan)
1588	Annibale Carracci: *Venus, Satyr, and Two Cupids* (Uffizi)
1592	Carracci: *Virgin of St Luke* (Louvre)
1594	Ludovico Carracci: *St Hyacinth* (Louvre). The Carracci are a typical embodiment of the transition from the Renaissance to the Baroque

Central Italy

1250–60	Government of the "primo popolo" in Florence		
1250	† Friedrich II		
1260	Battle of Montaperti (defeat of the Guelfe under Siena's command)	1265	* Dante Alighieri († 1321) *Divine Comedy* (1307–1321)
1266	Battle of Benevent	1266	* Giotto di Bondone († 1337): frescoes in the *Upper Church of Assisi* (1296–1300)
1269	Battle of Colle di Val d'Elsa (Victory of the Guelfe)	c. 1285	Cimabue: *Madonna Rucellai* (Louvre)
		1295/00	Giotto: *Stigmatization of St Francis* (Louvre)
1309–77	Papal Exile in Avignon	1304	* Petrarca († 1374)
		1311	Duccio di Buoginsegna: *Maestà* (Cathedral Museum, Siena)
		1313	* Giovanni Bocaccio (1375): *Decamerone* (one of the first poetic works of the Early Renaissance)
		1316	Simon Martini: *frescoes in the Palazzo Publico*, Siena
		1319	Sack of Assisi (city laid under interdict until 1352). End of St Francis's influence on the artistic development of the occident
1329	Florence conquers Pistoia		
1334	Orvieto: the Monaldeschi come into power		
1335/36	Siena subjugates Massa Marittima and Grosseto	1335	Giotto is entrusted with supervision of the construction of the *Campanile* of the Cathedral of Florence
1340	Plague – collapse of Florentine and Sienese banks	1336/42	Simone Martini: *Road to Calvary* (Louvre)
1348	The Black Death (Pisa and Florence)	1348	Pietro Lorenzetti, Maso di Banco, Bernardo Daddi, and others die in an epidemic
1351	Florence conquers Prato		
c. 1355	Hunger, poverty, and uprisings in Tuscany – social upheaval		
1360–80	War between Florence and Pisa	1359	Andrea Orcagna: *Burial and Assumption of the Virgin* (marble sculpture in *Orsanmichele,* Florence)
1361	Florence conquers Volterra		
		1365	Giovanni da Milano: *Lives of the Virgin and St Mary Magdalene* (frescoes in the *Rinuccini Chapel of Santa Croce,* Florence)
1371	Workers' revolt in Siena		
1375	Perugia declares independence: 100 years of conflict and violence		
1378	Beginning of the Schism – decay of Papal and ecclesiastical authority	c. 1375	* Gentile da Fabriano († 1427)
		1377	*Facade of the Cathedral of Siena*

Date	Historical events	Date	Art events
1385	Siena: fall of the reform government	1385	Spinello Aretino: *frescoes* in *San Lorenzo*, Arezzo
1389–1464	Cosimo (il Vecchio) de' Medici (pater patriae)	c. 1385	Sienese art begins to decline
1406	Florence subjugates Pisa	1414–19	Gentile da Fabriano: *frescoes in the Broletto* of Brescia
		1416/20	* Piero della Francesca († 1492)
1417	End of the Schism	1417/18	Donatello: *Pazzi-Madonna* (Berlin)
		1418	End of the Council of Constance
		1418–36	Filippo Brunelleschi: *Cathedral Cupola* (Florence)
		1423	Masaccio: *frescoes* in the *Brancacci Chapel* (Santa Maria del Carmine)
1424	War between Florence and Milan	1424	L. Ghiberti: completion of the *North Door of the Baptistry* (Florence)
		1425	Work commences on the *East Door* (Door of Paradise)
		c. 1425	Donatello: *Baptistry Font* (Siena)
		1427	† Gentile da Fabriano
		1428/31	Masolino: *St Jerome and St John the Baptist* (London, N.G.)
		1431	Fra Angelico: *Last Judgement* (San Marco Museum, Florence)
1432	Battle of San Romano (Florence victorious over Siena, Lucca, and Milan)	1433	Domenico di Bartolo: *Madonna of Humility* (Pinacoteca Nazionale, Siena)
1434	The Medici come into power in Florence (until 1494)	1434	Brunelleschi: completion of the *Cathedral Cupola* in Florence
		1435	Fra Angelico: *Deposition* (San Marco, Florence)
1439	Council of Florence between Western and Orthodox Church	from 1439	Together with the Greek language, Classical Greek philosophers and poets gain entry to Italy – Johannes Bessarion in Florence – beginning of the Humanist movement
		1440	Piero della Francesca: *Baptism* (London, N.G.)
1443	Urbino becomes a duchy	1445	* Filipepe, Alessandro di Mariano, known as Sandro Botticelli († 1510)
1444–82	Federigo de Montefeltre governs in Urbino	1445	Fra Angelico: completion of the *frescoes in San Marco* (begun in 1436)
		1445–62	Piero della Francesca: polyptych of the *Madonna* (San Sepolcro, Museo Civico)
1449	Dissolution of the Council of Basle		

		1446	Donatello: *David* (Bargello, Florence)
		1451	Piero della Francesca in Rimini: *frescoes* in the *Tempio Malatestiano*
		1452	* Leonardo da Vinci († 1519)
		1452	Completion of the *Door of Paradise* in the Baptistry, Siena
		1452–1564	Piero della Francesca: *frescoes* in San Francesco, Arezzo, *Legend of the True Cross*
1453	Conquest of Constantinople by the Turks	1453	Donatello: equestrian statue, *Gatta-melata* (begun in 1444)
		1458	Leon Batt. Alberti: construction begins on the *facade* of *Santa Maria Novella*, Florence
		1459	Benozzo Gozzoli: *Medici Family as the Magi* (Palazzo Medici-Ricardi, Chapel)
1462	Francesco Sforza appoints the Montefeltri of Urbino and the Malatesta of Rimini common rulers over the Marches	1465	Sandro Botticelli opens his own workshop in Florence
		1468	Luciano Laurana begins with the construction of the *Ducal Palace* of Urbino (facade by Francesco di Giorgio Martini)
1469–92	Lorenzo de' Medici (il Magnifico) (*1449) "The Golden Age" – literature and art flourish in Florence	1470/75	Andrea Verrocchio: *Baptism* (Uffizi)
		1471	Cennini opens the first printing office in Florence
		1472/73	Francesco di Giorgio Martini: *Coronation of the Virgin* (Pinacoteca Nazionale, Siena)
		c. 1475	Antonio Pollaiuolo: St Sebastian (London, N.G.)
		1475	* Michelangelo Buonarotti († 1564)
		1475	Andrea della Robbia: *Virgin and Child with Cherubim* (Bargello, Florence)
1478	Pazzi conspiracy in Florence – Lorenzo's brother Giuliano is murdered	c. 1480	Ghirlandaio: *Portrait of an Old Man and a Boy* (Louvre)
		c. 1480	Publication of Vitruvius's *De architec-tura* – with a profound influence on the development of architectural style
		c. 1480	Hugo van der Goes: *Portinari Altar-piece* (Uffizi)
		1480	Botticelli: *Birth of Venus* (Uffizi)
		1481/82	Pietro Perugino: *Christ Giving the Keys*

1482	† Federigo de Montefeltre – his son Guidobaldo joins the governent		*to St Peter* (Sistine Chapel, Vatican)
		1482	Leonardo goes to Milan (until 1499)
		1483	* Raphael († 1520)
		before 1485	Lorenzo di Credi: *Annunciation* (Uffizi)
		1485	Ghirlandaio: *Adoration of the Shepherds* (Sassetti Chapel, Santa Trinità, Florence)
		before 1490	Piero della Francesca: *Madonna with the Duke of Urbino as Donor* ("Brera Madonna") (Brera, Milan)
1492	† Lorenzo de' Medici	1492	Perugino opens a workshop in Florence
		1492	† Piero della Francesca
1494	Expulsion of the Medici from Florence	1495	Pinturicchio: painting of the *fresco cycles in the Borgia Apartments in the Vatican*
		1496	Erection of the equestrian statue of *Colleoni* in front of the church St John and Paul (model by Verrocchio)
1498	Execution of Savonarola	1497/99	Michelangelo: *Pietà* (St Peter's, Rome)
		1498	Botticelli: *Calumny of Apelles*
		1499–1502	Luca Signorelli: frescoes in the Cathedral of Orvieto (incl. *End of the World*)
		1500	Perugino (from 1499 back in Perugia) works on the *Collegio* Cambro
		1500	* Benvenuto Cellini († 1571)
1502–03	Exile of Guidobaldo in Mantua and Venice – expulsion of Cesare Borgia from Urbino	1501–04	Michelangelo: *David* (Piazza della Signoria, Florence)
		1503–05	Leonardo: *Mona Lisa* (Louvre)
1503	† Pope Alexander VI – appointment of Julius II († 1513)	1503	Mariotto Albertinelli: *Visitation* (Uffizi)
		1504	Michelangelo: *Doni Tondo* (Uffizi)
		1505	Leonardo: cartoon for the *Battle of Anghiari*
		1505/10	Piero di Cosimo: *Madonna and Child with St John as a Boy* (Liechtenstein)
		1506	The humanist Pietro Bembo (1470–1547) resides in Urbino

		1506	Raphael: *Madonna del Granduca* (Palazzo Pitti)
1507	† Cesare Borgia	1507	Pinturicchio: frescoes in the *Cathedral of Siena, Piccolomini Library*
		c. 1510	Leonardo: *Anna Selbdritt* (Louvre)
		1510	† Sandro Botticelli
		1510–11	Raphael: frescoes in the *Stanza della Segnatura* (Vatican)
1512	Florence: end of the Repulic – return of the Medici	1512	Michelangelo: ceiling frescoes in the *Sistine Chapel* (begun in 1508)
	Siena: † Pandolfo il Magnifico	1513/14	Raphael: *Sistine Madonna* (Dresden)
		c. 1513	Raphael: *Madonna della Seggiola* (Palazzo Pitti)
1513–21	Pope Leo x (Giovanni de' Medici)	1513–16	Michelangelo: *Moses* (St Peter's, Rome)
		1516/17	Raphael: Portrait of *Baldassare Castiglione* (Louvre)
		1518	Raphael: *Betrayal of Christ* (Pinacoteca Vaticana)
		1519	† Leonardo da Vinci (in Cloux, near Amboise, France)
		c. 1520	Andrea del Sarto: *John the Baptist* (Liechtenstein)
		1520	† Raphael
		1521–34	Michelangelo: *Medici tombs* (Medici Chapel, San Lorenzo, Florence)
1522	Plague in Rome	1523/25	Jacopo Pontormo: *Deposition* (Santa Felicità, Capponi-Chapel, Florence) Typical of early Mannerism
		1524	Andrea del Sarto: *Lamentation* (Palazzo Pitti)
		1526	Sodoma: *St Sebastian* (Palazzo Pitti)
1527	Sack of Rome by the troops of Charles v (Sacco romano)	1527	Destruction of Raphael's art school
1529	Imperial troops in Florence	1528	Publication of the *Cortigiano* by Castiglione
1530	The Medici again govern in Florence	1535–41	Michelangelo: *Last Judgement* (Sistine Chapel) Mannerism's point of departure
1534	Perugia becomes a Papal state		
1537–74	Cosimo i Duke of Tuscany – from 1564 he leaves governmental matters to his son, Francesco	1540/45	Angelo Bronzino: *Luxuria* (London, N. G.)
		1540/43	Benvenuto Cellini: *Salt of Francis* i

1540	Erection of the fortress of Paolina – Perugia comes definitively under Papal rule	after 1541	Andrea del Castagno: *frescoes* in *Santissima Annuciata* (Florence)
		1545/54	B. Cellini: *Perseus* (Loggia dei Lanzi, Florence)
1546–63	Council of Trent – point of departure of the intra-ecclesiastical revival movement	1546	Michelangelo assumes supervision of the construction of *St Peter's, Rome* Excavations in Chiusi and Arezzo awaken interest in Etruscan culture (chimaeras, orators, minerva)
1555	Augsburg religious peace		
		c. 1560	The "heathen" Renaissance loses momentum – the decrees of the Council of Trent are also reflected in the arts
		1564	† Michelangelo, in Rome
1569	Pius x appoints Cosimo i Grand Duke		

Venice and its sphere of influence

1204	Venice conquers Constantinople under the command of Doge Enrico Dandolo	1204	Byzantine "acquisitions" form the basis of the *Treasury of San Marco* (including the *bronze horse* above the vestibule of *St Mark's Basilica*)
1259–1387	Reign of the Skaliger in Verona	c. 1300	*Paolo Veneziano († before 1362), active from 1333–58
		c. 1305	Giotto: frescoes in the *Capella Scrovegni*, Padua
1310	Establishment of the Council of the Ten in Venice to restrict the power of the Doge	c. 1350	Polyptych depicting the *Coronation of the Virgin and Scenes from the Life of Christ* (Accademia, Venice)
1338	Padua acknowledges Venetian sovereignty – prosperity under the Carrara		
1350–88	Francesco II Vecchio Carrara governs in Padua	1361–68	Petrarca resides in Venice
1378	Genoa and Padua unite against Venice	1371	Lorenzo Veneziano: polyptych depicting the *Annunciation with Saints* (Accademia, Venice)
1381	Definitive victory of Venice over Genoa – end of the Hundred Years' War	1377/79	Alichiero Altichieri: *frescoes* in the *Capella San Felice* (St Antonius, Padua)
1389–1494	Conquest of the *Terra ferma* by Venice	1394	Nicolo di Pietro: *Madonna and Child Enthroned* (Accademia, Venice)
1399	Venice victorious over Padua		
1404	Venice subjugates Verona	1395	† Altichiero da Zevio, in Verona
1405	Padua placed under the immediate control of the Venetian senate. With the extension to the university, Padua becomes the educational centre of the Venetian realm		
1416	Victory of the Venetian fleet over the Turks – political and geographical balance with the port for a quarter of a century	1415/20	Jacobello del Fiore: *Robed Madonna between John the Baptist and John the Evangelist*
			Pisanello in Venice: paintings in the *Sala del Maggior Consiglio*
1418–20	Venice conquers Friuli and Istria	1424–30	Construction of the *Cà d'Oro* (Venice)
1423	Francesco Foscari (* 1372) elected Doge – F. leads Venice to the apogee of its power – F. is removed shortly before his death (1457)	1424–38	Giovanni and Bartolomelo Buon: construction of the *west wing* of the *Doges' Palace* (*Porta Della Carta* 1438–43)
		c. 1431–36	* Giovanni Bellini († 1516)
1426/28	Brescia and Bergamo fall to Venice	c. 1433	Pisanello: portrait of *Ginvera d'Este* (Louvre)
1432	Emperor Sigismund elevates Gianfrancesco I Gonzaga to Margrave of Mantua	c. 1440	Pisanello: *Vision of St Eustace* (Louvre)

1441	Venice conquers Ravenna	1446	Antonio Vivarini und Giov. d'Alamagna: *Virgin and Child with Sts Jerome and Gregory, Ambrose and Augustine* (Accademia, Venice)
		1447	Ricci: construction begins on *San Giorgio in Braida* (cupola of *San Micheli* 1500, Verona)
		1450	† Giovanni d'Alamagna
		1452	Jacopo Bellini settles in Padua – contact with Mantegna's art
1453	Conquest of Constantinople by the Turks under Sultan Mahomet II – impacts on Venetian trade	1453	Donatello: *Gattamelata* (Padua) Donatello leaves Padua 1454
		1458–1534	Antonio Gambello: *facade of San Zaccharia* (Venice)
		1459	Giov. Bellini: *Agony in the Garden* (London, N. G.)
1463	Venice faces the Turks alone	1462	Jacopo Bellini resides in Verona
		1469	First book printers' in Venice
		c. 1470	Giov. Bellini: *Pietà* (Brera, Milan)
		1474	Gentile Bellini in Constantinople at the Court of Sultan Mahomet II
		1475	Antonello da Messina: *Virgin Annunciate* (Palermo)
		1475/76	Antonello da Messina in Venice – profound influence on Giov. Bellini and other Venetian painters
1478–85	Term of Giovanni Mocenigo as Doge	1477	Bartolommeo Vivarini: polyptych for the *Arte dei Tagliapietra* (Accademia, Venice)
1479	Venice loses Negroponte, Skutari, and Morea to the Turks – tributary payments at the port	1479/90	Giov. Bellini: *Pala di San Giobbe* (Accademia, Venice)
		1480	Gentile Bellini: *Portrait of Sultan Mahomet II* (London, N. G.)
		1481–89	Pietro Lombardo: construction of *Santa Maria dei Miracoli* (Venice)
1483	Sixtus IV lays Venice under an interdict	1486	Carlo Crivelli: *Annunciation* (London, N. G.)
		1487–95	P. Lombardo: construction of the *Scuola di San Marco* (Venice)
		1490	Bart, Vivarini: *Madonna and Child* (Eremitage, St Petersburg)

		1490	Girolamo dai Libri: *Deposition* (Santa Maria in Organo, Verona)
		c. 1490	Vittore Carpaccio: *Legend of St Ursula* (Accademia, Venice)
1492	Discovery of America – with impacts on Venetian trade relationships	until 1494	Giovanni Mansueti: *Miracle of the True Cross at the Campo di S Lio* (Accademia, Venice)
		1493/94	Carlo Crivelli: *Coronation of the Virgin with Saints* (Brera, Milan)
		1495/97	Gio. Bat. Cima: *Madonna of the Orange Tree* (Accademia, Venice)
1501–21	Term of Leonardo Loredan as Doge	1496	Gentile Bellini: *Procession on the Piazza San Marco* (Accademia, Venice)
		1505	Giorgione: *Tempest* (Accademia, Venice)
1508	The Emperor of the Holy Roman Empire, the Pope Julius II, Naples, and other Italian states, together with France, all unite against Venice – Venice's political and economic power is challenged to its limits	1508	* Andrea Palladio († 1580)
		1508/10	Giorgione and Titian: *Venus* (Dresden)
		1510	Marco Basaiti: *Calling of the Sons of Zebedee* (Accademia, Venice – smaller copy in Vienna)
		1510/11	Giorgione / Titian: *Concert Champêtre* (Louvre)
		1512	Sebastinao del Piombo: *La Fornarina* (Uffizi, Florence)
		1512	Bartolommeo Buon (the Younger): construction of the *Campanile* (Piazza San Marco, Venice)
		1513	Palma Vecchio: *Assumption of the Virgin* (Accademia, Venice)
		1514	Giov. Bellini: *Feast of the Gods* (Widener Collection, Washington)
		1515	Giov. Bellini: *Lady at her Toilet* (Kunsthistorisches Museum, Vienna)
		1516–18	Titian: *Assumption* (Assunta) (Frari-Church, Venice)
		1516	† Giovanni Bellini
1519	End of the battle with the league – Venice a spent force	1516	Titian is summoned to Ferrara
1521	† Lorenzo Loredan	1523	Titian in Mantua (again in 1527)
1523–38	Term of Andrea Grittis as Doge	1525–30	Bandinelli: *Hercules and Cacus* (courtyard, Doges' Palace, Venice)
1527	Sack of Rome	1527	Pietro Aretino in Venice

		1530–35 Lorenzo Lotto: *The Adulteress*, (Louvre)
		1530/40 Giov. Girolamo Savoldo: *The Transfiguration* (Uffizi, Florence)
		1532 Giov. Antonio Pordenone: *St Lawrence of Giustiniani and Saints* (Accademia, Venice) – a remarkable example of so-called Protomannerism
		c. 1533 Lotto: *Lady as Lucretia* (London, N. G.)
1534–49	Pope Paul III (Alessandro Farnese)	1534–39 Titian: *Presentation of the Virgin in the Temple* (Accademia, Venice)
		1536 Titian: *Venus of Urbino* (Uffizi, Florence)
		from 1537 Jacopo Sansovino: *Palazzo Corner (Ca' Grande)* (Venice)
		1537–84 J. Sansovino: *library* (Venice)
		c. 1540 Perino del Vaga: *Holy Family* (Liechtenstein)
		c. 1542 Titian: *Christ Crowned with Thorns* for Santa Maria delle Grazie in Milan (Louvre; later version in Munich)
1545–53	Term of Francesco Donà as Doge	
1546–63	Council of Trent – the intra-ecclesiastical revival also has a major impact on artistic production	1546 Titian: *Pope Paul III and his Grandsons* (Capodimonte, Naples)
		1549 Andrea Palladio: *Palazzo della Ragione* (Vicenza)
		1553 Titian: *Danae* (Prado, Madrid)
		1562–63 Paolo Veronese: *Marriage at Cana* (Louvre)
		1564–87 Jacopo Tintoretto: cycle in the *Scuola di San Rocco* (Venice)
		from 1566 Palladio: construction of *San Giorgio Maggiore* (Venice)
1568/69	Famine across much of Italy	
1570	Venice loses Cyprus to the Turks	after 1570 Giov. Bat. Moroni: *Portrait of a Priest* (Liechtenstein); an outstanding example of the portrait art of the School of Brescia
1571	Destruction of the Turkish fleet in the Battle of Lepanto (with the participation of Venice)	
1574	Fire in the Doges' Palace	1576 † Titian
1575–77	Plague in Venice (c. 50,000 die)	1577–92 Palladio: construction of *Il Redentore* (Venice)
1577	Fire in the Doges' Palace – destruction of the *Sala del Maggior Consiglio*	1579–80 Tintoretto: *Gonzaga cycle* (Alte Pinakothek, Munich)

		1580	Palladio: draft for the *Teatro Olimpico* in Vicenza
		c. 1580	Veronese: *Mars and Venus* (Metropolitan Museum, New York)
1585–95	Term of Pasquale Cicgona as Doge – increased levels of piracy in the Adriatic adversely affect Venetian maritime trade	before 1585	Veronese: *Triumph of Venice* (Doges' Palace, Venice)
		1588	Antonio Contini: construction of the *Rialto Bridge*
		1588	† P. Veronese
		c. 1592	Leandro Bassano: *Susanna at her Bath* (Alte Pinakothek, Munich)
		1592–94	Tintoretto: *Last Supper* (San Giorgio Maggiore, Venice) Completion of *Paradise* (Sala grande, Doges' Palace, Venice)
		1594	† Tintoretto

Selected Bibliography

Dictionaries

Dictionnaire des Peintres et Sculpteurs, E. Bénézit, Paris 1966.
Dictionary of the Italian Renaissance, London 1981.
La Pittura in Italia, Il Quattrocento, Milan 1986.
La Pittura in Italia, Il Cinquecento, Milan 1987.
La Pittura in Emilia e in Romagna, Milan 1995.
The Oxford Dictionary of Art, Chilvers et al (eds.), Oxford 1997.

General works

Ames-Lewis, Francis and Mary Rogers (eds.), *Concepts of Beauty in Renaissance Art*, Hants, England, Brookfield, VT 1998.
Andres, Glenn M. et al, *The Art of Florence*, New York 1988.
Barash, Moshe, *Light and Color in the Italian Renaissance Theory of Art*, New York 1978.
Barolsky, Paul, *The Faun in the Garden: Michelangelo and the Poetic Origin of Italian Renaissance Art*, University Park, PA 1994.
Baskins, Cristelle Louise, *Cassone Painting, Humanism, and Gender in Early Modern Italy*, Cambridge, New York 1998.
Baxandall, Michael, *Giotto and the Orators: Humanist Observers of Painting in Italy and the Discovery of Pictorial Composition, 1350–1450*, Oxford 1971.
Berenson, Bernard, *The Italian Painters of the Renaissance*, New York 1952.
Blunt, Anthony, *Artistic Theory in Italy, 1450–1600*, London, New York 1962.
Brown, Patricia Fortini, *Art and Life in Renaissance Venice*, New York 1997.
Burckhardt, Jacob, *The Civilization of the Renaissance in Italy*, Oxford 1995.
Burke, Peter, *The Italian Renaissance: Culture and Society in Italy*, Princeton 1999.
Chambers, David, *Patrons and Artists in the Italian Renaissance*, London 1970.
Chastel, André, *The Studios and Styles of the Renaissance: Italy 1460–1500*, London 1966.
Chastel, André, *The Flowering of the Italian Renaissance*, New York 1965.
Christiansen, Keith, *Painting in Renaissance Siena, 1420–1500*, New York 1988.
Clark, Kenneth, *The Art of Humanism*, London 1983.
Cole, Bruce, *Italian Art, 1250–1550: The Relation of Renaissance Art to Life and Society*, New York 1987.
Cole, Bruce, *Masaccio and the Art of Early Renaissance Florence*, Bloomington, Ind. 1980.
Dunkelman, Martha Levine, *Central Italian Painting, 1400–1465*, Boston 1986.
Emison, Patricia A., *Low and High Style in Italian Renaissance Art*, New York 1997.
Freedberg, S.J., *Painting in Italy, 1500 to 1600*, New Haven, London 1993.
Gilbert, Bennett, *The Art of the Woodcut in the Italian Renaissance Book*, New York, Los Angeles 1995.
Gombrich, E.H., *Norm and Form: Studies in the Art of the Renaissance*, Chicago 1985.
Hager, Serafina (ed.), *Leonardo, Michelangelo, and Raphael in Renaissance Florence*, Washington, DC 1992.
Hale, J.R., *England and the Italian Renaissance: The Growth of Interest in Its History and Art*, London 1996.
Hartt, Frederick, *History of Italian Renaissance Art: Painting, Sculpture, Architecture*, New York 1979.
Henneberg, Josephine von, *Architectural Drawings of the Late Italian Renaissance*, Città del Vaticano 1996.

Hollingsworth, Mary, *Patronage in Sixteenth-Century Italy*, London 1996.
Holmes, George, *Art and Politics in Renaissance Italy*, Oxford 1993.
Jacobs, Frederica Herman, *Defining the Renaissance Virtuosa: Women Artists and the Language of Art History and Criticism*, Cambridge, New York 1997.
Karpinski, Caroline, *Italian Printmaking, Fifteenth and Sixteenth Centuries: An Annotated Bibliography*, Boston 1987.
Kemp, Martin, *Behind the Picture: Art and Evidence in the Italian Renaissance*, New Haven 1997.
Kurz, O., *Bolognese Drawings of the XVII and XVIII Centuries at Windsor Castle*, London 1955.
Lemaitre, Alain J., *Florence and the Renaissance: The Quattrocento*, Paris 1993.
Lengyel, Alfonz, *The Quattrocento: A Study of the Principles of Art and a Chronological Biography of the Italian 1400s*, Dubuque, Iowa 1971.
Macioce, S., *Il gotico internazionale*, Art Dossier, Florence 1989.
Paatz, Walter, *The Arts of the Italian Renaissance: Painting, Sculpture, Architecture*, New York 1974.
Paoletti, John T., *Art in Renaissance Italy*, New York 1997.
Partridge, Loren W., *The Art of Renaissance Rome, 1400–1600*, New York 1996.
Pietrangeli, C., *The Sistine Chapel*, New York 1986.
Posner, Kathleen Weil Garris, *Leonardo and Central Italian Art, 1515–1550*, New York 1974.
Reed, Sue Welsh, *Italian Etchers of the Renaissance and Baroque*, Boston 1989.
Richardson, Brian, *Print Culture in Renaissance Italy*, Cambridge, NY 1994.
Rosand, David, *Painting in Sixteenth-Century Venice*, Cambridge, NY 1997.
Rosenberg, Charles M., *Art and Politics in Late Medieval and Early Renaissance Italy, 1250–1500*, Notre Dame 1990.
Rowland, Ingrid D., *The Culture of High Renaissance: Ancients and Moderns in Sixteenth-Century Rome*, Cambridge, New York 1998.
Schultz, Bernard, *Art and Anatomy in Renaissance Italy*, Ann Arbor, Mich. 1985.
Sheard, Wendy Stedman and John T. Paoletti (eds.), *Collaboration in Italian Renaissance Art*, New Haven 1978.
Shearman, John K.G., *Only Connect: Art and the Spectator in the Italian Renaissance*, Princeton 1992.
Stephens, John M., *The Italian Renaissance: The Origins of Intellectual and Artistic Change Before the Reformation*, London, New York 1990.
Stinger, Charles L., *The Renaissance in Rome*, Bloomington, Ind. 1998.
Summers, David, *Michelangelo and the Language of Art*, Princeton 1981.
Thomas, Anabel, *The Painter's Practice in Renaissance Tuscany*, Cambridge, New York 1995.
Toman, Rolf (ed.), *The Art of the Italian Renaissance*, San Diego 1995.
Torriti, P. *Arte a Siena*, Art Dossier, Florence 1987.
Tuena, F.M., *Il Tesoro dei Medici*, Art Dossier, Florence 1987.
Vasari, G., *Le vite de' più eccelenti architetti, pittori, et scultori italiani, da Cimbue insino a'tempi nostri*, Florence 1550, Turin 1991.
Welch, Evelyn, *Art and Society in Italy, 1350–1500*, Oxford, New York 1997.
Welch, Evelyn, *Art and Authority in Renaissance Milan*, New Haven 1995.
Williams, Robert, *Art, Theory, and Culture in Sixteenth-Century Italy: From Techne to Metatechne*, Cambridge, New York 1997.
Wittkower, Rudolf, *Idea and Image: Studies in the Italian Renaissance*, London 1978.
Wölfflin, Heinrich, *Classic Art: An Introduction to the Italian Renaissance*, Oxford 1980.

Museum Catalogues

Ancona: *Pinacoteca Nazionale* (Marchini).

Baltimore: *Italian Paintings, XIV–XVIIIth Centuries from the Collection of the Baltimore Museum of Art*, Baltimore 1981.

Chicago: *Italian Paintings Before 1600 in the Art Institute of Chicago* (Christopher Lloyd), Chicago 1993.

Florence: *The Uffizi (All Paintings)*, 1971.
– *The Uffizi* (L. Berti), 1993.
– *Palazzo Medici-Ricardi (B. Santi)*, 1983.

London: *National Gallery – Complete Illustrated Catalogue*, 1995.
– *National Gallery* (Michael Wilson), London 1982.

Los Angeles: *Italian Panel Painting of the Early Renaissance in the Collection of the Los Angeles Museum of Art* (Susan L. Caroselli), Los Angeles 1994.

Milan: *Pinacoteca di Brera – Scuole lombarda e piemontese*, Milan 1988.
– *Un museo da scoprire (Pinacoteca del Castello Sforzesco)*, 1993.

New Haven: *Early Italian Paintings in the Yale University Art Gallery* (Charles Seymour, Jr.), New Haven 1970.

Padua: *Il Musei Civici agli Eremitani*, 1992.
– *Esplorando il Santo* (D. Bobisut & L. Gumiero), Padua 1995.

Siena: *Palazzo Pubblico, L'Arte a Siena sotto i Medici, 1555–1609*, Rome 1980.
– *La Pinacoteca Nazionale di Siena* (P. Torriti), Genua 1980.

St Petersburg: *Paintings in the Hermitage* (C. Eisler), New York 1990.

Udine: *La Galleria d'Arte Antica (La Pinacoteca)*, Udine 1994.

Washington: *National Gallery of Art – Early Italian Painting*, 1969.
– *National Gallery of Art – Late Italian Painting*, 1969.
– *National Gallery of Art* (Ross Watson), London 1979.

Exhibition Catalogues

1969 Hayward Gallery, London, *Frescoes from Florence*.

1980 Florence, *Il primato del disegno*.

1980/81 Allentown Art Museum, Allentown, PA, *Beyond Nobility: Art for the Private Citizen in the Early Renaissance*.

1988 Metropolitan Museum of Art, New York, *Painting in Renaissance Siena*.

1993 National Gallery of Art, Washington, DC, *Raphael and America*.

1993 Museo e gallerie nazionali di Capodimonte, Naples, *Raffaello, Michelangelo e bottega: i cartoni farnesiani restaurati*.

1996/97 Uffizi, Florence, *L'officina della maniera*.

1996/97 Casa del Mantegna, Mantova, *Pisanello e l'arte delle armature nel Rinascimento*.

1997/98 National Gallery of Art, Washington, DC, *Lorenzo Lotto: Rediscovered Masters of the Renaissance*.

1997/97 Grand Rapids Art Museum, Pietro Perugino: *Master of the Italian Renaissance*.

Single Artists

Andrea del Sarto – Natali, Antonio, Florence 1989.
Antonella da Messina – Barbera, Gioacchino, Milan 1998.
Beccafumi – Torriti, Piero, Milan 1998.
Bellini, Giovanni – Tempestini, Anchise, Milan 1997.
Botticelli, Sandro – Santi, Bruno, Florence, New York 1991.
– Caneva, Caterina, Florence 1990.
– Pons, Nicoletta, Milan 1989.
Caravaggio – Puglisi, Catherine R., London 1998.
– Seward, Desmond, New York 1998.
Castagno, Andrea del – Horster, Marita, Ithaca, NY 1980.
Cimabue – Bellosi, Luciano, New York 1998.
Cozza, Francesco – Trezzani, Ludovica, Rome 1981.

Crivelli, Carlo – Zampetti, Pietro, Florence 1986.
Donatello – Avery, Charles, New York 1994.
Duccio di Buonisegna – Jannella, Cecilia, Florence, New York 1991.
– Stubblebine, James H., Princeton 1979.
Francesco di Giorgio Martini – Toledano, Ralph 1987.
Gaddi – Peruzzo 1987.
Gentile da Fabriano – De Marchi, Andrea, Milan 1992.
Giotto – New York 1999.
– Flores d'Arcais, Francesca, New York 1995.
– Bellosi, Luciano, Florence, New York 1981.
Ghiberti – Goldscheider, Ludwig, London 1949.
Ghirlandaio, Domenico – Kecks, Ronald G., Florence 1998.
– Micheletti, Emma, Florence, New York 1990.
Giorgione – Pignatti, Terisio, New York 1999.
– Anderson, Jaynie, New York 1997.
– Lucco, Mauro, Milan 1996.
Giulio Romano – Cambridge, New York 1998.
Guercino – Mahon, Denis, Washington, DC 1992.
Leonardo da Vinci – Plain, Nancy, New York 1999.
– Brown, David Alan, New Haven 1998.
– Vezzosi, Alessandro, New York 1997.
Lippi, Filippo – Filippina, Cecilia, Prato 1994.
Lorenzetti – Rutigliano, Antonio, New York 1991.
Lotto, Lorenzo – Cortesi Bosco, Francesca, Milan 1997.
– Humfrey, Peter, New Haven 1997.
Mantegna – Camesasca, Ettore, Florence, New York 1992.
– Lightbown, R.W., Berkeley 1986.
Martini, Simone – Jannella, Cecilia, Florence, New York 1989.
– Martindale, Andrew, New York 1988.
Masaccio – Savelli, Divo, Florence 1998.
– Fremantle, Richard, New York 1998.
Masolino – Roberts, Perri Lee, Oxford, New York 1993.
Matteo di Giovanni – Gengaro, M., Siena 1934.
Michelangelo – Condivi, Ascanio, University Park, PA 1999.
– Goldscheider, Ludwig, London 1996.
– Bull, George Anthony, London, New York 1995.
Palma il Vecchio – Peruzzo 1988.
Paolo Veneziano – Muraro, Michelangelo, University Park, PA 1970.
Parmigianino – Gould, Cecil H.M., New York 1994.
– Di Giampaolo, Mario, Florence 1991.
Perugino – Scarpellini, Pietro, Milan 1991.
Pisanello – Milan 1996.
– Woods-Marsden, Joanna, Princeton, NJ 1988.
Piero della Francesco – Calvesi, Maurizio, Milan 1998.
– Lavin, Marilyn Aronberg (ed.), Washington, DC 1995.
– Levy, Bernard Henri, Paris 1992.
Raphael – Hall, Marcia, Cambridge, New York 1997.
– Beck, James H., New York 1994.
– Guillaud, Jacqueline, New York 1989.
Reni, Guido – Spear, Richard E., New Haven 1997.
– Pepper, D. Stephen, New York 1984.
Titian – Cole, Bruce, Boulder, CO 1999.
– Ridolfi, Carlo, University Park, PA 1996.
– Manca, Joseph, Washington, DC/Hanover, NH 1993.
– Biadene, Susanna (ed.), Munich/New York 1990.
– Caroli, Flavio, Milan 1990.
Uccello – Roccasecca, Pietro, Milan 1997.
Borsi, Franco, New York 1994.

Charts

KEY

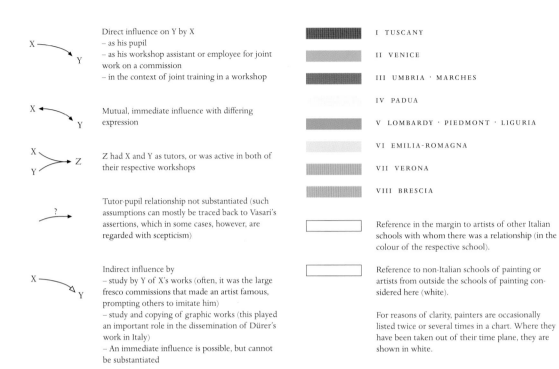

Direct influence on Y by X
– as his pupil
– as his workshop assistant or employee for joint work on a commission
– in the context of joint training in a workshop

Mutual, immediate influence with differing expression

Z had X and Y as tutors, or was active in both of their respective workshops

Tutor-pupil relationship not substantiated (such assumptions can mostly be traced back to Vasari's assertions, which in some cases, however, are regarded with scepticism)

Indirect influence by
– study by Y of X's works (often, it was the large fresco commissions that made an artist famous, prompting others to imitate him)
– study and copying of graphic works (this played an important role in the dissemination of Dürer's work in Italy)
– An immediate influence is possible, but cannot be substantiated

Influence by X on Y can be substantiated only in earlier or later productive years

I   TUSCANY

II   VENICE

III   UMBRIA · MARCHES

IV   PADUA

V   LOMBARDY · PIEDMONT · LIGURIA

VI   EMILIA-ROMAGNA

VII   VERONA

VIII   BRESCIA

Reference in the margin to artists of other Italian schools with whom there was a relationship (in the colour of the respective school).

Reference to non-Italian schools of painting or artists from outside the schools of painting considered here (white).

For reasons of clarity, painters are occasionally listed twice or several times in a chart. Where they have been taken out of their time plane, they are shown in white.

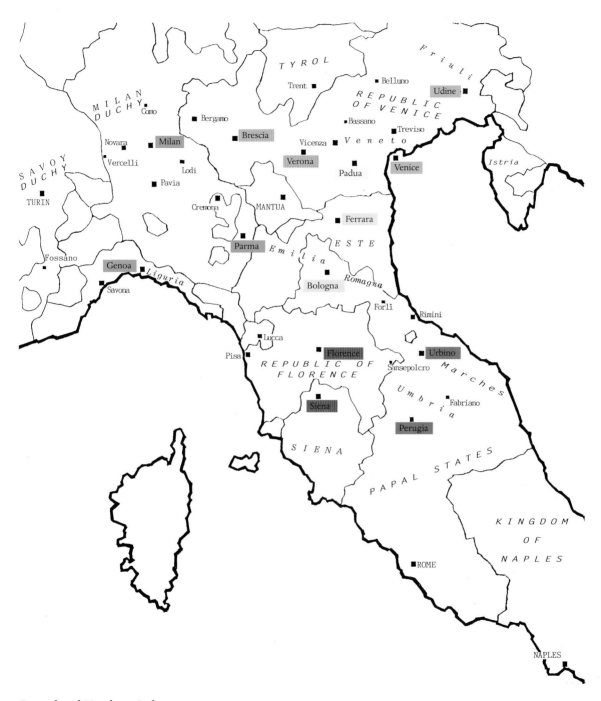

Central and Northern Italy
in the second half of the
fifteenth century

I Tuscany

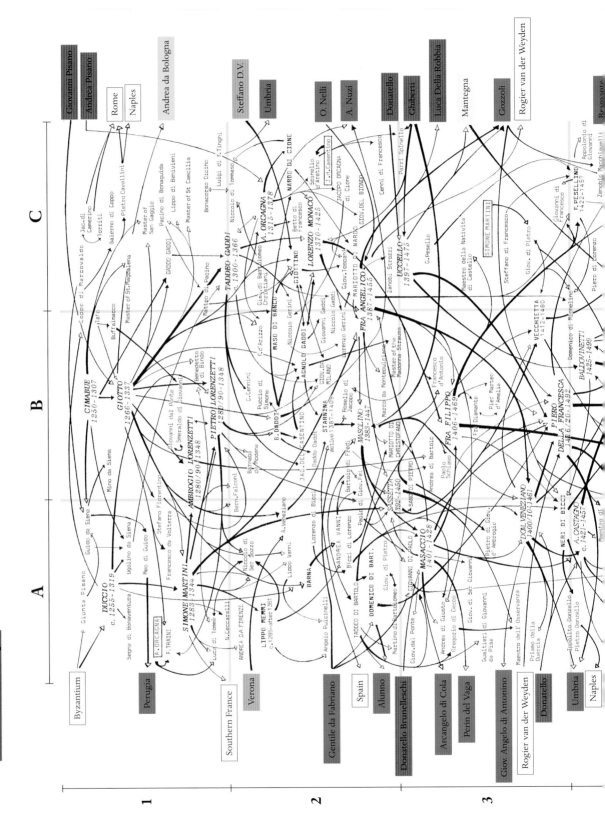

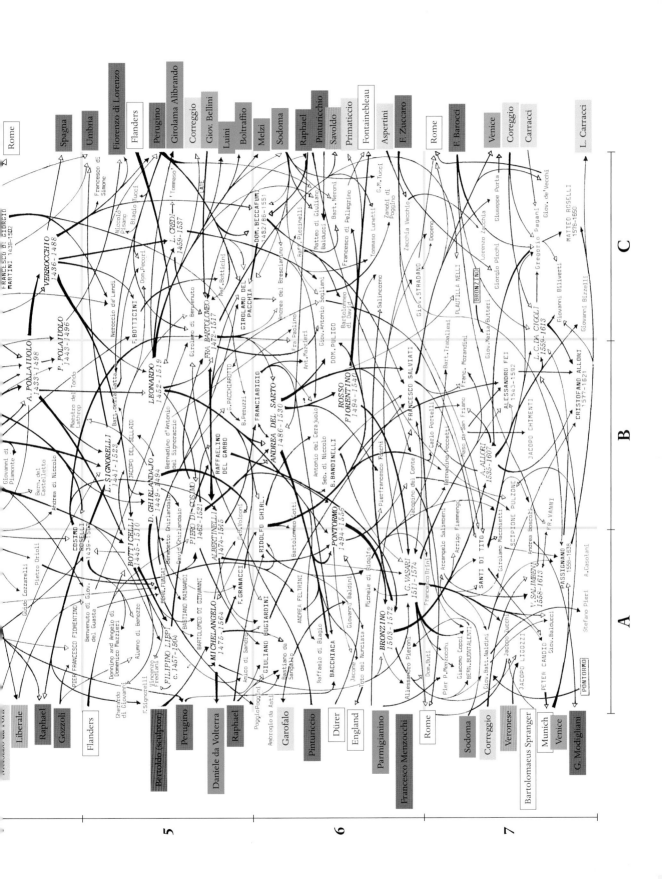

II Venice

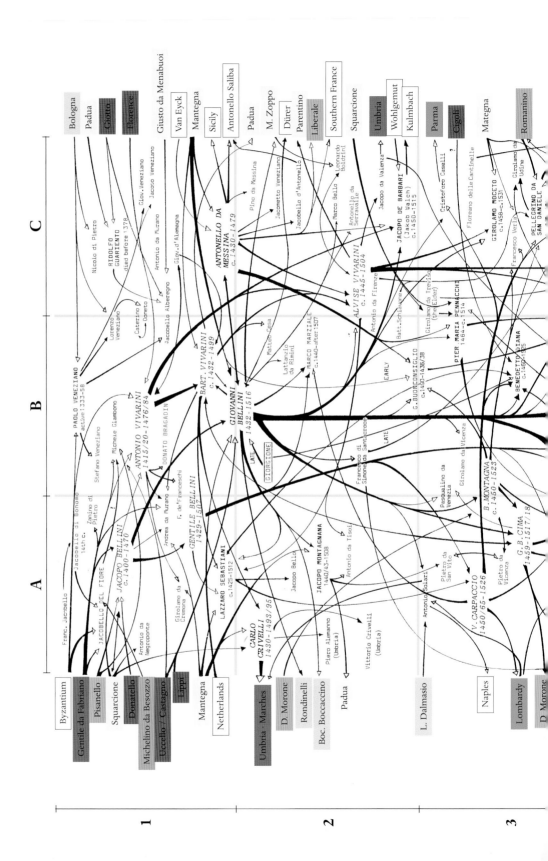

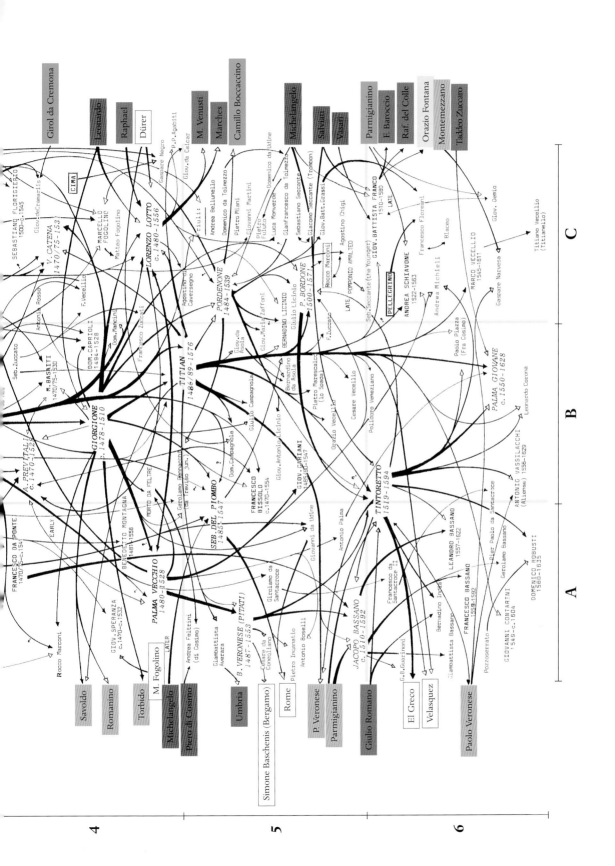

III Umbria · Marches

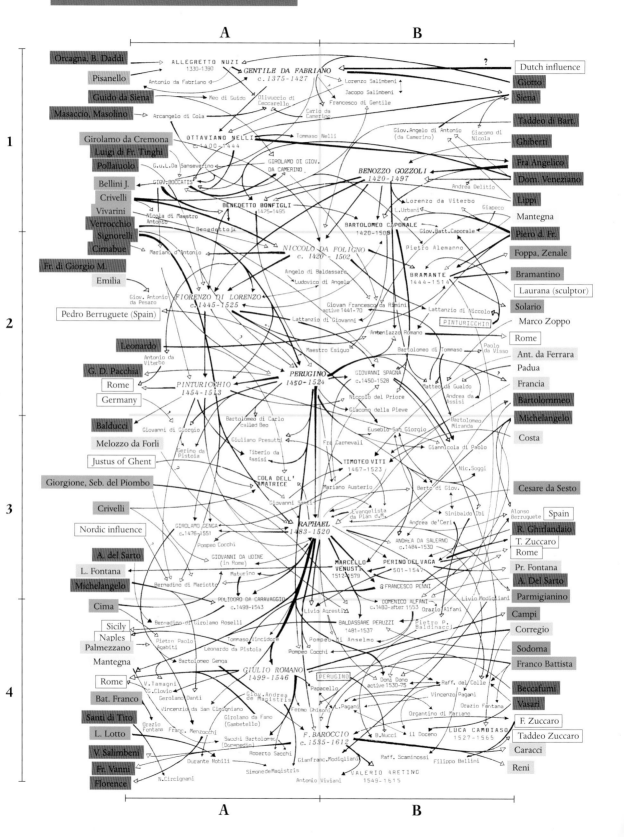

IV Padua

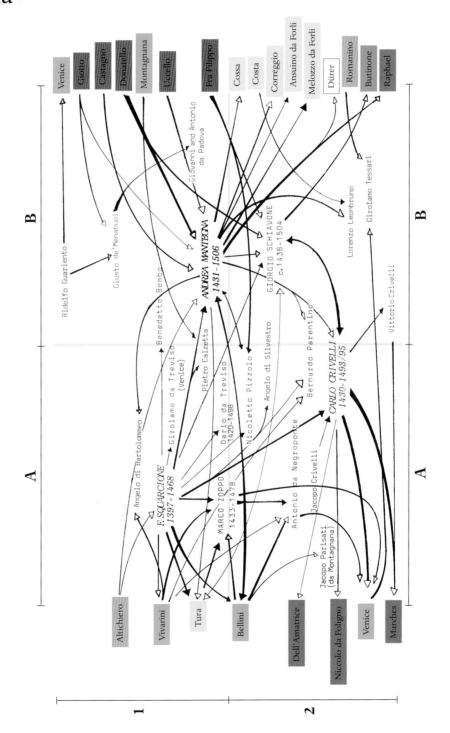

V Lombardy · Piedmont · Liguria

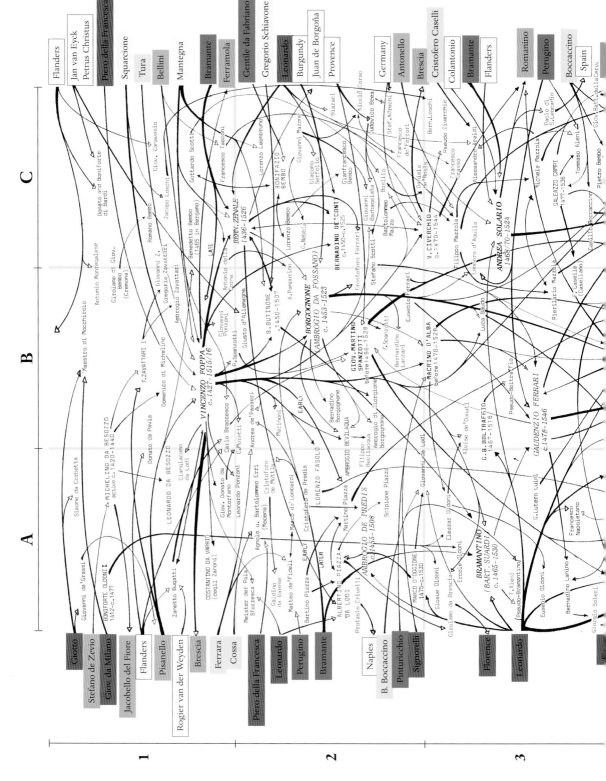

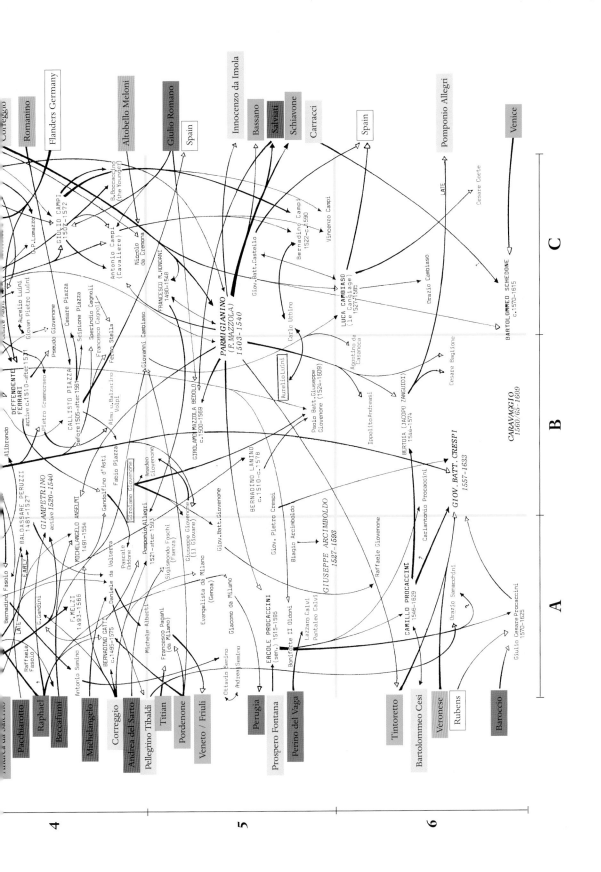

VI Emilia-Romagna

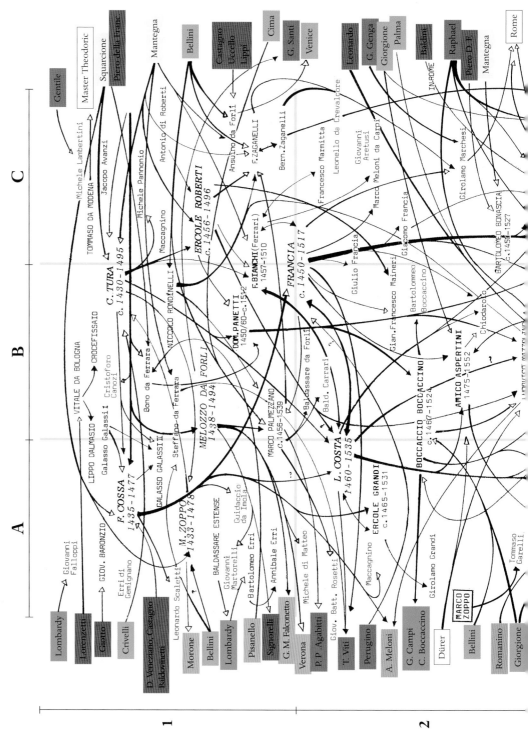

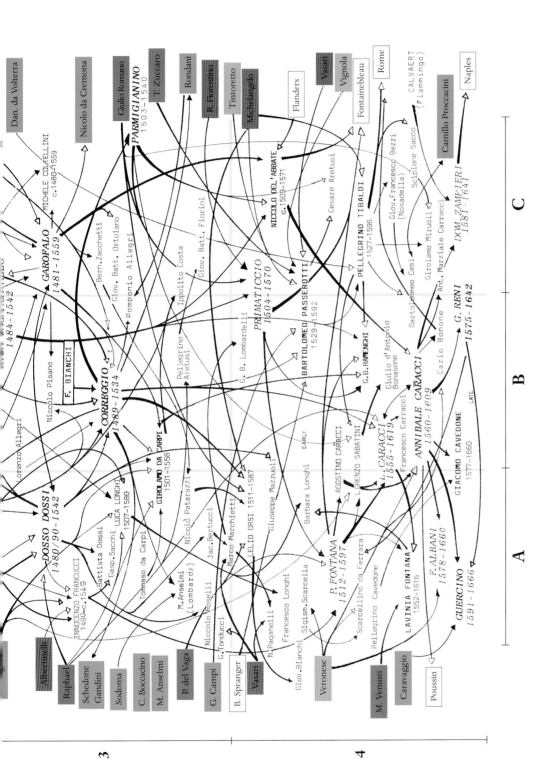

Dan. da Volterra

Nicolo da Cremona

Giulio Romano

T. Zuccaro

Rondani

R. Fiorentino

Tintoretto

Michelangelo

Flanders

Vasari

Vignola

Fontainebleau

Rome

MICHELE COLTELLINI
c.1480-1559

GAROFALO
1481-1559

Bern.Zacchetti

Giov. Batt. Ortolano

Pomponio Allegri

Giov. Batt. Fiorini

NICCOLO DEL'ABBATE
c.1509-1571

Cesare Aretusi

Giov.Francesco Bezzi
(Nosadella)

Scipione Sacco

CALVAERT
(Fiammingo)

Naples

Camillo Proccacini

1484-1542

Lorenzo Allegri

Niccolo Pisano

F. BIANCHI

CORREGGIO
1489-1534

Pellegrino
Aretusi

Ippolito Costa

G. B. Lombardelli

PRIMATICCIO
1504-1570

BARTOLOMEO PASSEROTTI
1529-1592

G.B.RAMENGHI

Giulio d'Antonio
Bonasone

PELLEGRINO TIBALDI
1527-1596

Bartolommeo Cesi

Girolamo Miruoli

Ant.Marziale Carracci

Carlo Bonone

G. RENI
1575-1642

DOM.ZAMPIERI
1581-1641

DOSSO DOSSI
1480/90-1542

INNOCENZO FRANDUCCI
1490-c.1549

Battista Dossi

Gasp.Sacchi

LUCA LONGHI
1507-1580

Tommaso da Carpi

GIROLAMO DA CARPI
1501-1556

Nicolò Patarazzi

LELIO ORSI 1511-1587

Marco Marchietti

Giuseppe Mazzuoli

EARLY

AGOSTINO CARRACCI

LORENZO SABATINI

L. CARACCI
1555-1619

Francesco Carracci

ANNIBALE CARACCI
1560-1609

LATE

GIACOMO CAVEDONE
1577-1660

PARMIGIANINO
1503-1540

Raphael

Schedone

Gandini

Sodoma

C. Boccacino

M. Anselmi

G. Campi

B. Spranger

Vasari

M. Venusti

Caravaggio

Poussin

Albertinelli

M.Anselmi
(Lombardy)

Jac.Bertucci

Niccolo Roselli

G.Tronducci

M.Paganelli

Francesco Longhi

Sigism.Scarcella

Giov.Bianchi

Veronese

Barbara Longhi

P. FONTANA
1512-1597

Scarcellino da Ferrara

Pellegrino Cavedone

LAVINIA FONTANA
1552-1616

F.ALBANI
1578-1660

GUERCINO
1591-1666

A

B

C

3

4

VII Verona

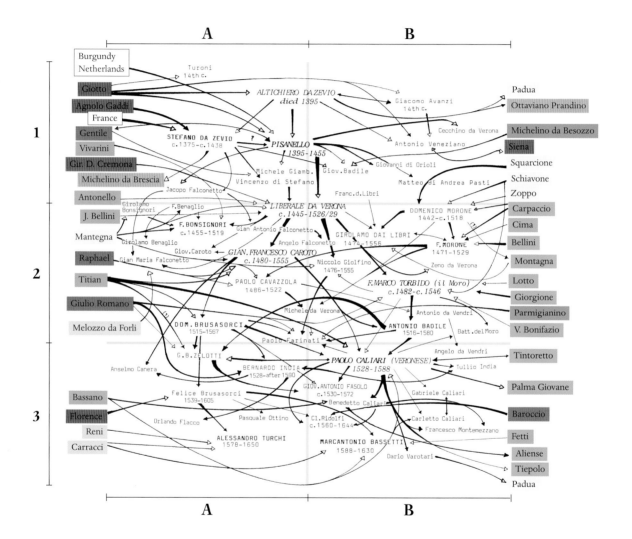

A   B

Burgundy
Netherlands

Giotto

Agnolo Gaddi
France

Gentile

Vivarini

Gir. D. Cremona

Michelino da Brescia

Antonello

J. Bellini

Mantegna

Raphael

Titian

Giulio Romano

Melozzo da Forli

Bassano

Florence

Reni

Carracci

Turoni
14th c.

ALTICHIERO DA ZEVIO
died 1395

Giacomo Avanzi
14th c.

STEFANO DA ZEVIO
c.1375–c.1438

PISANELLO
1395–1455

Cecchino da Verona

Antonio Veneziano

Michele Giamb.
Vincenzo di Stefano

Giov.Badile

Giovanni di Orioli

Matteo di Andrea Pasti

Jacopo Falconetto

Girolamo
Bonsignori

F.Benaglio

F.BONSIGNORI
c.1455–1519

Franc.d.Libri

LIBERALE DA VERONA
c.1445–1526/29

DOMENICO MORONE
1442–c.1518

Girolamo Benaglio

Gian Antonio Falconetto

GIROLAMO DAI LIBRI
1474–1556

F.MORONE
1471–1529

Gian Maria Falconetto

Giov.Caroto

Angelo Falconetto

GIAN.FRANCESCO CAROTO
c.1480–1555

Niccolo Giolfino
1476–1555

Zeno da Verona

PAOLO CAVAZZOLA
1486–1522

F.MARCO TORBIDO (il Moro)
c.1482–c.1546

Michele da Verona

Antonio da Vendri

DOM.BRUSASORCI
1515–1567

Paolo Farinati

ANTONIO BADILE
1516–1580

Batt.delMoro

G.B.ZELOTTI

Angelo da Vendri

Anselmo Canera

BERNARDO INDIA
1528–after 1590

PAOLO CALIARI (VERONESE)
1528–1588

Tullio India

Felice Brusasorci
1539–1605

GIOV.ANTONIO FASOLO
c.1530–1572

Gabriele Caliari

Benedetto Caliari

Orlando Flacco

Pasquale Ottino

Cl.Ridolfi
c.1560–1644

Carletto Caliari

Francesco Montemezzano

ALESSANDRO TURCHI
1578–1650

MARCANTONIO BASSETTI
1588–1630

Dario Varotari

Padua

Ottaviano Prandino

Michelino da Besozzo

Siena

Squarcione

Schiavone

Zoppo

Carpaccio

Cima

Bellini

Montagna

Lotto

Giorgione

Parmigianino

V. Bonifazio

Tintoretto

Palma Giovane

Baroccio

Fetti

Aliense

Tiepolo

Padua

1

2

3

A   B

VIII Brescia

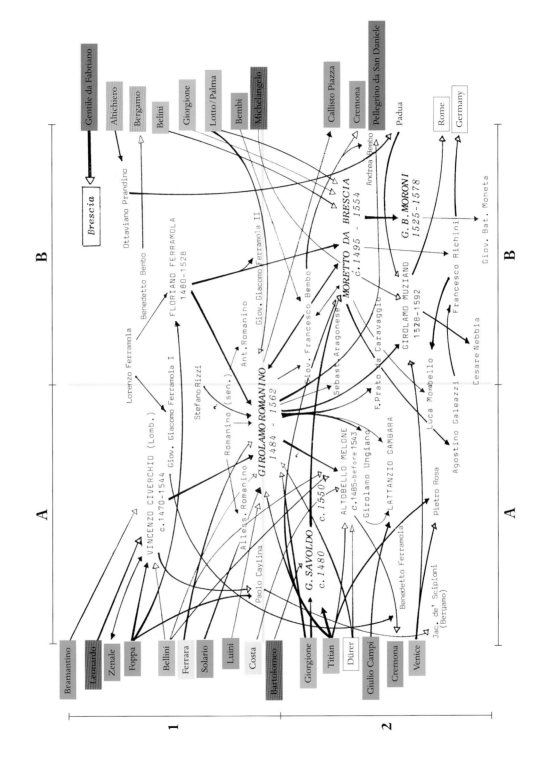

Brescia

Gentile da Fabriano

Altichiero

Bergamo

Bellini

Giorgione

Lotto/Palma

Bembi

Michelangelo

Callisto Piazza

Cremona

Pellegrino da San Daniele

Padua

Rome

Germany

Ottaviano Prandino

Benedetto Bembo

Lorenzo Ferramola

FLORIANO FERRAMOLA
1480-1528

Ant.Romanino

Giov. Giacomo Ferramola II

Andrea Bembo

G.B. MORONI
1525-1578

VINCENZO CIVERCHIO (Lomb.)
c.1470-1544

Giov. Giacomo Ferramola I

Stefano Rizzi

Romanino(sen.)

GIROLAMO ROMANINO
1484 - 1562

Giov.Francesco Bembo

Sebast.Aragonese

MORETTO DA BRESCIA
c.1495 - 1554

GIROLAMO MUZIANO
1528-1592

Francesco Richini

Giov. Bat. Moneta

Alless.Romanino

Paolo Caylina

G. SAVOLDO
c.1480

ALTOBELLO MELONE
c.1485-before 1543

(Girolamo Ungiano)

LATTANZIO GAMBARA

F.Prato da Caravaggio

Luca Mombello

Agostino Galeazzi

Cesare Nebbia

Pietro Rosa

Benedetto Ferramola

Jac. de' Scipioni
(Bergamo)

Bramantino

Leonardo

Zenale

Foppa

Bellini

Ferrara

Solario

Luini

Costa

Bartolomeo

Giorgione

Titian

Dürer

Giulio Campi

Cremona

Venice

B   A   A   B

1   2